RUDY ECKHARDT

The TRUTH of LOVE and FEAR

The TRUTH of LOVE and FEAR ®

MANIFESTING REALITY

Original Concept "Manifesting Reality"-Nov. 1998

Author:

RUDY ECKHARDT

META-CREDO PTY LTD

Initial concept Nov 1998
Re-Write Inspired Oct 2008

Editors
Andrea Eckhardt
Rudy Eckhardt

Original Cover Design

Nagui Henein

© 2015 Rudolf Eckhardt
© 2013
All Rights Reserved.

No part of this publication may be reproduced, stored in a retrieval system, or transmitted, in any form or by any means, electronic, mechanical, photocopying, recording, or otherwise, without the written permission of the author.

First published by Dog Ear Publishing
4010 W. 86th Street, Ste H
Indianapolis, IN 46268
www.dogearpublishing.net

ISBN: 978-1-4575-1666-5

This book is printed on acid-free paper.

Printed in the United States of America

Introduction

This book was written to bring knowledge and awareness into your life by allowing you to see the illusions by which you live in order to recognize the truth of who you really are.

The truth, you will realize, is actually very simple compared to the illusion or lie by which you live. In the absence of our awareness of the truth our experience of reality appears to be very complicated causing us to be deceived by our perception of reality.

The answers we come to when we begin to question reality confuse us. Should we accept our inner experience of reality or the one we share with others, as the truth of what is real? Or, should we accept the reality created by our intellect and logic or that by our emotions and feelings as true? If you are confused you are not alone.
The intention of the book is to give answers to questions about consciousness; life and living you may have never thought to ask. Answers that relate to concepts that right now control every aspect of your life experience.

Your life is about Being and not about Doing. This book will show you how you can **be** a powerful person rather than just engage in acts of power. You will see that true change is very different from only changing your feelings, behaviours or attitude. Imagine, changing the thinker instead of the thought or changing the doer instead of what he or she does.
It will educate you about love, fear and guilt and how it influences your mind and controls your behaviour. It will lead you to a new understanding of the nature of unconditional love, acceptance and trust and explain the potential of your personal power and the lack of it in your life. It will challenge your present way of thinking and cause you question your perception. Be warned because it will change how you see yourself and the way you see your life as you have lived it so far. It will alter your perception of your past, present and future.

The concepts you will be exposed to are both spiritual and psychological in nature because our mind and spirit are one. You have the opportunity to get a perspective of yourself and your life that is presently hidden from your awareness. This information will reveal insights into the process of living life that will give you a new perception of yourself, others and the world.

Our attachment to our individual fears contributes to the collective of fear and distrust that humanity lives with every moment of every day of which the consequences are evident all around us. If we were only prepared to recognize them for what they really are we might initiate an effort to deal with fear on a large scale and eliminate much of humanities self-created suffering. Taking individual responsibility for your issues by addressing your fears makes a significant contribution to changing the collective. You are the place where all change in the world has to start and this makes taking responsibility for what you manifest in your life an act of much greater importance than it may seem. As long as the emotion we call fear is in control of how we manifest our lives individually we will not change the outcome to which our collective fears are taking us. The absence of unconditional love and acceptance, rejection and exclusion, abandonment and guilt, powerlessness and the absence of control are such influential negative forces in our emotional lives that they determine our human destiny.

A little about me:

Even though I have not been one to hide from truth or to avoid confrontation with my own issues it has taken me time to understand the deeper meaning of existence and the process of by which I and others live our lives. My introduction to a series of books written by Jane Roberts — beginning with Seth Speaks — in my early thirties was the beginning of insight into the nature of my own consciousness. This caused me to experience life ever more consciously. I was then given the opportunity to learn kinesiology and work with clients in my early forties. I was attracted to find solutions for emotional issues rather than the body and was therefore not completely satisfied with the results of the method I had learned. Through searching I had an insight that I developed into a methodology that proved to be extremely effective in resolving psychological issues by creating true change. This book is an explanation of the philosophy that evolved from this therapy and how you can explore this for yourself.

Resolving the emotional issues of my clients from about 1990 until now has given me enormous scope to learn and understand human consciousness. My intense desire to achieve positive outcomes for my clients prompted me to apply myself without fear or preconceived limitations. In other words I would do and still do for each client what ever it takes to ensure they achieve real change. This approach has allowed me to discover new aspects of human consciousness and its experience of its own reality.

The existence of this book is therefore also a product of the contribution made by everyone that trusted me to work with them. All my clients have made me realize that nothing we achieve is ever achieved alone.

Besides my clients there others to whom I want to express my gratitude. I also thank those who have provided emotional support through the years: The loving and unfailing support from my partner Andrea, my daughter Nikola and my friend Nagui who designed the book cover. My close friend and retired chef Roger, Emma, Glenn, Frank, Duane, Henry, Carlos and all of my clients, many of whom I count as friends. Special thanks goes to my friend Saxon for his support and faith in my work and for inspiring me to rewrite the much longer initial version of this book.

TABLE OF CONTENTS

The Masterpiece by Andrea Eckhardt xvi

Chapter 1

Fear, Illusions and the True Nature of Love 1

Trapped by History..2
Obvious Deception..3
What is Life and Who Controls It?...4
The Battle for Personal Change 5

Chapter 2

Love 10

What True Love Is Not 11
The True Nature of Love 12
Love and Fear 13
Unconditional Love 15
Conditional Love is Fear...16
Our History of Fear 18
Our Higher Purpose 20

Chapter 3

The Beginning of Everything 23

Controlled by Illusions 24
Your Relationship with Everyone and Everything 26
Your Innocent Arrival 27

The Beginning of Fear 29
The Loss of Our Authentic Self 31

Chapter 4
The Influence of Conditional Love 34

Trapped by Conditional Love 36
Unseen Influences..37
The Nature of Your Sense-Of-Self...39
Trusting Fear 41

Chapter 5
The Power of Belief Systems 44

How Fear Conditions the Mind..46

Chapter 6
The Origin of Emotional Reality 50

The Inception of Feeling..51
When Fear is in Control 51
Living Life Conditionally 53

Chapter 7
The Power of Intent 56

The Intent of Fear 59
Controlled by Guilt 60
Aggressive Control...61
Destructive Criticism...61
Master of Your Intent 63

Chapter 8
Relentless Needs..64

The World to Exploit 67
Partners in Conflict 68
Conditional Relationships 71

Chapter 9
The Illusion of Being Free..73

Becoming Strategic 74
Conflict with Your Self 78
Lost in Behaviour 80
Depending on Strategies 84

Chapter 10
Our Greatest Fear...86

In Fear of Love 86
Trapped in Conditional Love...88
Fear, Illusions and Unhappiness......................................90

Chapter 11
Your Emotional Body..94

How the Body Meets Your Spirit 94
When the Body Speaks...96
Mind Rules The Body 99

Chapter 12
Creator of Your Own Reality..100

Deceived By Conditional Reality...................................102

The Habit of Victimhood..105
Life Without Fear..108

Chapter 13
Responsibility Without Blame 109

When Guilt Dominates 114
Conditional Parenting 115
The Roots of False Guilt 118
The Source of False Guilt 120
Embarrassment and Shame..123

Chapter 14
Conditional Relationships 125

Attractions and Desires..126
Developing a Conditional Sense-of-Self...................................129
Blinded by Illusions...131
Misled by Feelings and Attractions 133
Trapped in Conditional Love...135
Who is to Blame?...138
The Story of: "Suspicious Distrust" and "the Convincer 140
The Story of: "Never Enough" and the "Tireless Provider".....142
Without Feelings Where is Love?..145
Change Without Fear 147
Emotional "Genetics" 150
Empowered being..151

Chapter 15
The Quest for Happiness 153

Happiness Without Fear..156

Finding Happiness Within 157
Happiness by Avoiding Suffering 157
Happiness in Relationships 159

Chapter 16
Power Without Fear 161

The Beginning of Powerlessness 163
Living in Powerlessness 165
From Powerlessness to Anger to Violence 168
Control Without Power 170
Dominant Control 171
True Personal Power and Control 172
Collective Powerlessness 173
The Story of Fear 174

Chapter 17
Transcending Fear 176

Victimised by Beliefs 178
The Origins for Negative Events 179
In Life and Death 180
Emotional Suffering 182

CHAPTER 18
Fantasy and Imagination 184

Suppressing your Creative Self 185
Escape from Reality 187
Lost in Fantasy 188

Chapter 19
Living Your Unconditional Potential 190
Defined by Fear 190
The Lies Fear Creates 193
The Battle for Control over Your Mind 194
Dependence on Strategies 199
Strategic Relationships 199
False Needs and Expectations 201
How to Be Authentic 203
Transcending your Illusionary Self 204

Chapter 20
Our Conditional Mind 206
Deciphering Your Truth 210
Owning Your Issues 212
Understanding Life's Purpose 213
From Issues to Negative Beliefs 215
The Elements of Negative Beliefs 216
Cause, Context and Consequence in Negative Belief Systems 217
The Ultimate Intent of Your Beliefs 219

Chapter 21
Uncovering Self-Deception 227
Negative Life Events 229
Conditioned by fear 230
A New Perspective 233

Chapter 22
The 'Power' of Harmonious Intent 236
Creating Harmony from Within..239
Conscious Harmonious Intent..241
Unconscious Creators 242
Evolving Your Consciousness 246
The Creator Within 247
Confronting Change 248

Chapter 23
The Voice of Your Authentic Self..253
The Right to Be Authentic 255
Being Authentic..257
Escape From Illusions 258
Love Without Fear..262
Conflicting Needs and Expectations 263

Chapter 24
Unconditional Being..266
Your Evolution 270
Fearless Self-Questioning 272
Your Authentic Truth...273
Unnatural Behaviour 275
Generational Transference..276
Not Becoming your Parents 277
Your Reality is YOU 282

Chapter 25
Living Unconditional Love 289
Positive Interventions..289
Awake to Truth 291
The Essence of Being...293

The Masterpiece

Spirit is carved from the wastelands of my mind.
It takes its form while gathering my woes,
my tears my hopes and wishes.
With tools in hand it shapes for me my dream.
It smoothes away the sadness to reveal the soft edges.
It grinds away the despair
to expose the velvet texture of my bliss.
Spirits' mallet pounds away at the indentations
left by the footprints of my fears.
Standing back, Spirit inspects
what has come forth from this chaos
Changes are made allowing my hidden emotions
to be shown the way out of their abyss.
Now the carved sculpture stands for all to see
in the splendour that is SPIRIT
and the Grace that is me.

By Andrea Eckhardt

07-07-13

CHAPTER 1

Fear, Illusions and the True Nature of Love

What would it be like to be the person you were always meant to be, living the life you always dreamt of? How would it feel to live without fear, confident in yourself, trusting your direction in life and clear of what you want to achieve? To have the capacity to determine your destiny and create a life that is representative of your potential.

Reality is that for many, life is not what they thought it would be. It often feels as if success does not come as easily as failure and our partner is not the person we thought they were. At work we struggle to be noticed and rewarded for our achievements and at the same time hope that our failures go unseen. We may move from one relationship to another to find the person we hope will make us happy. We spend our lives chasing dreams and fulfilling expectations that are not even our own. We try to fulfil an idea of happiness and success that ultimately does not give us a sense of completion and wholeness we hoped for. More than often, life becomes a struggle between our desire to fulfil a fictitious idea of what our lives should be and the emotional issues that stop us having it. In the meantime, experiencing our emotional issues can be so persistently painful, intrusive and debilitating that we often choose medicate ourselves with alcohol, drugs or sex or what ever else we can find so that we can still have "a good time".

In order to feel better about ourselves we avoid our issues by engaging in mental distractions. We self-medicate to create an illusionary world of love, self-significance or power to escape the person we fear that we are. We want solutions, but not knowing where to look or how to find the answers, we practice a variety of behaviours to avoid our fears and negative feelings. The truth is that we do not really know ourselves at all or not well enough. *Our belief and understanding of who we are, is generally a mixture of our habitual behaviours and feelings coupled to likes and dislikes we do not even know the origin off.* We tend to assume that our insecurities and fears are an intrinsic part of our personality. We certainly do not realize that all of this and more form the foundation of why and how we create the life we experience. Whilst we recognize the effect that life has on us through our feelings, we have no idea how we are implicated in the process that creates the experience in the first place.

How would your life be different if you were totally in charge of every aspect of your life experience? You may believe that this would only be possible if you were in control of everything and everyone around you. How else could you have everything the way you want it to be?

The truth is that you were born with the capacity to be in control of your own existence so that you can manifest a life that is an expression of your authentic self and fulfils your potential. The real problem is that the only one that stands in the way of achieving this is you and the fears you hold. Without your fears and insecurities you would become the creator of your own reality and life experiences. *Your relationships, aspirations and happiness will be under your control if you were to release the program of fear that presently runs your life.*

Trapped by Your History

Partially driven by what we have learned from our parents and reaffirmed by the life experiences we have and common consensus, we generally believe that we are powerless to change our life. At the same time, we are usually stubborn in adhering to the solutions we have learned in order to escape our negative experience of life. Convinced that we can only avoid our emotional and life issues if we change **how we behave, what we do and how we think**, we set about to try and control our behaviour and modify our thoughts and feelings. Unfortunately, it is unlikely that we can maintain our effort to stop ourselves from experiencing our issues and problems by trying to consciously replace our behaviour, feelings or thoughts with positive ones. Somehow no matter how hard we try our issues and the negative emotions that go with them always return. Once old negative feelings return we quickly fall back into emotional habits and behaviours that take us back into the same life experiences we sought to escape.

It becomes easy to justify your issues when most of the people you know have a very similar experience of their lives. We are easily distracted by the pressure of having to provide in order to have a roof over our heads, to meet the financial responsibilities of our family and deal with problems of everyday life. Living can than feel like a struggle with infrequent moments of joy or space for ones own needs and self-fulfilment.

Our issues can make the task of having to take responsibility for our own life and for those who depend on us stressful and overwhelming. Having to become the success we believe we should be can be daunting. Fame, money, wealth, happiness and abundance always seem to be one decision, one step away or the preserve of others who always appear to be more fortunate than we are. The examples of those who reach these pinnacles of success appear all around us but somehow achieving the same for ourselves eludes us. Usually when we try and understand why and how we did not succeed we tend to blame others or circumstances. We come to the conclusion that we somehow should have done it differently or that we were disadvantaged or deceived by others. Our perception of the outcome can convince us that we are failures or just inadequate or plain unlucky. Often, we have no choice but to accept our failures and perceived shortcomings because the answers we arrive at do not lead us to solutions. Frequently, limited by our perspective, with our dreams still in our eyes, we will try again in the hope that this time, by doing it differently, we will succeed. The problem is that we do not recognise that we are changing what we do but not the person who is doing it.

Obvious Deception

Your traditional approach to resolve your emotional issues will cause you to miss what is most important. The reason you missed it is that it is almost too obvious for you to recognize and understand its significance. It is truly a case of not seeing the wood for the trees. First of all, you have not realised that without exception, ***YOU are the common factor in every event — negative or positive — in your life***. The intensity with which you are involved with everyone and everything around you distracts you from the awareness that *you* are the central force in everything that has happened to you in every moment of your life.

You have been and will always be the central figure in every one of your life's failures or achievements whether they are socially with friends, at work or play. If each negative emotional event in your life were a crime, you would definitely be arrested as the prime suspect. Even though you may as yet not understand how, your presence at every event points to you being the instigator of your own life experiences.

It should also be obvious however that you and others are not aware how and why you manifest these negative experiences. It seems illogical that you would consciously choose to create a painful or fearful life. The fact is that you make conscious effort to do exactly the opposite in order to avoid drama and negative experiences. However, your attempts to avoid creating negative emotional experiences is likely to be limited to changes in your strategies or behaviours even though the outcome is often inconsistent and unsatisfactory. Characteristically, life still keeps returning you to the same old negative patterns.

One of the primary limitations to our self-understanding is that the person whom we believe ourselves to be represents who we actually are or are meant to be. You may be aware of the fact that you are very reactive and affected by everyone you have to deal with. You may worry about what others think of you and how they judge you. You may feel insecure about making decisions that others may judge and criticise or you may be aggressively dominating and controlling. Confrontation with authority or the opposite sex may terrify you. You may be easily offended and upset by the way others treat you or take a confronting and aggressive approach to avoid being invalidated or negated. You may actively avoid groups of people because you fear not knowing who to be and how to respond or you need to have people around you for support for fear of being alone. You feel powerless or insignificant in the presence of dominating, aggressive or confrontational personalities or be dominating in order to feel significant. The truth is none of these fears are representative of who you really are.

The world and the people in it appear to have an enormous control and influence over your life and how you can live it. Somehow, it feels that the external emotional forces — the attitudes, behaviours, needs and negative emotions expressed by others and circumstances —dictate how you will or can behave, feel and think and consequently influence your decisions and choices. Now, while in the midst of your emotional issues, controlled by the belief that others are the cause for your issues, it is understandably difficult to know where to begin to look for solutions.
The question is: Why is my life not my choice?

What is Life and Who Controls It?

The more precise question is: What is the nature of life and who and what determines how you will live it? Does it seem to you that others are always better off, more successful, have less problems than you do? Do you feel that you exist to serve those around you and that they control your choices and decisions and your turn never seems to come? Are you angry and resentful with others over the slightest thing?

You may have frequently asked why you life is so different from that of others. Why do others not feel the same way in the same circumstances and with the same people as I do? How come I attract certain personalities and situations in my life? Why can I not achieve my goals and do my life experiences always fall short of my expectations? Why do negative things happen to me when I try so hard to do the right thing? Why am I not treated as being special and significant the way others are? Why is what I say not listened to and taken seriously by others? Why do I feel that I do not matter to anyone? Why do I fear how others see and judge me? Why do I believe that I am not good enough?

These questions and others will have crossed your mind at one time or another. What were the answers you came up with to explain the quality and nature of these beliefs, feelings and thoughts? What explanations did you arrive at to understand the reasons for your negative life experiences?

Did you blame yourself because of guilt or did you hold others responsible, circumstances or the world in general? Finding fault with yourself and then labelling yourself with all of your perceived shortcomings is not just self-destructive. It is a way to give your self a seemingly irrevocable excuse for what is wrong in your life. By blaming everything on yourself, you have made yourself into a victim of who you think you are. You might believe that this absolves you from responsibility because you are convinced you cannot help being who you are because it feels unchangeable. Of course if everyone else is responsible for your ills because you believe yourself to be a victim and with that, you excuse yourself from any responsibility for your life's miseries.

When it seems obvious to you that others are in control and have power over you; what can you possibly do? How can you be in control of your life when you are subject to forces created by others such as the rules and expectations, control and needs? When we are confronted with an issue we are usually quite certain of cause. Our understanding and interpretation of events appears to make it clear who or what is responsible for creating our negative emotional experiences. By coincidence, we generally go to great length to prove that others or the world are responsible and conveniently exclude ourselves.

We do not realize that our feelings and reactions are the same as those of our parents when they showed us with their behaviour that this is the way that life functions. They taught us that our lives are subject to others and the world but this mindset will never resolve our emotional struggles. We do not understand why we feel and think the way we do, the reasons for many of our choices and attractions and why we cannot stop negative events happening in our lives. Our conditioning is so comprehensive that most of the time we do not even question, let alone try to understand the nature of our own consciousness.

Most of all, we are frustrated by our inability to change our life: To turn our failures into successes, find a relationship that will bring us joy and happiness, to feel and think positively about ourselves and the world. We feel trapped in the fear-based negativity of our mind, by life situations we feel powerless to change. We feel victimized by negative outcomes we believe we have no choice but to live with. We try to find what we need to do to change our lives but usually, no matter how hard we try to implement these changes, in the long term we still falter and fail. We find ourselves going back to old patterns and behaviours, to old feelings and attitudes and frequently back to the same old negative experiences.

There are four fundamental questions we need to answer:
- Is it true that our lives are a controlled by outside forces and are we therefore subject to our environment and the people we associate with?
- Can we change who we feel and believe we are?
- Are we responsible for creating our own life experience individually and collectively?
- Do we have the capacity to transform our lives by changing **who we are** rather than by **what we do**?

Most people believe that they are sometimes in control and at other times subject to others and circumstances. They also tend to think that their sense of power depends on the situation they are in and people they are with. Once you have accepted that we cannot be responsible for our life experiences you have given away the power over your life. In fact, you have chosen to become a victim of the environment and subject to the whims and will of others. The truth is that accepting being responsible for your experience of life or be the victim of your life is a challenging choice. We are generally guilty of choosing explanations that are emotionally convenient for us. For one they are taken to be proof of our innocence and secondly because they provide justification for the actions and choices that brought about undesirable circumstances in our life.

The alternative is to consider the idea that we create our own experiences by being the active instigator of every one of our life events and encounters. If this is true than we must also accept responsibility for the consequences of everything that we manifest.

The good news is that if **we are the instigators of our life experiences than as the origin, we also have the power and control to change the life we manifest and experience.**

In other words, by accepting our role as the creators of the experience of our own existence we automatically empower ourselves with the capacity to change our selves. If we accept that we are subjects of others and our environment we also have to accept that as victims we are therefore largely powerless in life.

The question is: Whether it is really possible to change ourselves and thereby change our life or are we destined to spend our lives battling external forces that appear to control our existence? Do we have no choice but to accept a life in which we cannot avoid disappointment, pain and suffering and so on? Or, could it be that we need a completely new understanding of the nature *who we are* as a consciousness. Can we learn to understand *what it means to change who we are* so that we create a positive life?

The Battle for Personal Change

Considering the rows of self-help books lined up on the bookshelves of just about any bookstore in the world, we are not short on advice on how to change our lives. It is not for me to list them individually but they can be broadly divided into three areas.

The most common advice is based on the principle that you need **to do** things differently to have a solution to your problems. The message appears to be that there are the things you **have to do** to have the life you want or to have the things you want out of life". The second most common strategy is achieving change in life through disciplined practice: meditation, some styles of martial arts and yoga. The third is change through exercising control over your thinking, emotions or attitude, which often also involves some form discipline.

All of these have the potential to have some level of success in getting positive personal results but that does not mean you have arrived at an enduring solution for your emotional issues. Changing what you do through consciously and strategically altering your actions and choices does actually not address the core of your issues. It can in the short term change exactly what it intents to change — *how* you behave, *how and what* you choose and do and *how* you express yourself. While this can create good and positive results at the time, it is also likely to be temporary. You will only maintain a level of success if you remember to diligently and consciously apply all of your advice and instructions in all circumstances where your issues appear. These strategies are extremely vulnerable to failure should there be any changes in the elements that act as a trigger for the emotional issues they are supposed to be a solution for.

Change through discipline and practice can be powerful but requires consistent commitment and dedication by the practitioner to be effective. Generally, the intent of practice is to develop a disciplined mind with the capacity to surrender to a neutral state of being to achieve inner change through self-realization and an expanded consciousness. The most immediate result this practice provides is a sense of emotional release, inner-peace and harmony, which for many can only be maintained by continued practice.

The most referred to form of change, which appears to be also the least understood is **self-change — to change the self you believe you are**. The problem with this idea is that whenever it becomes part of a discussion, process or concept, it is reduced from a *'being' solution* to a *'doing' solution*. Generally, the conclusion is that we have to engage in a new set of strategies or coping behaviours to overcome our emotional issues in life. In reality, that still does not represent a change in 'who you are'.

Changing **who you are — changing your inner-identity** — requires an understanding of the nature of our consciousness and the process it uses to manifest its own reality experience and the reasons why. This also needs us to look at the nature of our mind and the beliefs that make up our sense-of-self. So that instead of changing **what we do and how we do it** we will actually change the nature of who we believe we are — our sense-of-self. So far, our contracted perception of ourselves and reality has stopped us from recognizing who or what is responsible for the perception we have of ourselves. Because of this, we cannot fathom the reasons for the negative experiences we consequently have.

You may wonder why it is more important to change "**who you are**" rather than "**what you do**" if what you do gets result even if it can be inconsistent. First of all, your doing is generally a strategic response after the negative event has already happened or a pre-emptive strategy to prevent your fear becoming reality. In other words you have already become the victim or you going to battle before the war has been declared. You do not realize that by using your behaviours you are not addressing the reason why these events are happening in the first place. Y**ou are dealing with symptoms of your problems and not the causes**. The problem with only dealing with the symptoms is that the similar negative events are likely to repeat themselves again and again.

Just imagine that you not only understood the causative factors for your issues but you also released them so that they are no longer a part of you. Without these elements being present in your sense-of-self you would no longer manifest these negative events in your life. **By changing yourself — your inner-identity — you are dealing with the origin for your negative experiences.** The transformation of who you are has the effect of changing your perception and feelings, choices and decisions, your relationships and thereby your life. This is the exact outcome we should expect from **true personal-change**. We need to develop an understanding of who we are as a consciousness and the process of living life that we all engage in without exception. This process is ultimately responsible for creating the emotional life experiences we manifest — every moment of every day.

However, you can only change who you are if you know what exactly it is you have to change and how. This requires a new understanding of the true nature of your **sense-of-self** or ego — i.e. ***who you believe yourself to be, both its negative and positive qualities**.* You will need to know how you acquired this negative inner-identity and why you hang on to it. You will also need to develop a clearer insight into your feelings and emotions, to understand what drives them and why you are so hooked on responding to them beyond reason and common sense.

Before you can incorporate these new concept and alter your perception of yourself, others and life you will need to change many of the commonly held beliefs about the way our consciousness and psychology functions. This will change your perception of way life functions as a process and create a deeper understanding of the dynamics in relationships. You will come to realize new truths about yourself and the world in which you exist but let us take it one step at the time

Chapter 2

LOVE

With the whole world in pursuit of feeling and experiencing love, it seems strange to think that most of us are actually in fear of love. To even suggest that there might be something in us that actively avoids love would seem a paradox. Yet issues with committing to, receiving and giving **unconditional love**, including trusting love are very common. The question is: "Why is that so if we all strive to be loved and have someone to love"?

To understand this, we need first of all to ask what is love really is and why it is so significant in our life. In general, society depicts love in a myriad of different ways that are in some respects caused by the limits in linguistic expression. We are presented with romantic love, sexual love, family love, religious love, love for your country, love for the objects we own or wish to own and so on. Whilst our concept of love in all of these is obviously not the same, we have lost the true perspective of what love is because we apply the same word to mean different things. If you add our individual differences in perception to this, it becomes very difficult to find a shared acceptable definition for what love really is (or isn't). The power and significance of love is undeniable and so regardless of what definition we arrive at, there is no doubt that love is central to our life and part of every relationship.

The state of absolute love is unconditional and if clearly understood, can form the basis by which we can determine the true nature of love and help us define emotional standards to live by. Our awareness and understanding of unconditional love will also clarify the nature, motivation and intent of our own consciousness. From this, we will be able to develop a new appreciation of what the meaning and significance love has in our personal lives and our relationships. Evolving a deep inner-relationship with unconditional love will not only serve our own sense of being but will also have a profound effect on the way we impact others and the environment that is our world. Our perception of love is reflected in the language we speak, as each language is a manifestation of the mindset of population using it. Some languages are limited in their capacity to define love in its various forms while others have developed the vocabulary to give expression to the different applications of love. Often we resort to metaphors and stories to try and explain the nature and value of love.

The significance of love for all mankind is testified by the fact that almost all religious and spiritual belief systems have it as their core value in one form or another. On a personal level love forms the foundation for every intimate human relationship. In the final analysis you will find that it is the link that binds all human consciousness together, regardless of nationality, race or religion or any ideas or belief systems created by man.
Love is the most influential emotional force in existence and thereby represents an immense and irresistible power.
If you doubt this then consider the effect and consequences on the human consciousness when love is absent. There is proof on all levels that human consciousness cannot exist without love. Through personal transformation we create the opportunity to realize that '**Unconditional Love**' is the essence of who we are and central to everything in our existence.

What True Love Is Not

Amidst the many definitions we give love one would imagine there to be one that approaches its true nature yet there is no general consensus. Our understanding of what love is will be clearer if we begin by excluding everything that love is not.

- ***True Love is Never Conditional*** (if it is, it becomes something entirely different).
- True love is not our need or needful attachment to others, objects, power and control.
- True love does not need, demand or expect reciprocation.
- True love does not expect nor require sacrifice of any kind.
- True love cannot be acquired by force, coercion or manipulation.
- True love does not set out to fulfil the needs of others.
- True love is not conditional to self-sacrifice or by putting others before self.
- True love is not acquired or created through lies, deceit and misrepresentation.
- True love does not exploit the weaknesses in others.
- True love has no need to dominate or control through aggression or power.
- True love does not require you to surrender your voice, power or control.
- True love is not found by being a victim, self-deprecation, and self-abuse or self-harm.
- True love does not manifest in response to over-responsibility and misplaced guilt.

- True love is not driven by servitude or submission or subjugation.
- True love does not require you to be inferior, worthless or insignificant in respect to others.
- True love is not given or acquired through judgment, criticism and blame.
- True love does not demand your sacrifice, suffering, and pain.
- True love will not be a part of you if you live in fear of abandonment and rejection, exclusion and loneliness.
- True love is not acquired through embarrassment and shame.
- True love will not be a part of you if you believe you do not belong and are not wanted.

After reading this list, ask your self if any of these conditions are a part of your sense of being in life and if so, why and how did you come to accept them as your sense of yourself.

The True Nature of Love

- ***True Love is Unconditional.***
- True love is fearless, without any angst.
- True love accepts unconditionally.
- True love trusts unconditionally.
- True love gives unconditionally and feels entitled and deserving to receive.
- True love is always self-responsible for the state of its own being and its manifestations.
- True love will always seek to exist in harmony with its core sense of being.
- True love is always spontaneous, open and free in its self-expression.
- True love immediately knows and recognises conditional love, lies, deceit or falseness.
- True love is free to be and act within the awareness of consequence and responsibility to other consciousness.
- True love always has and gives choice.
- True love respects the nature of others and does not impose itself.
- True love is confident, aware and conscious of itself.
- True love is always empowered without the need for power.
- True love empowers others.
- True love is and will always be truthful.
- True love seeks to fulfil its own potential and supports others to fulfil theirs.

- True love is never critical or judgemental.
- True love is always responsible to the nature of its own being and the consequences its actions bring forth.
- True love ensures others accept responsibility for nature of their being and the outcomes this creates in their lives.
- True love has the intent to support others in evolving their spirit without taking away the experiences they manifest in their life.
- True love recognises emotional disharmony in others as easily as harmony.
- True love has harmonious intent for oneself and in relation to others and the environment.
- True love teaches and allows others to learn for themselves without criticism or judgment.
- True love is optimistic, creative and expansive in its intent

There are likely to be a number of statements in this list you find challenging to accept but you will learn that the reasons for your resistance lie within the nature of your own ego or sense-of-self.

Love and Fear

Love and fear are at the opposite ends of the scale of our emotional range. The fear referred to is not the fear we have when our physical safety is threatened. This fear is emotional in nature and brought about by emotional issues — the fear of speaking our mind, living our truth, being spontaneous and so on. Emotional fears of this kind are a product of negative states held by our mind and even though in the real sense they cannot physically hurt or kill us, our response to them is characterised by worry and stress, anxiety and avoidance, aggression and anger and powerlessness and so on. Just remember those moments when you reacted aggressively or defensively to an emotional confrontation, criticism or someone's imposition on you. There are many who have issues with asking for things we are actually entitled to or become shy and withdrawn when put in a position where we are expected to speak our truth. Others have a need to be aggressive and demanding to get what they want for fear of never getting it. Of course we always have a million excuses and justifications for our behaviour but the question is: "Why do we behave this way and what are our fears really about"? What can be so terrible and fearful about telling someone how you really feel and think? Are they going to fall apart, get angry or is it you who cannot cope? Or perhaps you need to ask yourself why you have to put your needs and expectations aggressively before every one else's?

Ask yourself: "How real and valid are these fears that dominate your perception and determine your behaviour'?
The reality is that these fears are not a threat to our physical survival although many would feel this to be the case in the moment of the experience. Although we have the sensation of our fears being real they are actually a product of illusions held as a truth by our minds. You will learn that all of our negative emotions and feelings, perceptions and behaviours are based on illusions that a product our fears. We do not realize that we actually depend on these same fears to keep us emotionally safe and secure.

Fear as an emotion is represented by a state of hyper awareness, alertness and vigilance, manifested by our sense-of-self to keep us safe from perceived threats. The reality of any fear depends on the actual reality of the threat and therein lays the real problem because your perception is determined by your fears. It must be obvious by now that our mind has trouble discerning an illusionary threat from one that will actually endanger you. When our emotional fears are triggered, they generally cause us to experience a high degree of stress, frequently with physical discomfort and as such our fears feel very real. We do not realise that our emotional response puts us in contradiction with unconditional love, acceptance and trust because of the fears that now dominate our mind. Fear also drives our attachment to these illusions and this causes us to depend on our fears for our emotional survival. Once fear controls our feelings, thoughts and behaviour, we become unaware we no longer trust unconditional love to support us.

Living your life in response to your fears will cause you to feel that love is **conditional** just as it will be for *acceptance* and *trust*. Conditional love is very different from unconditional love in that it requires you to meet conditions that are set by yourself or by others before you become deserving or entitled to love. Your response to these conditions is underpinned by **the fear** that you may not be able to meet them. Should you manage to meet the conditions you believe you have to meet, you will have avoided the realisation of your fears but your belief that love is conditional will ensure that your fears are maintained. The problem is that once conditional love becomes the only love you know you will begin to trust and accept that the conditions you believe you have to meet are normal. This can result in a life in which you constantly have to prove to others that you are worthy of their love, acceptance or trust or you will become a victim of your need for love. This makes you dependent on how others treat you and behave towards you and hooks you into a cycle of having to engage others using specific strategic behaviours to get their love, attention, approval or endorsement and so on. Their response to you will either prove to you that you are lovable, acceptable and wanted and so on or that you are not.

Your incessant behaviour and attitude is driven by the belief that if you fail, your fear of being unlovable will become reality because you are trapped in the illusion that this is who you are. You now live in fear that if you cannot meet the conditions you believe exist you will be rejected and excluded. Your fears will become a source for manifesting stressful and negative encounter with others no matter what behaviour you choose to employ.

Once these fears become a part of who you are — your sense-of-self — you live in constant fear of losing love and being unacceptable and so on. These fears translate into fear of abandonment, rejection, judgment, criticism, exclusion, shame, ridicule, powerlessness, insignificance and more. Your fears will reaffirm the necessity to be in a state of constant psychological vigilance and engage in strategic behavioural games that you believe are essential for your emotional survival. Ironically, once you rely on your fears to protect you from the consequences they imply, you will begin to depend on fear so completely you cannot live without them. Because of this, you will lose the innate trust and expectation that unconditional love, acceptance and trust will support you in life in the first 8 to 10 years and with it your authentic self.

Unconditional Love

So far we have referred to unconditional love as being central to our being but there is much more to love than this. Unconditional love is in fact the essence of our spiritual self — it is the eternal reference point for our consciousness that allows it to be aware of the nature of its inner-identity and the experiences it creates. The nature of each and every spirit is unique and different from another. Each contains the capacity to manifest using its immense creativity supported by fantasy and imagination. Each has unique talents and abilities, an inexhaustible imagination, innate wisdom. Each has the capacity create and manifest, to learn and evolve. Each is endowed with resources that allow it to manifest and create its own life and experience it through its senses. Together with its innate intellect, the capacity for reasoning and conceptualisation, we form intent to make the decisions and choices with which we create our life. Beyond this there are faculties and capacities yet undeveloped, suppressed or unused of which we get occasional glimpses through ourselves or others. The potential of many these is yet to be revealed to us. This gives each and every consciousness an almost infinite variety of pathways through which to channel the innate potential of its being.

Our present level of psychological and spiritual development has limited our capacity to understand the true nature and power of unconditional love in respect to our consciousness and thereby the process by which we manifest and experience life. Our sense-of-self or inner-identity is so strongly connected to our superficial interpretation of reality and other consciousness that we cannot comprehend our lack of self-awareness and understanding. Our dominant focus is on the behaviour of others, how they speak and what they say to us. We respond to others without being necessarily aware of the deeper motivations within them or within our selves. Their behaviour and attitude in respect of us comes to define how we see ourselves and who we are. As a result we cannot differentiate who we truly are from the emotional experience we are engaged in. We are so used to being in a conditional relationship with everyone in our world that *unconditional* love, acceptance and trust are strangers we do not even recognise.

We have the tendency to use the word love indiscriminately for our partners, objects or activities. The manner in which we use the word love often implies that a person or even an object has the power to create the kind of love we feel for it. Without realizing we put the capacity and responsibility for what we feel outside of us. We can confuse the attraction for someone to be true love or acceptance when what we feel is actually products of our neediness to be loved, wanted or accepted or to be sexually desirable. Over time, we have structured our perception to convince us that others are responsible for the way we perceive them and ourselves. By accepting this as being true, we unconsciously give our emotional power to others and thereby endow people or objects with powers and qualities they cannot possibly have. As a consequence we live life depending on others to feel loved and accepted. We remain in constant fear that failing to meet the conditions we believe exist to qualify for love, acceptance and being wanted, we are at risk of being rejected or judged.

Unconsciously we have given others control over our emotional life and at the same time feel totally responsible for the success or failure of the relationship. In doing so we have allowed ourselves to become subject to their whims, issues and insecurities. Should they do or say anything that is interpreted by us as a judgment or rejection, we likely to feel unacceptable and unlovable because we believe we are not what we are expected to be. Since we do not recognise our own part in this drama, we are likely to be either in denial of our own complicity, hold them responsible or go into self-effacing blame. The reasons for these potential reactions are explained further on.

Conditional Love is Fear

You may ask: Why *"being unconditional"* is so significant and why is it so important to strive to live your life in an emotionally unconditional state? Is it something that anyone can achieve and live by in all situations at all times?

We are all born with the innate expectation that the essence of our spirit — unconditional love acceptance and trust — will continue when we begin our experience of life through our interaction with our parents. Although our parents may have the conscious intent to love us unconditionally, they are prevented from doing so by the conditions they themselves have in respect to love in the form of their own fears and insecurities. Their fears translate into expectations and behaviours that are interpreted by the child as being the conditions to their love and acceptance and these will eventually dictate the way it will live its life. Its naïve acceptance of the parent's conditions becomes the source for emotional issues that will affect many aspects of a child's life and becomes a source for unhappiness and pain.

Consider this: If we were to be suddenly in the presence of absolute unconditional love, we may expect that we would feel wonderful but we would also automatically feel the expectation to respond in kind by being totally unconditional ourselves. This would demand we let go of all of the defensive and protective mechanisms developed over a lifetime of fear in which we have learned to trust completely. While some may be able to surrender all their fears, most will feel totally overwhelmed by the prospect of having to give up the fear-based strategic tools they are convinced they need for their emotional survival. We identify so intensely with the conditions we believe exist for love, acceptance and trust that letting go of these beliefs and supporting strategies is like giving up who we are. Unconditional surrender to love will require us to accept love as the only valid emotional force that we will trust to support us in our existence and in living life. This means living life in the complete absence of fear, without any defensive or coping strategies and fear based needs. For many, this is so confronting that it is very likely that their fears will win the day. However the power of unconditional love is such that even though fear may triumph in the moment it will always win out in the long term but not necessarily in the way you might think.

We experience unconditional and conditional love as a paradox in the beginning of our life:

- We learn to distrust and reject our authentic and unconditional essence through the emotional pressure created by our issue bound parents. Our physical dependence on them gives us no choice but to accept the conditional relationship unconsciously offered by our parents.
- The conditions we accept become our inner-identity, which will determine our perception and strategic behaviour and become the source for our negative feelings, needs and. thoughts. We use our learned strategic behaviour to meet these perceived fear-based conditions.

- As we mature, the negative life experiences our conditional state of mind manifests act as emotional triggers for an innate yearning for the lost oneness with the essence of our being —unconditional love, acceptance and trust.
- Unaware of reasons for our negative life experiences and having become dependent on our fear-based strategies, needs and feelings to get love, acceptance and trust, we now fear letting go of them.
- As long as we live in fear of letting go of the fear-driven mindset that causes us to maintain **conditional** love, acceptance and trust in our lives, our fears will prevent us from accepting **unconditional love** as our truth.

Unconditional love is to our consciousness what thread is to a tapestry — it is its core and foundation but also forms the patterns that define it. Just like the tapestry could not exist without thread, our spirit would not exist without unconditional love and the elements it contains. From the beginning of our existence, even before we breathed the air of our new physical experience, it is already our most compelling inner frame of reference. *From birth, we are innately aware when we are being unconditionally loved and accepted, wanted and trusted and also immediately sense when we are not.*

Our History of Fear

Conditional love is a learned aspect of our emotional mind because we are born with the expectation to exist in a state of unconditional love and the innate entitlement to experience, give and receive **unconditional love**. Our mind forms its sense of itself i.e. its ego in the first 8 to 10 years of our life at which time our parents and family are our most intense influence. Our mother and father grew up subject to the influence of their parents and culture, which defined their state of mind. You have become the recipient of this generational legacy of emotional distortions, which you — just like your parents — have accepted as the truth of who you are. It evolved in you to become your definition of who you are to yourself and who you believe you are to others. Without realising you have formed behaviours as a strategic means to deal with the conditions your mind has accepted as reality. From here on in you are more who you believe yourself to be rather then who you are authentically.

Our learned fears are not static states in our mind but are active propositions that have the intent to manifest the reality they represent for you. They will actively steer our behaviour and attract events, people and conditions that reflect fear's intended nature. If for example you fear confrontation, you will do your best not to upset any one even if it means that you have to suppress what you want or your truth. Your fear will control how you communicate by altering the manner and tone of your speech in an effort to avoid creating any negative reaction in others. Unconsciously sensing your fears they will feel safe to confront you with their demands or criticism for example because they feel that you will not stand up for yourself. Unconsciously your passive fearful state of mind attracts very confrontation you seek to avoid. Your fear sets you up to be an easy victim. Even though our passive strategic behaviour has the intent to avoid confrontation in reality it acts as an attraction for those who are only brave enough to be aggressive with someone who is passive and fearful like you. Your state of mind will lead you to compromise how you are in the world and how much of your emotional self you are prepared to express and expose to others.

The sense-of-self we form by internalising the fears and insecurities of our parents separates us from who we are truly meant to be — our authentic self. If we do not change **who we are,** we will in many ways become our parents, have similar relationships by choosing similar partners and become the same parents to our children as they were to us. We will perpetuate an emotional generational cycle that already existed before we were born. Our choice to change **who** we are will also become a decisive act of breaking a generational cycle of emotional issues.

There is a lot more to this than you might think. You are likely to be unconscious of much of what is negative in your sense-of-self even though it controls how you see the world and how you make your choices. Without the awareness of what negative aspects of your sense-of-self you cannot know what drives your decisions and choices, why you are attracted to certain personalities and the reasons for your negative emotions and feelings. Without recognizing **how you** are the creator of your life experiences, you live with the idea that you are largely powerless in life and that others and the world are in control.

It is crucial in our understanding of ourselves that we recognize that once love or any other state like acceptance or trust is conditional, we enter a state of emotional powerlessness, distrust and neediness and become *fear driven.*

Without the innate security that unconditional love, acceptance and trust provide, we live in fear that we are not able to meet the conditions that we now believe exist before we are deserving and entitled to love, acceptance and trust.

Conditional love creates internal conflict because it contradicts our innate expectation to be unconditionally loved, wanted and accepted and trusted.

Inner-harmony depends on being in a state of unconditional love, acceptance and trust with our selves — our spiritual essence.

This contradiction in our emotional dialogue can only be resolved if we accept that to begin with **we are at the core of our very nature, unconditionally lovable and acceptable, wanted and trustworthy**. Finding personal resolution for this inner conflict and thereby transcending our limited mindset makes the process of living life our greatest human and spiritual challenge.

Our conversation about conditional love also covers every other emotional aspect of human relationships such as conditional self-expression, acceptance and trust and so on. Conditional love causes everyone to look for love and acceptance from others in an attempt to find the harmony and fulfilment they lack within. When we eventually do find love in relationships, we often discover it is not what we expected it to be. Most live with the naive assumption that the love from a partner will resolve their inability to love themselves.

Reality paints a very different story. In most relationships — instead of finding love and harmony — partners experience emotional difficulties and conflict with each other. When two people are attracted to each other there is obviously a lot more going on than what meets the eye.
If they are not aware that they bring their personal fears and insecurities into the partnership, the love, acceptance and trust between them will usually be conditional in its very nature. Their fears force them into particular behavioural strategies, designed to protect them from their fears being realised.

The person who is exposed to the strategies of their partner is expected to respond in a way that satisfies the fears held by them because if they do not they will be made responsible for how the strategic partner feels. If for instance one partner has a strategy to avoid criticism and judgement than the other cannot hold them responsible without risking conflict. To avoid this they have to change their behaviour to accommodate the partner's insecurities in order to make them feel safe. If they do not, they will be blamed and held responsible for how the strategic partner feels.

Our Higher Purpose

Feelings are like the alarm system of your mind. They are the communication your spirit mind uses to make you aware that there is conflict and disharmony between its essence — unconditional love — and the mind set that is your sense-of-self OR that both are in harmony.

This means that inner-disharmony will create negative life experiences, which will be sensed as negative feelings.
Inner- harmony will create positive life experiences, which will be sensed as positive feelings.
All feelings have the capacity to dominate your senses and thereby your mind. Your current state of perception and understanding is biased to believe that the event or the people that triggers your negative feelings are also responsible for them. Your most likely initial response will be to find fault with them and prove yourself innocent. In that moment it will not occur to you that you must have had a significant part to play in the creation of the event just like all the other participants. Your behaviour may be effective in temporarily influencing others to believe in your innocence but this will not stop it from happening again. The power that you may exercise by convincing another does nothing to release the causes within your mind responsible for your creation of the event.

The nature of spiritual reality is that you are responsible for creating and manifesting your experience of life — every relationship and event in your life. ***Nothing happens by accident or misfortune***. Accepting that you are the creator of your own experience of reality and therefore responsible also gives you the power to change your life by ***changing yourself***. It is this capacity for self-change that gives you control over your life. Once you have chosen to confront the negative aspects of your sense-of-self, understand them and released them, your life will automatically change in everyway.

Your feelings and emotions, perception and awareness will change the moment you do and as a consequence so will your decisions and choices. You will not lose you identity but naturally who you belief yourself to be, will be different — without fear. In the absence of your negative beliefs your true nature will begin to emerge layer by layer. You will become aware of this through how you feel in different situations and the changes you experience with others and how they relate differently to you. Releasing self-limiting beliefs is a decisive step, which will require you to discard your old fears and ultimately demands your faith in the innate integrity of the essence of your spirit. Each change brings transformation to your sense-of-self causing it to become more representative of your authentic self as it aligns itself progressively with unconditional love, trust and acceptance. Each cycle of change will bring you closer to being who you were always meant to be and provide greater freedom to fulfil your potential.

The power of intent plays a central part in your process of change. Intent is the central force in the beliefs that create your experience of life. The beliefs that make up your sense-of-self hold intents that control the manner in which you inhabit your life. By understanding the source of your intents — your self-beliefs — you can begin to take charge of your life. Change will not come by just wanting or wishing for it but you can make the first decisive step by consciously creating the intent to change by accepting responsibility for your present state of life whatever it may be. The intent created by conscious effort will begin to draw your energy and you mind into a pattern that will support the changes you need to make. Your intent will manifest a path along which the whole process can find reality.

Although it may seem we are no longer talking about love we are.
We can only create harmony in our selves by releasing the negative beliefs rooted in fear that separate us from being in a state of unconditional love. The capacity and the propensity to achieve this inner state of harmony is an innate in our being but once it gets lost, its recovery becomes an unconscious life quest.

> *The life journey we all take has the profound intent we evolve into conscious creators in harmony with our essence.*
>
> *Our search for Unconditional Love to experience the oneness with our Origin is the Core Inspiration for All Consciousness.*
>
> *It is the fire that fuels our creative expression and the fulfilment of our potential being.*

Chapter 3

The Beginning of Everything

The sensation of living and being alive begins with the first awareness of our embryonic consciousness of our self, our first breath, our first emotional sensation and first physical contact. We are at the very centre of our own experience of being conscious and alive and only we, through all of our senses, can know what it is like for us. No one can say what being 'us' is like because without exception, we are unique from one another and therefore our experience of conscious existence is individual and exclusive.

We create our experience of life from the way our consciousness translates the input from our senses — our emotional, physical and meta-senses. Each contributes to create a unique mosaic of emotional, intellectual and physical sensations that we come to call life. Living in a physical reality, we are most aware of our physical senses and they demand our greatest attention but that does not indicate that they are the most pervasive influence. That honour goes to our meta-senses, which are a part of the spiritual self, even though it feels furthest removed from our daily awareness. Its consistent influence has the ultimate intent to provide us with a sense of inner-harmony and oneness with all consciousness within the emotional framework of unconditional love, acceptance and trust. This part of our inner being is the key to our emotional and physical health and wellbeing and to evolving our consciousness to its potential. It plays a leading role in the how and why we create the kind of life we will live.

Our physical senses are our connection with material reality but how they are experienced will be different from person to person. The interpretation of the information that comes through our eyes and hearing, touch and taste and so on, will depend on what emotions the experience generates in us — how it makes us feel. Significantly, this can also give us the belief that our perceptions and feelings are totally produced by external forces.

It therefore appears that the most immediate and most powerful influence over our life are our emotions, as they seem to act as an irresistible force, driving our actions, reactions and choices. Our response to our fear-based emotions are mostly unchecked by our intellect and reasoning and therefore generally do not create the best outcomes. The expression of our emotions and behaviour creates an identity by which we know ourselves and others know us. It provides us with so called personality traits such as being shy or aggressive, withdrawn or extrovert, which in turn allows others to pigeonhole us as a certain type of personality. There are lots of reasons why our feelings and emotions have such a defining influence over us and this is particularly so when they are negative.

Controlled by Illusions

You could say that our emotions rule our life and this even applies to the most logical and intelligent of individuals. Often science-focused intellectuals tend to reject anything emotional, intuitive or instinctive in the belief they can only trust their logical reasoning as sound basis for understanding, analysis and choices. The exclusion of anything that cannot be scientifically quantified by their standards of objectivity restricts access to other vital and natural elements of their consciousness. This is in spite of the fact that major new discoveries are usually the product of intuition, fantasy, imaginations, dreams and inspirations. Frequently, the need for logic and supposed objectivity is driven by distrust of their own emotions, intuition and feelings. That does not mean however that our intellect with its capacity for reasoning and logic is not significant. Each aspect of our consciousness is meaningful within its purpose and needs to be used in balance with all others. Nothing is redundant in the expression of our consciousness, emotionally, mentally or physically. Trusting some and excluding others is indicative of an imbalance in its expression and this will ultimately manifest as issues in our lives.

Feelings and emotions can be divided into two extremes: on one side we have unconditional love of which trust, acceptance and belonging or being wanted are key elements. On the other there are all kinds of fears. Fear as a product of being excluded or separated from unconditional love, acceptance and trust will cause us become conditional in giving and receiving love. It is not possible to be in both emotional states simultaneously about the one thing — you cannot be critical about something and than say that you are accepting of it. Fear of every kind prevents us from being unconditional. In fact it is the very reason why we readily accept negative or painful emotional conditions as a part of life. If, for example, you have the fear of being rejected, you will also believe that there are conditions attached to your acceptance — you may than believe that you have to be good looking, smart or rich for instance.

Our feelings and emotions play an inescapable part in every aspect of our life — relationships, work, and leisure. Our capacity to deal with life becomes restricted when our emotions are negative and dominate our senses. If we were to give free expression to our negative emotions we run into trouble because they will potentially trigger negative responses in others — anger, shame and blame and so on. When you get angry or frustrated for example it is because you have emotional triggers for anger and frustration within you that can be activated by a situation or person in your environment. Once your angry feelings overtake your senses you are likely to be unaware of what is happening within you. Your attention will be totally consumed with what you believe to be the external causes for your feelings. In these moments you do not understand the reasons for your behaviour and responses. But, invariably our **behaviour is a response to our feelings**.

Not knowing the source for our feelings we tend accept that they are a dependable justification for our actions and choices. In the belief that our feelings tell us the truth, we find it easy to blame outside influences as the reason for our negative and positive feelings and the behaviour that follows. As a consequence, the idea that we may be the originators of our own life experiences is not even considered. A beautiful sunset can make us breathless with awe or be totally ignored. You can be deeply moved by a certain piece of music or be irritated by it. How is it we are all not equally affected by the same experience? There is more to this than the fact that we are unique from one another.

If we feel powerless and diminished because someone is abusing us and putting us down then it seems logical that they must be responsible for what we feel and react. Similarly, it is commonly believed that if one partner rejects another that the partner who does the rejecting — the aggressive one — is responsible for the suffering of the other — the passive one. It seems like an open and shut case. We usually believe that **one did it to the other** or vice versa. The result is the one who was left behind is judged to be the victim and the one that left the aggressor.

Our understanding of who is responsible for what we feel seems to indicate that our interactions with others generate our feelings. Should that be true, we should also have the power to make others feel the way we want but we know that this is not possible. We cannot deliberately make someone love, want or trust us when they have no intent to do so. The only way that might be achieved if we were to manipulate their perception of us by convincing them that we are the opposite of what they believe we are. However, emotional manipulation is not the same as directly creating feelings in someone and neither would constitute a genuine and sincere relationship. We are rooted in the habit of blaming others for our pain and suffering, anger and resentment and so on and consequently do not look for other explanations for our negative emotional experiences. Once your perception is locked into this mode it is difficult to realise that you are living in illusion

If others do not create our feelings and emotions then how and why do feelings become a part of us? What is the source of our feelings and why do they become such an intense experience when we go through negative situations involving others?

Our Relationship with Everyone and Everything

Whether we are aware of it or not, we are in a constant relationship with everyone and everything in the world —through our mental, physical, emotional or meta-senses. This becomes intense experience when we become involved in relationships with others, particularly if they are intimate. All of our relationships whether with the world in general or with people specifically are always subjective. The nature of our consciousness does not allow us to have purely objective relationships because we do not function in the absence of our emotional self, even though in some situations we like to believe that we can.

Our relationships range from the connection with our partner or child to that with a flower or a sunset, from friends and business colleagues to our pets. Our most significant relationship however, is the one we have with ourselves. It is not possible to connect with something without your emotions colouring the experience. It is not a conscious choice but a reflection of how human consciousness relates to itself and consequently to everything around it.

Regardless of whether we are attracted to or repulsed by something, or even indifferent to it there is always a deeper emotional reason for ***how and why*** we relate to it the way we do. We are generally not aware of the emotional filters that shape our perception and colour the way we see our selves and others. We need to become aware what these filters are and why they are a part of us in order to become aware of the true nature of who we believe we are. Developing this level of emotional and mental clarity demands that we make changes in our sense-of-self — ***who we believe ourselves to be***. The beliefs combined with our innate and unique nature, form our sense-of-self and ultimately determine our self-perception and how we see others. The belief systems that form our sense-of-self are at the core of why and how we create and experience our lives in our individual way.

Our judgment, responses, reactions and choices are not necessarily spontaneous or even a conscious choice. Much of what drives us in life is a product of what we have learned in childhood through our parents, our culture and other environmental influences. The sense that your feelings, thoughts, responses and choices are normal is a result of your inability to remember that you once were different from who you believe yourself to be right now.

The memory of who you truly are — the authentic and original nature of your being — has for most long left conscious memory.
How is it that we no longer know who we authentically are and meant to be? How and when did the true nature of who we are get lost?

In the absence of being and living as our authentic self, *we live life as aggressive or passive victims of an emotional environment of our own making.* Many struggle to find truth, meaning and happiness in their existence. It is not like that all the time but to a greater or lesser extent, we do not live life to the fullness of our potential. To discover the answers that can lead us out of this process, we need to look at the beginning of our existence, without judgment or guilt.

Your Innocent Arrival

We come into this world as unique spirits, as consciousnesses with innate and unique potentials, qualities and capacities that give us the capability to manifest a life that fulfils our aspirations and potentials. An attraction to rhythmic patterns and structures might lead to music or mathematics. A creative desire to build things may point to architecture, design or organisational talents. The possibilities are endless but it will commonly depend on the nature of the outside influences at the beginning of your life whether any of your innate capacities, talents and abilities will find realization.

Born as an individual consciousness with an innately unique nature, talents and abilities you have no awareness of what it all represents for you. You exist without knowing who or what you are and what you are truly capable of. In the absence of self-awareness and without a history of life experience, we lack a proven sense of ourselves in which we can have confidence and trust. We need to understand what our inner-identity represents in us and why. The absence of this level of awareness of who we are as a consciousness contributes to our mental and emotional vulnerability to outside influences.

We arrive in life with the innate need, entitlement and expectation for love and attention, support and approval, validation and guidance to learn and understand who we are to ourselves, others and the world.

The realisation of the sense of who we are needs to be experienced in a framework of unconditional love and acceptance, trust and belonging.

Our deepest and most primary emotional expectation is that we are **unconditionally loved and accepted, wanted and trusted** by those responsible for raising us — our mother and father. This expectation will be a determining influence for every response, action and choice you will make in your life because it will be defining of who you will believe yourself to be. The influence of unconditional love is so powerful that it will rule everyone's life. Ultimately you find yourself existing in harmony with it or living in contradiction to it.

The origin for this expectation is in the innate quality with which our spirit is endowed. It is the core vibration that brought us, our spirit, into conscious and individual being. It describes the nature of the source from which we came and it is therefore intrinsic in our human spirit. Regardless of what we may do in life or what our goals are, **we will always strive to exist in a state of unconditional love acceptance and trust or if denied, feel forced to accept a conditional version of this.** This is not something you consciously choose nor can you refuse to respond its incessant influence within you because it will always make its presence known and felt in your life.

The enormous negative effect the absence of unconditional love has on us is first of all demonstrated by our lifelong pursuit to try and find love, acceptance and trust that is **not** conditional. Our fear of rejection, exclusion, shame, guilt, embarrassment, inferiority, powerlessness, helplessness, being denied and so on are all emotional derivatives of **the absence of unconditional love and acceptance, being wanted and trust** within us. The circumstances and conditions in which love becomes **conditional**, determine the nature of the fears that generate our negative emotions that then become an unavoidable a part of our life experience.

The love referred to is not necessarily the love we associate with intimate relationships or romance although this is also an essential part of our experience of love. This love is much more than the love for another individual. This love encompasses **everything that is** and can only be experienced through your inner-self. **This love is unconditional in all respects to everyone and everything and can only begin by loving yourself unconditionally.** Once you release the fears that separate you from unconditional love, accept and trust you will be able to have an unconditional relationship with yourself and the world. Fear is at the foundation of all of your issues and by releasing the reasons for them you are creating ever-greater harmony within yourself.

We can only realize the nature of our issues if we recognize what they are and how they affect us. An emotional issue is much more than just a bad feeling or a horrible experience. On deeper levels every emotional issue is a product of fear. Even though it may be difficult to make the connection at this stage of your awareness, **all fears are essentially a result of being separated and excluded from unconditional love, acceptance and trust.** This is important to remember when you try to understand your issues and discover their origin.

It is a simple truth that every human being innately seeks to feel and experience unconditional love, acceptance and trust. When a child has no alternative but to accept conditional love as a substitute there will be unavoidable negative emotional consequences for its future. Whenever we do accept **conditional love, conditional acceptance and conditional trust**, they create inner-emotional conflicts, which manifest as emotional issues with oneself, others and the world. Our conditional relationship with love becomes the conditional relationship with our self. This forms our inner-identity that acts as a negative filter on the expression of our consciousness.

This raises the question; "How does this happen to us and why?"
To understand how we have come to be who we are today with all of our issues, we need to go back into our personal history — our childhood. **The external influences on the first 8 to 10 years of our life** shape the inner-foundation that will **determine the way we perceive ourselves and the world for the rest of our lives.**

The nature of our ego or sense-of-self is crucial to the way we will live and experience the rest of our lives. To take it one step further, how our sense-of-self evolves in childhood will be the source from which we will create our daily reality. What follows will explain exactly how that works and what the consequences are.

The Beginning of Fear

At birth, we have the innate expectation for unconditional love, acceptance and trust to continue just as it was a part of our spiritual state and then physically experienced as we grew in our mother's womb. For that to be a part of our new reality it is necessary for our parents to be unconditional in every aspect of their being and self-expression.

Before we go any further we need to try and understand what the actual capacity of the nature of unconditional love might be if it were the natural emotional and mental state of our consciousness.

The full extend of unconditional love is literally godlike in its magnitude and capacity and at this stage of our being beyond our capacity to conceive.
It is difficult to imagine what it would be like to be a state of unconditional acceptance of everything that is, in the absolute absence of all fears, no matter whether they are physical or emotional. Nothing, not even death, pain or any other kind of loss would generate fear or revulsion. Once you achieve that state of mind, your capacity to love, accept, trust, give and receive could become infinite in its capacity.

The underlying intent of your life journey is to fulfil the potential of your unique being. It is not likely that you will achieve this absolute "godlike" state in your lifetime and it is not necessary that you do. It is important that you hold the expansive destiny of your spirit in your awareness and appreciate the journey that will take you there. Regardless of it being a conscious choice or not, you are on this journey right now. The construct of the process by which we create and manifest our lives does not allow us to opt out. The reality is that if you are conscious, than you are also on the path of evolving your spirit self.

The origin for your fear based conditions start at home with your mother and father. Their inherited fears and insecurities are unintentionally passed on to you. If your mother and father were truly unconditional in every aspect of their being, you would have learned to be just like them. Should they have any fears and insecurities however, you will take them on as if they are your truth. Through being exposed to their fears and emotional issues you will form the nature of who you believe yourself to be — your sense-of-self.

The expression *sense-of-self* will be used throughout this book to make a distinction from the word ego, which has taken on a different meaning for many. (Someone with an ego is often deemed to be superior to others) Your sense-of-self is who you believe yourself to be — the inner picture you hold of your self to yourself, consciously or subconsciously.

From the moment of birth, the actions and reactions of a child are spontaneous and mostly driven by their physical needs. Even though helpless and powerless to fend for itself, it has no direct fears for its emotional or physical survival as long as it senses that its connection with its mother is secure. Throughout the first 9 months after inception, it was taken care of unconditionally by the mother's body. It is a period where the mother's body gives priority to physical needs of her unborn child, putting her own second. From the time of birth, it has the innate expectation for this unconditional experience — in the form of unconditional love acceptance, trust and support — to continue. With this expectation as its only innate reference point, a child begins to develop its sense-of-self through the emotional experiences it is exposed to through its parents and family environment.

There are a number of mental and emotional forces within its spirit that it must respond to because they are an inseparable part of the nature of its being. Besides the underlying drive to exist in harmony with unconditional love, it also seeks to create from its innate qualities and manifest its unique and different potentials. It is naturally driven to learn, to express itself in physical reality coupled with a strong drive to survive on both an emotional and physical level. A child wants to learn in any way it can — through the acquisition of knowledge, skills, experimentation, exploration and discovery — using all of its resources and senses. Motivated by the impulse to develop its capacity to exist independently, with an infinite mental, physical and emotionally curiosity and an irrepressible desire to learn.

You might say that the only condition a small child has for its relationship with its parents is that it will be raised, nurtured and guided with unconditional love, acceptance and trust and to be validated as its authentic self. In many ways there are no other expectations as it spontaneously and fearlessly launches itself into life. In a sense, it is the very reason, why young children get themselves into so much trouble with their parents. They act and express themselves without fear, judgment and expectations while the parents have conditions — justified or based in fear — for what they are prepared to accept from their child or not. It is also the reason why children need unconditional and unbiased guidance and support so that they do not have the feeling that they are being judged or unjustifiably restricted by those they depend on for their emotional and physical survival.

Unfortunately this is rarely the experience a child has. Most people are not aware enough or prepared to accept responsibility for their own emotional issues and to deal with them before they become parents. In fact, most do not like to admit that they have any emotional issues at all, let alone accept that they have affected their children negatively.

The Loss of Our Authentic Self

A child naively expects that unconditional love; acceptance and trust will be a consistent part of its new emotional environment. When its parents unconsciously set specific conditions for the child to be deserving of love or to be accepted it cannot understand the reasons and motivations for this. It senses the absence of unconditional love like you would a missing step on a staircase in the dark. As an adult, you have the advantage of your past experience with staircases and therefore you are able to determine that it is the staircase that is faulty but a child cannot.

The child does not have past experience, awareness or insight to draw on. It feels that its spontaneous authentic self has failed to meet the conditions that it has to fulfil if it is to be loved and accepted. Unable to determine who or what is responsible for this feeling, it concludes that it must be to blame. Believing that the fault must lie with **whom and what it is** it searches for an explanation within its very limited experience and knowledge. Lacking the awareness to separate *who it is* from its negative emotional experience, it assumes that something must be wrong with *who it is*. Limited by its lack of self-awareness a child cannot do anything other than believe that the conditions the parents set are a statement of disapproval, rejection and judgment of *who it is*. It is blind to the fact that the parent's conditional behaviour is a product of their issues.

Exclusion from unconditional love through rejection and judgment may seem to be insignificant but it has the capacity to create deep and fundamental trauma and fears in child and adult alike. Born without fear, with the innate trust and confidence that it can unconditionally depend on its fundamental emotional and physical life support systems — its parents — the child now plunges into a new and unknown emotional state — **fear**.

Imagine unconditional love to be an intrinsic part of your being without which your existence has no core intent or focus. The conditions set by your parents cause you to be separated from it, because you can no longer trust them to be your emotional support any more. This creates a chasm between your sense of being and unconditional love you expect which then becomes like a distant island. You have now lost trust and therefore access to your core essence and the only option you have is to build a bridge across the void to find love within the conditions your parents have set. It feels that this is the only way you can experience love even though you do not realize that it is conditional. Now love, acceptance and trust have to come from outside of you — from others. You feel that your innate entitlement to receive it, as an intrinsic part of your sense-of-self, can no longer be trusted or depended on. The kind of love you ultimately settle for is totally dependent on the conditions that your parents and in the future others set for you.

As adults, we can easily relate to our fear for our physical survival but our emotional survival fears are more difficult to grasp and understand. The most likely explanation for this is that we live and express ourselves with different levels of emotional fear most of the time. Many of these fears are in a general sense shared with others allowing us to normalise them as an acceptable and common part of the human psyche. We often use this as a way to justify our feelings and thereby our issues. It is not uncommon for someone to say; "But no one likes to be alone" or "Everyone fears rejection" or "Everyone has troubles in their relationships" and so on. Though there may be truth in these statements, it does nothing to solve our personal emotional issues.

Each time the spontaneous authentic child feels that its spontaneous and natural being is invalidated, judged or rejected more fears are internalised. Before long the authentic self is pushed aside, dismissed and distrusted. In the absence of trust in its authentic self, it will not have a chance to unfold its potential through its progress in life. A fear based conditional self has taken its place not just as an emotion but also as a part of its sense-of-self. The authentic-self and its spontaneous self-expression have now become something to fear and suppress to avoid the repercussions the child has learned to expect.

Something truly dramatic has happened to the child psyche but it went completely unnoticed by its parents. No one seems to be able to see the destruction of the unconditional and authentic self of the child and the appearance of fear. How could this happen and why?

Chapter 4

The Power and Influence of Parenting

*As a child, your sense-of-self is shaped
by the emotional environment created by your parents
When you become a parent
your sense-of-self will become the environment
that shapes the minds of your children.*

There is no escaping the fact that parents are a major influence in the psychological and emotional development of their children. Their responsibility is not just in being the caretakers and providers but also in establishing certain values, standards and principles for their children to live by. **Self-discipline and responsibility, accountability and a strong sense of consequence are essential qualities for a productive and positive experience of life.** The personality of the parents represented by their behaviour and attitude is the most immediate influence on their child. Other elements such as the values set by their religion, culture and nationality or their absence all play a role but are initially always presented through the personalities of those involved with a child.

Parents have a much greater influence on their children than most would be willing to accept and many are resistant to the idea that they may have a decisive responsibility for the way their child turns out. Their good intentions are usually confused with the actuality of the emotional paradigm they created with their fears and insecurities. They usually do not realize the influence they have on their children when they play out their relationship dynamic between each other in their presence.

Most parents would not be able to tell what part of their child's personality represents its authentic self and what part it has taken on from them and the family environment. The main reason for this lies in their lack of awareness of the nature of their **own** issues. Obscured by their fears and issues, they are unlikely to know their own **authentic nature** therefore do not recognize it in their own children. Not conscious of the origin of their issues, parents are unaware that their perception is distorted, which makes having an objective and clear perspective extremely difficult if not impossible.

Many couples already become parents when they are still in the infancy of their relationship with each other. Not only do they have little or no real awareness of the true nature of their partner, each has not as yet a true understanding of them selves. The problems generally begin when we choose to commit ourselves to someone without knowing what drives our own attraction and choice. We are convinced that our attraction is love when we have no understanding of our own internal relationship with love acceptance and trust. ***It is an illusion to think that you can know someone else if you do not even understand yourself.***

The absence of the extended family structure also makes it unlikely that a young woman is aware of the demands that being a mother will place on her and what she will have to change in her life as a consequence. Similarly, the boy who is to become the father is often not ready for the responsibilities of fatherhood, not to mention the change in emotional focus that will occur in his partner as a result of becoming a mother.

We need to be clear that this is not about the lack of good intentions or the desire to bring a child into the world. Their own issues and those with others and the world will ultimately determine the experience their child will have of itself and the world it perceives. Parents raising their first child will discover that it is as much an emotional challenge and learning curve for them as it is a testing time for their child.

For example, should a mother feel powerlessness in life, be generally insecure and fearful, she would have a tendency to worry and be anxious. As a consequence her behaviour with her baby may appear to be very protective and caring but she is unconsciously creating an environment driven by her fears and worries. A first time father, who resents losing the attention of his partner because of the time she gives to her child instead of to him, is unconsciously competing and his child will sense this.

The change a newborn child brings into a relationship can bring up issues in each individual and these can become the source for conflict between them. The emotional state that this will cause in each of them will shape the emotional environment of the family and also become part of the child's emotional experience. The assumption made by many is that because the arguments are not about the child or directed at it that this therefore should not be an issue. They do not recognize that their child develops specific conclusions to protect itself through being exposed to emotional or physical conflict. Even if it is not the target, the experience of physical or verbal aggression and abuse will have a life-changing impact on the formation of a child's mind.

Trapped by Conditional Love

Our emotions and feelings dominate and control nearly all of our actions, responses and choices. As emotional beings, people do not change because they become parents. Parenting makes demands on them, which challenge their state of mind because of the issues they have. In many respects, they unwittingly replicate the family environment they grew up in even though it may not have been their intent. This becomes even more complicated when you consider that the partner they chose is likely to be an emotional representation of one or both of their parents. When all these elements are activated through parenthood the consequences this will have on the child become unavoidable.

Initially a child does not know how to be anything other than itself and it therefore expresses itself without an emotional agenda — spontaneously and unconditionally. The parent however cannot make the same claim. They have already made the same journey with their parents that their child is about to make with them. When they grew up, they were exposed and influenced by the fears, issues and problems of their parents. Just like their child, they did not have a frame of reference to understand what they were exposed to and why and therefore assumed that it was normal. Now they can all but act and react to their emotional fears and insecurities because they feel as if they are a natural and unchangeable part of their personality. They therefore accept the negative emotions and feelings this brings up without thinking to question their own behaviour. In addition they are convinced that their negative feelings, reactions and experiences are caused by others or outside forces. By accepting this as the truth they do not only avoid responsibility for their own life experiences but also how the expression of their fears affect their children. They do not realise that thereby they teach their children to believe that they are also the victims of others and their environment.

Through their experience of childhood, the sense-of-self of an individual has two aspects:
Part One is the original and authentic self that was disapproved of by their parents.
Part Two is the mind that holds beliefs that it has to meet the conditions set by the parent's fears and insecurities.

Each parent, just like every child, came into the world with the full capacity of their spontaneous life force and potential and the innate expectation of unconditional love, acceptance and trust intact. Between birth and adulthood they learned to suppress it and now they are no longer who they were originally meant to be. Without the parents undergoing personal change, the destiny of their child is in fact written by their own emotional family history.

Unseen Influences

We have an incredible list of descriptions for all of our fears, issues and insecurities depending on their nature and origin.
Being unlovable, unacceptable, unwanted, mistrust, distrusted, not good enough, anger, resentment, rejection, exclusion, abandoned, judged, criticised, self-critical, guilty, jealousy, envy, embarrassment, shame, impatience, aggression, self-doubt, doubt, inferiority, worthlessness, being without value, insignificance, not of any consequence, undesirable, unattractive, ugly, powerless, helpless, weak, insecure, blamed, accused, deceived, manipulated, suspicious, disbelieving, and there are more.
All are negative emotional states that can be a part of us for because of the absence of unconditional love. The common base for all of these negative states is always fear. Even though we may only feel our issues in specific situations or with certain people, they have never the less become a typical emotional part of our mind and consequently our sense-of-self.
The question is: How have these negative emotional states become such a persistent and intrinsic part of us and why do we keep experiencing them in the same situations and with the same people usually in the same way?

A child sense-of-self is formed by the endorsement or disapproval of its authentic self within the framework of its innate expectation to be unconditionally loved, accepted, trusted and wanted. A child will perceive an abrupt or aggressive criticism or dismissal of its needs as a rejection of its innate expectations and will potentially experience it as a personal rejection. The emotions it feels in that moment do not harmonise with its need for unconditional love and acceptance and instead creates the feeling that it is being rejected or abandoned. In that instant it can sense that its innate expectation for unconditional love and acceptance is denied and instead feels the separation from unconditional love, acceptance and trust. Limited in its capacity to reason and discern who is responsible for what, it believes itself to be the cause for what is it experiences. Over time a child will come to the inevitable conclusion that there must be something wrong with it for it to be judged, blamed or rejected by its parent. Its innate expectation and need for unconditional love and acceptance is now challenged by feelings of fear.

The child's dilemma lies in its innate need to trust in unconditional love, acceptance and trust as its core inner-value versus the more direct and physically experienced support, protection and care promised by its parents which is coloured by fear. It has to choose between the physical experience and its as yet unconfirmed sense of being. Even though the love and acceptance from its mother and father are conditional, they are tangible and fulfil immediate physical if not emotional needs. Imperfect as they may be by being conditional, they still provide support for their child's emotional and physical survival even though it will be distorted. The child's immature state assures that it has a need to depend on the emotional, psychological and energetic bonds that exist between mother and child. The conditions placed on the expression of its spontaneous and authentic self makes a child feel threatened that love and acceptance (support) will be withdrawn. It is almost inevitable that its need for emotional and physical survival will cause it to choose to accept the conditions created by its parent's fears and insecurities. Unfortunately, this choice is not without deep emotional and potentially physical consequences and these are likely to affect a child over its lifetime.

We need to dispel the idea that only gross acts of verbal abuse, violence, aggression, exclusion, manipulation can have a negative emotional impact on a child. This idea creates the illusion that if we were never subjected to anything remotely violent or abusive, our childhood must have been 'normal' and this is simply not true. Based on this assumption we should not have any issues if we had a 'normal' family with 'normal' parents who gave us a 'normal' upbringing. This also implies that if you do have issues you must have been born with them.

This perspective creates a number of problems on what to do if you experience emotional issues in your life. If you have convinced yourself that you do not have any issues and others are to blame you can be sure that you are wrong. If you believe that you were born with them it follows that they must be an indivisible part of you, you would be wrong again. If you believe and accept that you were not born with your issues and you acquired them from others as you grew up, you are right. Since you issues are learned, then you can also 'unlearn' them and this makes a real and permanent resolution is possible.

Take a family where both mother and father have an issue with expressing their emotions because they have learned as children that it is embarrassing, inappropriate and confronting for others. They therefore see the display of both joyful exuberance and negative emotions as highly inappropriate and undesirable. As a result, each parent does not only do their best to avoid making an emotional spectacle of themselves but also actively suppresses the emotional voice of their children. Their children learn very early to contain and suppress exuberant joy and happiness and other feelings emotions. Particularly emotions that are negative or aggressive in nature because they are most feared by their parents. When still very young, their spontaneous self-expression was already unwelcome and made wrong. The rejection of their naïve emotional self was felt as a rejection of **who they are as a consciousness**. It would have felt as if there was no choice but to accept the conditions for emotional expression set by their parents.

A child will interpret these conditions to mean that openly expressing its emotions — negative or positive — make it unacceptable, an imposition, shameful even aggressive. Convinced that it will only be worthy of its parent's acceptance and love if it does not confront and burden them with its emotions a child will begin to suppress itself. It feels no longer free to give a voice to its true feelings and its fear and insecurities. Unconsciously, the child will develop a deep critical distrust of its own emotions and the innate impulse to give expression to itself because it becomes convinced that they make him or her unacceptable. It is in constant fear that it will be guilty of being an embarrassment and provoke judgment and rejection. It is not difficult to imagine that it will grow up to be an emotionally closed and inaccessible adult whose sense of guilt and shame prevents it from being emotionally present and expressive.

No one in this family yelled and screamed or used any physical violence. In fact it was quite the opposite; both parents never made a display of what they really felt and on the surface they seem to get on really well. Without any form of open conflict or affection to point at, it may seem that there is nothing in childhood that we can hold responsible for the issues their children experience as adults.

Yet, the reality is that there was an intense emotional conflict fought by the child's unformed consciousness. Without a voice, without power and influence its innate entitlement of freedom of self-expression fights with feelings of guilt and shame. From the outset, it fought a losing battle but its loss will become a lifelong quest for the recovery of unconditional love and acceptance, trust and feeling wanted. Once it has moved from childhood through teenagehood into adulthood, *it will unconsciously seek to return to a state of inner harmony with unconditional love, acceptance and trust*. This will be an overwhelming force in its life, an intent that will underpin all of its self-expression, actions and choices and the challenge it seeks to overcome.

The Nature of Your Sense-Of-Self

Our sense-of-self or ego is central to the function of our mind and consciousness and therefore appears in many of the explanations that are given here. We think that we know who we are until we scrutinise our conclusions and then realise that much of what we believe to be true is in reality just a collection of assumptions and beliefs. You may wonder whether it really matters if something has a basis of truth or that it is enough that you believe it to be true. You will discover that the difference can in fact be life changing. If your beliefs do not reflect the true nature of your spiritual, emotional and physical reality, everything that flows from these beliefs will distort your experience of reality. The perception of your self and the world, behaviour and judgement, choices and emotions and so on will in many ways be illusionary. The beliefs that support your issues will delude you into living life under the spell of illusions. Questioning the nature of your belief systems is like asking; *what is real about me and what is not?*

Let us go back to the family where the parents cannot cope with negative and positive emotional expression and therefore passively suppress this in their children. These children are made to believe that negative emotions such as discontent, disagreement, unhappy feelings and even exuberant joy and happiness are undesirable, bad and embarrassing emotions to reveal and display. Lacking the capacity to understand or judge, they are left no choice but to accept the reasons for their parent's judgement. Even though these distorted values only operate within their family, daily exposure to their parent's consistent fearful behaviour acts to cement this attitude as an emotional reality.

Living by these illusionary beliefs will have severe consequences for their future. It will alter their sense of who they are, their perception, the nature of their awareness, their emotional self-expression, their decisions and choices and their intent in life. Generally, they will not be conscious that they are playing out their childhood history. It will affect their relationships and their choice of partner who needs to be similarly afraid of being confronted with emotions. Their fear and guilt for openly expressing their emotions will also be experienced in the work place and in friendships. Deeper analysis of the environment and people they will be attracted to would show that they are likely to choose people who have similar issues.

The influence and power that fear has over us is the primary reason for our readiness to accept the conditions placed on us at an early age. Unable to understand what the underlying intent behind the behaviour of our parent is, we accept and feel guilt or powerlessness in our relationship with them. Should we not conform to the conditions as expected, we sense the potential for rejection or abandonment. This implies separation from the unconditional love we innately depend on for emotional balance and inner stability and believe should be ours to receive. **The realisation that unconditional love, acceptance and trust can be withdrawn becomes the fundamental cause for our fears.**

Our individual interpretation of the conditional behaviour of the parent makes the fear we experience unique to us, as are the beliefs we take on. The circumstances, particular consequences and the intent in which the fear is wrapped become the foundations for the negative beliefs that will shape our sense-of-self. With the understanding that our authentic self does generally not meet our parent's expectations we feel we cannot trust it anymore and begin to reject and suppress its presence in us. The conditions we accept form our belief systems that become our identity. Not only do we then begin to accept a distorted sense of who we are but **we also set ourselves up for what can become a lifelong inner-conflict — our illusionary and distorted sense-of-self versus our unique and authentic self.**

A family dynamic promotes the expression of unique standards and values, concepts and convictions and so children are exposed to a wide variety of belief systems that are potentially conditional. Collectively, these negative belief systems create an emotional environment that will shape their view of themselves and how they believe they need to be in the world. They are unlikely to have a clear recollection later in life as to how they came to be this way in the first place. Most will accept that because they feel worthless they actually must be or if we feel dumb it proves we lack intelligence. We are so convinced that what we feel represents the truth about us.

If for instance our parents show disappointment in us because we fail to meet their expectations than we will accept that we are responsible for being the disappointment. If our parents cannot express love and affection in an emotionally tangible way to us, we are very likely to believe that we are unlovable, unacceptable and undesirable. Should our parents resent being parents because are more concerned with themselves, each other or work, we are likely to accept the belief that we are insignificant, uninteresting and that we do not matter. Not only do we believe that we are what we feel but we will also develop behaviour that is a product of the negative sense-of-self we identify with. It is very likely that your parents experienced their childhood in a similar emotional family environment to the one they present you with. The strategic behaviours we adopt are an extension of our negative beliefs and come to define our external personality. Our feelings and behaviour commonly make up who we believe we are and are expressed without a question or thought.

Trusting Fear

Ideally, in the early period of our life, we evolve our inner-identity from the innate and unique elements of our authentic self under an umbrella of unconditional love and acceptance and so on. This would create an environment where we can freely express our potential and allow us to evolve the full capacity and power of our consciousness. However, this is generally not the case.

Raised with the fears and insecurities of your parents, you create a sense-of-yourself that has its roots in fear. These fears will be very real and because you feel them and manifest them in your life. The experience they create will convince you that they are based in truth. When you begin to trust your negative beliefs to be true, you are deceiving yourself that the experiences you create have a real foundation. What you manifest, as a negative experience, **will feel very real but is ultimately illusionary** because the beliefs that underpin it have no foundation in truth. Fear is an extremely powerful emotion that implies that we are in some kind of danger and therefore it will consistently demand our attention, making it central to our focus in life. It urges us to respond to its call by implying we will risk our emotional survival if we were to ignore it.

For convenience we can divide our sense-of-self into two different areas. The authentic unique nature of who we are and the belief systems it attains through its experience with our parents, family and the world. All beliefs we accept will either harmonise with the core nature of our authentic self and thereby have their validity endorsed or prove to be in contradiction with it. The relationship that develops between you and your parents will become conditional for you, if they are controlled by their fears and insecurities. The conditions you perceive exist in order to be loved and accepted will cause you to suppress and distrust your authentic sense-of-self. You will change your behaviour in order to accommodate your parent's fears and become acceptable to them. Acceptance of their fear based conditions will seem to be the only way you can ensure a level of emotional and often physical support.

This state of mind will create inner conflict because your initial expectations — to be unconditionally loved, accepted and trusted — were not met. You are pushed into a state of inner-disharmony and conflict because your primary expectations were invalidated by your parent's fear-based conditional behaviour. This leaves you with little or no choice but to accept their fear based reality as your truth. In accepting responsibility for their fears you will formulate your emotional experiences into understandings or beliefs that will determine the sense you will have of yourself — who you will come to believe you are. This newly realized negative part of your sense-of-self puts you into conflict with your self and it will become the source for fearful, negative and painful experiences and feelings. You must resolve your inner-disharmony in order dissolve your fear and pain and thereby become who you were meant to be. Your constant sense of being in fear and un-fulfilled will cause you to try and find inner harmony throughout your life — to be at one with unconditional love. How you do this will be decisive in your personal growth.

The reasons that your parents are not perfect as people are the same as why **you** are not. They were exposed to the same negative forces in their childhood, which they have unknowingly played out on you. It is therefore pointless to blame your parents and hold them responsible for your issues because if you are a victim of their issues then they were a victim of their parent's issues. Since *you are the only one that has the power to change who you are*, you must accept responsibility for the negative events you have created through the beliefs you hold. You actually do not have a choice if you do not want to live with your emotional issues — your fears.

Do not think that your negative beliefs attached themselves to you; *you have attached yourself to them*. They became your means to overcome your fear of rejection, exclusion, being unacceptable, not good enough, unlovable, distrust and so on. Unconsciously you have made them your life support system and a part of your sense-of-self. You can only transcend your issues by accepting them and acknowledging that your beliefs are your responsibility.
Trying to change others will not change you and blame and accusation will only serve to keep you locked in your illusionary fears and an issue filled life.

Chapter 5

The Power of Belief Systems

The power that our beliefs have over our minds is quite incredible but mostly not well understood. The extent to which they control our lives is difficult to recognize and accept because their influence is so seamless and invisible. By the time we are in our teenage years we have already learned to suppress and dismiss the innate and spontaneous expression of our authentic self.

We do not realize that many of our likes and dislikes, behaviours and responses are a product of our negative belief systems. None of this would be of any concern if it were not for the fact that on balance many of our beliefs are founded in fear. We therefore tend to behave and respond more out of fear than self-trust. The reason negative beliefs are such a powerful influence on us lies in their capacity to convince us that we cannot survive the consequences that our fears imply exist.

One of the main reasons why we do not recognize our fears for what they really are is that *they feel as if they represent who we are* — our identity. Fear creates the illusion that it is keeping us safe from the disastrous consequences implied by our negative beliefs. If, for example you have the fear that others will not like you, you will anticipate rejection and exclusion. You might do anything you can to make them like and accept you by pleasing them and not presenting your self as the person you think you are. Instead you try to be what you believe others want you to be to make yourself acceptable.

The question is; does it really matter and is it worth the stress and anxiety it creates in you and will it really make an actual difference in your life? When fear is a major driving force in the beliefs that form our sense-of-self, it changes our presence in the world. It alters *our perception of who we are* and our belief of *who we are to others*. Once our negative beliefs control us it is difficult if not impossible to differentiate *who we really are from who we are not* because of the influence fear has over us.

We have all woken up from an upsetting or terrifying dream in a sweat with our hearts racing even though we were safe in our beds. We know that these terrifying dreams are manifested by our minds and are thus our creations but when we are dreaming it feels very real. They affect us emotionally and physically as if we are living a real threat or drama. The physical response to a dream experience or for that matter an illusion exposes that we are convinced that what we are going through is real. We may on reflection dismiss our dream episode as just a dream but we cannot dismiss our physical and emotional response to it.

We do not realize that the fear-based beliefs that we have learned rely on to save us from our fears are also responsible for producing our negative life experiences. Our fears stop us from recognizing that the reality that we create with our fears are actually are founded in illusions. The powerful influence that fear has over our perception and emotions convinces us that what we hear, see and feel must represent the truth and therefore reality. The potential consequences portrayed by our fears insure that they will never be ignored. As a result we lose the capacity to distinguish emotional illusions from reality.

Negative beliefs have the capacity to be so overwhelmingly persuasive in their influence on our perception that alternative choices remain invisible to us. The potency that fear gives to a belief invalidates any other option for understanding, feeling and perception. As part of our sense-of-self, our beliefs determine for us who we are and thereby shape the perception of the nature and value of our being. Fear alters our inner-identity so that our self-expression, perception and emotional priorities no longer support the authentic nature of our sense-of-self. Instead it will be in conflict with the core values of our consciousness — unconditional love acceptance and trust.

If, for example, you hold the belief that you do not matter then in your perception of yourself, you do not matter to yourself and you will believe that others think you do not matter. Through your behaviour you will either try and convince others that you do matter and are significant or you will accept your insignificance as the truth of who you are and live your life accordingly. The same applies if you believe you are worthless, powerless, unlovable, unwanted and so on. Each of these negative beliefs form your sense of your self and become representative of how you live your life, conduct relationships and deal with difficulties and obstacles. The beliefs that make up your sense-of-self will determine how you are generally present in the world — in a positive and in a negative sense.

We acquire our negative sense-of-self generally in the first eight to ten years of our childhood. We will begin to define who we are by what we are told about ourselves as early as the first 4 or 5 years of life. If criticism at home has made us to believe that we are dumb, a disappointment or inadequate, our self-confidence will be affected as soon as we start school. Our lack of self-trust will convince us that we will not be able to understand the lessons we are taught. What we have learned from our family about who we are will cause us to anticipate rejection, failure and so on at a very early age. Take a girl, who is criticised for her appearance and has never been appreciated or praised by her parents for her unique presence and what she brings into the world. She will believe she has no value and nothing to contribute. She will feel and experience her low self-esteem as soon as she is exposed to her peer group. Lacking self-confidence as she matures, she is likely to suffer the consequences created by her negative self-beliefs on a daily basis in her friendships, work and intimate relationships.

How Fear Conditions the Mind

In a perfect world, our conscious spirit arrives in the world with a raft of qualities that represent our authentic and unique self. In the very first part of its life its original self is expressed without fear or self-judgement. Unconditionally and spontaneously revealing its truth by adding the dimension of its unique self to every form of self-expression. It fearlessly shows that although we have a central origin we are at the same time different from one another in often subtle, yet significant ways. Over the term of our life, our unique authentic self becomes a substantial aspect of our being because it demands fulfilment by the very nature of its existence in us. Fear stops this from happening.

We are exposed to the process by which we create our reality as soon as we open our eyes. Babies and young children lack the capacity to know the consequences of their judgement and choices. The opportunity to deal with our issues usually only presents itself later in life, when we have reached a level of emotional maturity and self-realisation. Logically, no child consciously chooses to grow up in the absence of love, conditional acceptance and trust but when this is the case, they will manifest the consequences of this throughout their lives.

A belief that forms a part of ***your sense-of-self*** can be negative or positive in respect to your idea of who you are. We are born with the innate expectation and need is to exist and express our authentic self in harmony with unconditional love, acceptance and trust. This congruency is crucial to the fulfilment of our innate potential and growth as a conscious spirit. When the beliefs that form our sense-of-self are founded in fear, we unconsciously choose to live our life conditionally — in fear. The result is that we will put the conditions we have learned to accept on the way we express our emotions and needs, choices and decisions and so on. We unwittingly severely restrict our field of creative expression thereby suppressing our authentic self and limiting the fulfilment of our potential. Our conditional sense-of-self will live in conflict with our authentic nature until we find resolution by releasing the fear-based negative belief systems that control us.

You can only live in harmony with unconditional love if the beliefs that form your sense-of-self are in congruence with it. Once your sense-of-self is in harmony with *the essence of your being*, it will seem as if you have no ego because one will be transparent to the other. Your sense-of-self and spiritual essence will essentially have the same core values and intent. Your self-expression, creativity, behaviour and choices will be spontaneous and without ulterior motives or fear. Your personal truth, feelings and emotions will have a voice free from fear of judgement and rejection and life can be lived as a self-responsible process. Each act of releasing fear-based beliefs will increase your inner-harmony, allowing you to reach this state progressively.

The most significant aspect of a parent and child relationship is the manner with which parents judge and then react to what is essentially their child's innocent and spontaneous behaviour. The intent for how they respond to their child will determine the experience the child will have of itself in respect to the event. Whether their child grows up with issues or without always depends on the issues and fears played out by the parents. The difficulty lies in the fact that if these were not dealt with prior to them becoming parents, it is almost inevitable that their parenting role will be contaminated by their fears. Their issues will become an intrinsic part of the relationship dynamic they develop with their children. It is an illusion to think that becoming a parent will somehow automatically release you from your emotional issues because you have the intent to love and accept your child no matter what. Once your issues have become part of your sense of self, they will dictate who you are and how you behave. You cannot help but play your fears and insecurities out in every part of your life, particularly as a parent and a partner.

Even though we are taught to not to trust our innate expectation to be unconditionally loved and accepted, this same innate need and desire to feel and experience love and acceptance, makes us accept a conditional version of this. We cannot imagine our existence without love and acceptance, being wanted and trusted and so we feel we have no choice but to accept the conditions we are presented with. The fears and insecurities our parents display in response to our unique and authentic self convince us that it cannot be trusted or depended on. We learn to believe and expect that if we were to give it free expression, it will provoke a negative reaction from our parents and later from others. The resulting fear of rejection and judgement causes us suppress our unique authentic nature to ensure that we never expose it. Instead, we learn to depend on negative beliefs — our fears — that tell us not only **<u>who</u> to be** but also **<u>how</u> to behave and express ourselves, <u>how</u> to be lovable, acceptable and trustworthy**. These behavioural strategies are subconsciously created and accepted in response to the negative emotional experiences with our caretakers in early life. They appear to hold the promise of keeping us safe from rejection and judgment and the potential for being loved and accepted. The actual effect on us is opposite to what we expect.

These are some examples: A parent who angrily reprimands his or her child because they are irritated by the noise they make whilst playing, does not realise that they are holding the child responsible for *their* feelings of annoyance. Instead of owning their annoyance and irritation, they blame the child and convince it that *<u>it is</u> the annoyance and irritation*.
A mother that blames her child for embarrassing her is not aware that *<u>she</u>* is not taking responsibility for her own shame and that she is making her child believe that *<u>it is</u> the cause for her embarrassment*. In accepting this, **her child becomes the shame and embarrassment**.
A father who criticises his son for not meeting his expectations does not see that as the creator of these expectations, he can only be responsible for fulfilling them and can therefore only be the cause his own disappointment. Instead **he blames his son for his feelings of disappointment**, thereby convincing his child that **<u>he is</u> the disappointment**.
A mother or father who has difficulty coping with life and just looking after them selves will be even more stressed having to look after their offspring. Their fears cause them to prioritise their need for fulfilment and security over that of their children. They will sense that their existence, and the expression of their innate needs and expectations are the *cause* for this stress and anxiety and conclude that they must be the cause. By accepting responsibility for their parent's fears and insecurities, **they also subconsciously accept that their innate needs and expectations as well as the expression their unique being are responsible for causing their parents stress and worry**.

To avoid the guilt their parent's issues create in them, they begin to suppress what are ultimately natural needs and expectations for a child to have. By doing so they try to be what they believe their parents expect them to be — children without needs and expectations, compliant and submissive. Not even their innate need for love and acceptance is allowed to find a voice in this environment and so this also needs to be suppressed. In their fear of being a burden to their parents, they often make a concerted effort to be emotionally and physically independent and self-sufficient. They grow up unable to express their needs and expectations or to ask others for help, support or advice. They avoid displaying issues or anything that might potentially upset their parents or others to avoid the guilt of being a burden — the cause for stress, anxiety or worry. This includes the fear of expressing love and the desire to receive it. As a result, they will inherit many of their parent's fears and insecurities, which later in life will become a negative emotional force in their relationships and parenting. This state of mind will deny them the capacity to live life to the fullest potential of their unique and authentic self.

Regardless of whether it comes from a place of inner-harmony or inner-conflict, a child will usually accept its parent's emotional expression and behaviour unconditionally as "truth and reality". A child lacks the experience and capacity to judge its parent's behaviour and attitude. When parents make their child feel wrong or judge it to be a failure it naively believes and accepts that it is responsible. It concludes that it is to blame for not meeting the conditions its parents set in their relationship. Most parents do not realise that their behaviour and attitude are a psychological mirror in which their children try to recognise and evolve who they are, their value and worth. If parents distort the relationship with their children with their own fears and insecurities they will unwittingly create erroneous perceptions in their children that become the conditional beliefs that will define their sense-of-self for the rest of their life.

Chapter 6

The Origin of Your Feelings

Our feelings are not just a product of random sensations generated by our mind, thoughts or behaviour. They have a definitive origin and reason for being a significant part of the emotional experience we call life. It is hard to imagine living life without feelings particularly when it often seems as if our emotions control every action and choice we make.

The influence our feelings and emotions have over our choices and behaviour is much greater than most of us would like to admit. No matter how objective we believe we are when it comes down to the line absolute objectivity is difficult to maintain. It is safer to accept that true objectivity does not exist for a human being than to assume that you can be objective. This way you are not deluding yourself and you have a chance to measure with clarity the true level of your objectivity.

The truth is that at the core of our being we are biased because of our innate expectation to be ***unconditionally loved and wanted, accepted and trusted***. Our spirit seeks constantly to be in balance between this innate intent and the state of our subconscious and conscious mind. This innate intent is like the force of gravity in that it creates a bias for our mind to incessantly seek harmony with these core values of our spirit. The result is that generally, all of our self-expression, actions and choices revolve around creating harmony between our mind and our spirit in our life. In spite of all of the fears and insecurities we have accepted as true and valid, we are still controlled by this intent and our desire to exist in this state of harmony. The effect of fear-based emotions causes us to search for the solutions for our problems in the world rather than within our self.

Some of our earliest awareness of feeling is the emotional sensation we have when we experience unconditional love etc.— ***harmony*** — or conditional love etc — ***disharmony***. Should we not feel unconditionally supported and accepted by the environment we arrive in we begin feel disharmony and instinctive fear for our emotional and physical survival. This is usually because our mother or father is playing out their fears and insecurities or perhaps exposure to other circumstances not directly under their control. We, in our naïve state, do not have the ability to understand or analyse what we is exposed to. Instead we will assume that the reason for discord is somehow our fault and by default, we accept responsibility in the form of guilt.

The Inception of Feeling

Fundamentally there are only three types of feelings — feelings that are generated by ***unconditional love and acceptance or*** those rooted in ***fear or conditional love and acceptance.*** We can also have feelings by being exposed to experiences to which we have no attachment. Every feeling will be a derivative of these. Given that our sense-of-self has a biased expectation to exist in harmony with unconditional love and our fears are in contradiction with that, we have all the elements for inner-conflict. The belief systems that make up our sense-of-self divide themselves in the same way —positive beliefs are in alignment with unconditional love and negative, fear-based beliefs set the stage for conditional love and acceptance.

Beliefs that resonate in harmony with unconditional love, acceptance and trust create positive events and generate positive feelings and reflect your innate intent and expectation to exist and be at one with the core values of your spirit.

Fear based belief systems manifest negative events and therefore generate negative feelings because they contradict the core values of your spirit. What you feel on the surface as anger, powerlessness, loss or loneliness and so on is on the deepest level of your being a result of your alienation from unconditional love, acceptance and trust. Your feelings create the perception that unconditional love and acceptance are unattainable.

When Fear is in Control

Once negative beliefs are a part of our sense-of-self they take control. The moment we experience a facsimile of the original experience that created them, the original fear will activate your negative beliefs and you will act them out. It is almost as if you have no choice in the matter. If for example, you have unresolved issues because of being raised by an abusive dominating father. It is then likely that you find yourself having the same experience with the partner you choose or perhaps your boss or co-worker. With them, you will react and act as if you are still the child that had this experience for the first time.

The truth is that we relive our childhood every time our fears take control regardless of what form our response takes.

Feelings are the first active emotional ingredient experienced in any relationship. Your belief systems are a pre-set program that determines every aspect of you potential expression and perception, including your feelings and emotions. Depending on how the nature of your beliefs have altered your perception and behaviour, they will determine whether you will be angry or laugh, feel offended or indifferent, feel helpless or motivated and so on. Your feelings and behaviours are mostly beyond your conscious control because you are mostly unaware of the emotional programs or belief systems that you hold. Feelings based in fear refuse to be suppressed and will always demand your immediate attention.

Once we become adults we will subconsciously seek out the same conditional relationships experienced in childhood. We then commonly recreate the same emotional relationship we had with our opposite gender parent with a potential partner. This has created the general understanding that girls will marry their father and boys their mothers. However, it is also possible to choose someone who carries the combined negative traits of both parents.

The truth is that is will only be the case as long as your mind holds on to a sense-of-self that is controlled by the negative beliefs from childhood. Once you release the beliefs that create the perception and feelings that drive your attraction to personalities that are a reflection of your own issues, your choice of relationships will change. Changing who you are will cause you to be attracted and attract a different kind of partner. Truly breaking with your past always requires you to change *your sense-of-self*. It will never be enough to just change your behaviour or strategies, feelings and thoughts.

We animate our life with the intentions inhabiting our consciousness and the resulting experiences appears to define who we are and re-affirm the nature of our sense-of-self.

It is in the nature of living — as a process of expressing our sense-of-self — that will cause us to be inevitably attracted and attract those people and situations that fit the nature of our intent. To counteract intent that is negative, we can try and evolve behavioural strategies and take on particular attitudes to avoid negative events and encounters in our life. However, our fear driven sense-of-self — the intent of our negative belief systems — will still continue to confront us. The negative life circumstances we manifest will always reveal the disharmonious part of who we believe we are — our personal fears. These can be experienced in every level of our life; in relationships, friendships, at work and at home. In the absolute terms there is there is no escape from this but in the moment it always seems as if learned behavioural strategies can save us. Relying on strategic behaviour only postpones inevitable re-occurrence of negative emotional or physical life experiences.

If for instance guilt were one of our issues, the type of the events and people that we will unavoidably attract will trigger guilt feelings that are specific to us. Our issues — negative belief systems — are individual because besides being unique from inception we are also raised by the unique nature of our parents. Each child will interpret an emotional event involving their parents through their primary individuality — their authentic and unique self. Each will translate their experience according to their original sense of being with which they will draw deeply personal conclusions. If the conclusions a child draws causes it to feel **separated from unconditional love and acceptance** it will feel rejection or abandonment by its parent. As a result **a child will experience the emotion that we call fear.**

Any emotional experience will come to shape a child's sense-of-self — who it believes itself to be. Exposure to harmonious experiences reinforces the child's inner-concept that it is unconditionally loveable, acceptable, trustworthy, wanted, included, significant and so on. Disharmonious experiences will do the opposite, causing it to feel unwanted, unacceptable, unlovable and so on.

Living Life Conditionally

How we will experience our fears later in life depends on our negative beliefs and the nature of the event that triggers it. For example, feelings of shame are a different fear than worthlessness, rejection or being a burden. Each carries their own intention. The situations that trigger them can vary markedly from person to person. The intensity of a negative emotional experience usually does not only depend on the intensity of your fears but also on the fears held by those that are the trigger for you.
When fears embedded in our beliefs are triggered by an experience, it will generate negative feelings that effect our perception and make it an emotionally negative event.
Positive feelings are a product of our positive or harmonious self-beliefs.

We usually respond to any issue by reacting to the feelings it initiates in us. We deeply resent and fear the feeling of being unlovable and unacceptable, insignificant or rejected or being of no consequence and so on. Believing that our feelings are the issue distracts us from searching for the real causes. We think that we can resolve our issue if we can stop feeling bad or upset and so on. You could compare the effectiveness of this to getting rid of the smoke without extinguishing the fire. In other words, the origin of your issue will still be there. You can be intermittently successful in dealing with your emotional issues by finding a way to make yourself feel better but it will never be a permanent solution. In fact it only makes understanding ourselves all the more confusing. We sabotage deeper exploration of our issues with our tendency to seek immediate and therefore usually short-term solutions to deal with what we feel.

Even though we are generally convinced that what we feel is responsible for how we experience our existence the purpose and intent of feeling and emotions is much more than that. Our feelings serve a higher purpose in evolving our spirit consciousness that we need to understand in order to know why it is a part of us. Without feelings our experience of living in physical reality would not be what it is right now regardless whether your feelings are positive or negative. When our feelings are rooted in fear they act like an alarm system for our consciousness.

Feelings serve the mind by alerting it to conditions that are either of a harmonious positive nature or a disharmonious and negative nature. Positive or negative feelings tell us whether our sense-of-self is in harmony with unconditional love — the core nature of our spirit — or in conflict with it. ***Without feelings, we would be completely unaware of the negative disharmonious state we hold in our subconscious mind.*** In the absence of this awareness we would ignorantly play out our fears without the possibility for resolution. We would not know that our fear-based beliefs control us and therefore never see the need to take responsibility for the consequences of their expression.

Negative feelings and the beliefs that create them do not define the true nature of who we are, even though it feels like that because we rely on our emotional and physical senses for the experience of being in life. For most of us, the feelings generated by belief systems that form our sense-of-self determine how we identify with ourselves. Fundamentally, all fear-based beliefs create negative feelings that will distort your perception of who you are.

Take for example someone who experienced abandonment or rejection in childhood. They are likely to believe that they are not wanted, undesirable and not good enough and therefore live in constant fear of rejection, judgment and criticism. They would approach every relationship with trepidation and caution to avoid a repetition of their past experiences. They will unconsciously look for a partner who would not do this to them — potentially someone who is also fearful of being rejected or abandoned themselves. The security that each will provides for the other lies in their dependence on each other's fear of rejection. In reality their mutual security is founded on illusions because neither can save the other from their fear of rejection. They have no choice but to remain in their own fear. Neither has the capacity to give themselves or each other what they really need — unconditional love and acceptance and being wanted and trusted. Initially though, their behaviour towards each other will give the impression that they are a perfect match for one another.

Our rejected friend may become emotionally cautious and withdrawn to avoid confrontation for fear of conflict and ultimately rejection. His partner of choice may present herself in apparent contradiction to his fears. She may give a lot of attention and affection, seemingly without fear and the more time he spends with her the safer he feels from his fears. He does not have to make any initial effort and thereby avoids exposure to potential rejection. She is not conscious that her behaviour is a strategy learned in childhood. Being the pleaser and compliant is the only way she knows how to get him to want, love and trust her — just like her mother did with her father. The deeper intent of their individual strategic behaviours is to avoid rejection and often guilt. He does it by being cautious, distrusting and non-confrontational and she does everything she can to prove that she loves him by pleasing him and meeting his needs to ensure he will not reject her. Their behaviours make them think they are very different from each other but their issues are in reality very much the same.

There are other emotional elements at play, which still have to be discussed in detail such as intent, needs and behaviour. On the surface, the behaviour pattern of this couple and the reason they chose each other was driven by their need for love and their mutual sexual attraction. However, their desire to be together is also driven and controlled by their issues. Their behaviours, which are the result of their issues, need to be complementary in order to fulfil the needs their fears have created.

Chapter 7
The Power of Intent

Intent exists literally within everything conscious. Every belief and concept, thought and idea, desire and wish, actions and choice holds intent at its core. It is usually easy to see the intent in an action or a choice but we do not always readily recognize it in our thoughts and beliefs and so on. Consciously formulated intents such as wanting to be the best at something, getting a positive result or just being on time are obvious. The power of intent, however, goes much deeper and further than you might think.

So why is the understanding of our intent so important to us?

Our consciousness relies on the power and influence of creative intent to manifest our lives in order to have emotional and intellectual experiences from which it can evolve.

At the same time it is also the very source for this intent. Innate qualities that are the inherent in consciousness underpin the very nature of our expression of life. Knowledge and experience from the past combines with our creative inventiveness in the present to form the basis for the nature of intent to manifest what we call life. Our strongest and most fundamental intents are that of emotional and physical survival, our innate desire to develop towards independence and to procreate. Our positive intents compete with and are distorted by the fear-based intent. Usually we are only aware of intent when we consciously formulate a path towards a specific goal. Otherwise it needs to be physically realized and emotionally experienced before we become conscious that we acted with intent. We express intent every moment of our lives without even realizing it regardless whether they are founded in unconditional trust and acceptance or in fear.

There is virtually nothing that goes on in our minds that does not contain intent: it is part of just about every belief and thought, every idea and concept that we hold and give expression to. Even though an intent may seem subtle, it acts like immense force on us and the world with the capacity to create not only our emotional and physical perception of reality but reality itself. Our intents will cause us to manifest and attract and be attracted to people, circumstances and events that reflect their very nature. If our intent is fear-based than we will over time find ourselves involved in situations and with people where these fears are being played out and realized. The idea that we create that what we fear is true but not really understood. The negative events we create will not necessarily go to their most extreme potential when manifested but if not dealt with emotionally this is exactly what ***could*** happen. This is not to say that every negative belief you hold will become equally present in reality as a physical event as they may only be actualized as an emotional experience. There are many different factors involved, which will determine the priority your consciousness sets for the manifestation of emotional life experiences.

The nature of our sense-of-self determines the life experiences we create.
The intent behind the positive or negative nature of the life experiences we manifest is to teach us how to be conscious creators.
This allows us to see who we believe we are in what we create.

We are totally responsible for the intent held by our beliefs regardless whether we are conscious of them or not. It follows that we are also responsible for the expression of these intents in life and the consequences of their manifestation in the world. It is the intent within our belief systems that makes us the originators of our life experiences, not just as individuals but also as a collective.

When intent is shared its capacity to manifest increases and so when many people have the same ideal the likelihood of it being realized increases exponentially. This is not only true for the positive concepts we want to realize but also for our collective fears and insecurities. When the intent of a collective becomes a choice that culminates into an action, it unleashes powerful forces that are greater than the numbers would have you believe. By the same token, in not dealing with or confronting a negative issue in society or the world as a collective, you unwittingly create psychological space that allows the reality of it to continue to exist. ***The ultimate power always lies with the individual's intent*** as part of a collective.

The power of intent is well known in the east where collective prayer and meditation may be focussed to influence disharmonious situations. Intent can be directed to achieve a specific outcome by influencing and changing a negative state. There are many stories about the power of meditation over negative situations or environments. Whenever people apply their minds to form a united intent amazing outcomes are possible. We may not have the capability to focus our minds like monks but this does not reduce our capacity to manifest our intent individually or collectively.

There are specific practices we can use to manifest positive and harmonious outcomes in life through intent. Meditation requires disciplined practice in order to focus the mind with the intent to achieve a certain outcome. There are many different styles of meditation that can be practiced to experience an empty mind or a mind with a specific intent. Moving your mind into a state where there is an absence of distraction or random thoughts is usually part of the process. Continued disciplined practice can produce enormously strong minds with the capacity for exclusive focus and positive outcomes.

The most effective way to manifest a positive life is to deal with all your fear based intent by releasing the source for their existence in you — your negative beliefs. The inherent intent within negative beliefs seeks to find fulfilment through our self-expression through our feelings of fear. This can be with others by capitalising on their fears, weaknesses and insecurities to manifest a shared experience where each is living through their fears. The absence of negative beliefs does not always automatically cause the mind to replace them with positive beliefs and intent. If the family you grew up in was intensely negative from the beginning, additional work may be needed to build a positive mindset. Generally, those who can already imagine a positive sense of being, the change to positive belief systems can occur almost seamlessly. Releasing negative beliefs at the source of a state of depression also has the potential to open the door to a positive and optimistic state of mind.

Every belief that makes up your sense of self, whether positive or negative, whether conscious or subconscious, holds intent.

The influential power of our belief systems resides in the intent it contains. If you want to overcome your issues this is highly significant. Through understanding intent you can recognize the positive or negative nature of your own beliefs. It is important to understand that your intent is an indivisible part of your sense-of-self when dealing with your issues,

The intent of unconditional love, acceptance and trust is **to be loved**, accepted and trusted and to be able to trust **unconditionally** and **to know and accept unconditionally that you are lovable, acceptable and trustworthy.**
The intent of the essence of your being — your spirit — is to love and be loved, accept and be accepted, trust and be trusted unconditionally.
This intent acts like an inner motivation and a reference point for your mind. It represents the innate positive value and standard that consistently informs us when our sense-of-self acts in harmony with our spirit and when it does not.

Our life experiences, strategies and feelings provide the evidence whether we manifest from unconditional love or fear.

This most profound of intents influences the expression of who we believe we are, whether we know it or not, whether we think about it or not and whether we believe in it or not. The intent within unconditional love cannot be turned on or off — it is a part of everything. *Any attempt to consciously control it through suppression or denial is futile because the force of its presence defines every other emotional state we experience.* All you would be doing is to create a new intent in conflict with unconditional love, the consequences of which will be negative for both mind and body.

The spell the innate intent of unconditional love holds over our being is like an encompassing force that steers our consciousness unfailingly towards harmony with the essence of our spirit — within ourselves, with others and the world. The essence of our spirit is by far the most powerful and positive force in our consciousness and it cannot be extinguished. Its intent will ultimately override all fears and insecurities and in time, even our innate drive for emotional and physical survival.

The Intent of Fear

It was explained earlier that we would experience fear if we are **conditionally** loved, accepted and trusted because it is our innate response to being separated from unconditional love and acceptance, being wanted and trust. The belief systems we form in response to our fears depend on our interpretations of the conditions we perceive exist. These than become a negative influential part of our mind by which we define who we are — our sense-of-self.

The intent of all of our fears is to make us trust that they will protect and save us from rejection and abandonment, powerlessness and helplessness, doubt and distrust and so on. Reality is that fear will keep us from finding and realizing unconditional love, acceptance and trust and with it, the true nature of our authentic self.

You are unconsciously taught to respond to your negative beliefs in a very specific way. Your parent's belief that you are responsible for their negative emotions teaches you that others are responsible for how you feel. Just like your parent expected you to change to accommodate their negative emotions — disappointment, irritation, anger and so on — you learn to hold others responsible in the same way. You become convinced that others need to change their behaviour or attitude towards you in order for you to feel safe from your fears and insecurities.

Controlled by Guilt

Instead of blaming others, you may have learned to accept responsibility for the negative experiences of others. As a result, your fear of being guilty compels you to suppress yourself emotionally to avoid being held accountable for what they feel. You do not realize that you unconsciously give others power over how you exist and express yourself and that their fear and insecurities now dictate your behaviour and self-expression. Your guilt has the intent to avoid blame and being held accountable for any negative experiences or feelings others may have. The suppression of your authentic self and true emotions will come at great cost to your own being and is harmful in the long term.

On the other side of the equation is the intent of the person who you feel guilty about. Your issue concerning guilt would have begun in childhood. One or both parents would have felt powerless and fearful and in fear of being held accountable or responsible for anything of a negative nature. Your exposure to their behaviour and emotions from very young makes you fearful of being responsible for how they feel even though you were too young to know how to be responsible for your own life. Y of responsibility for the fears and insecurities of your parent(s) forms the beliefs that become a part of your sense-of-self. If your mother or father cannot cope with their parenting role, for example, you may come to believe that: "I am burden to my parent because my needs and expectations make them impatient and resentful of me and I therefore have to suppress myself in order to avoid being the cause for what they feel because it is my fault they get upset or angry, disappointed or critical".

Parents who fear responsibility will act out whatever they have learned in their childhood in order to avoid being accountable. Often, one of those strategies is to act as if they are the victims of those they should be responsible for. They will manufacture justifications and excuses for not having the ability to be what they should be as a parent. When confronted and held accountable, their pattern of behaviour often takes them from denial to blame, followed by indignant anger and than to being unfairly victimized and powerless. Their final escape is to physically and emotionally withdraw as if the victim of their parental responsibilities. For the child or adult who tries to find resolution for their guilt feelings through emotional confrontation with their parents, this kind of outcome is generally extremely frustrating.

Aggressive Control

This applies to parents who hold on to a strict personal standards and values, rules and expectations they deem to be right. They commonly display controlling behaviour and anger with those who to not comply — their offspring and often their partner. The intent behind their behaviour is to avoid being challenged and proven wrong for fear of appearing inadequate or dumb and suffer a subsequent loss of power and control. To avoid this they need control over their environment, which in this case their family. Their deep-seated fears of powerlessness, embarrassment and being wrong drives their need to be in control over every aspect of their life-experience; particularly their own family. Commonly, they grew up with a parent who treated them similarly and their attitude and behaviour will almost guarantee that this overpowering behaviour will continue in the next generation. Some of their children will succumb to the aggressive dominating attitude and become ***passive powerless*** while their siblings may become just like the parent — ***aggressive powerless***. Their parents would in all likelihood react as if victims or completely deny the fact should their children confront them about their controlling behaviour. Often they will justify their behaviour by blaming their children for being difficult and therefore leaving them without any other options than to be aggressive.

Destructive Criticism

You are likely to be critical of your self and others if you have been raised by parents who are critical of you because you do not meet their expectations. Just as your parents pointed out your failings and shortcomings you feel the need to do the same with yourself and with others. Those who suffer from being self-critical and others have the subconscious fear that they are not good enough because they were criticised. They are now convinced that the only way to prove that they are better than that is by showing up what they believe to be the failings in themselves and others. It becomes a behaviour that seeks to prove to themselves and others that they are worthy the love, acceptance and trust they never felt from their parents. Your fear of failure and not being good enough requires you constantly monitor yourself to avoid potential failures. By finding fault with others you get the satisfaction of believing that you are right and they are wrong and in some instances superior.

Your need to be without fault or failure can be so strong that you convince yourself that there is only one way to achieve the right outcome and that every other way is wrong. You thereby totally ignore and dismiss the individuality of your own consciousness and that of others. Ultimately, your critical behaviour gives you no personal satisfaction because once you have accepted that you should be better than you are, you never will be. If what you achieve never feels good enough you will judge others in the same way and this will not make you friends.

Being critical of your self is learned and is likely to make you very sensitive to the criticism of others. If this is your behaviour, it is highly probable that one or both parents had high expectations or were critical perfectionists thereby placing their standards and values on you. In an effort to avoid being criticised, you may become a perfectionist, setting standards for yourself that no one, including you can fulfil. Your perfectionist attitude and a certain sense of superiority that flows from this can than become a perfect platform for criticism. You fear being unworthy of their love and acceptance if you cannot meet these expectations and standards. You become convinced that you will only be acceptable and valued if you are perfect.

Criticism and high expectations create fear of failure and with it stress and anxiety. You may not realize that you have started to do to yourself what your parents did to you: you have become a self-critical perfectionist who can never be good enough or satisfied with your own achievements. There are two phrases that are self-destructive if accepted as self-beliefs: "I should always be better then I am" and " I have to surpass myself".
Both of these imply that no matter what you have achieved it is never good enough because you can always be better. It also means that none of your successes are worthy of celebration because you should always have done better than what you did. If you live by this code you are bound to be unfulfilled, never content or happy. You will always be striving to reach a point of success and achievement that you move out of your own reach because of what you believe. This will eventually culminate into the conviction that you are not good enough and a disappointment to yourself and others regardless of your achievements.

Convinced that you are the imperfect one, you are likely to justify your self-criticism as if it is the only way you can evolve and improve yourself. Your behaviour in the world will often go to one of two extremes: You either believe you are imperfect and not good enough and accept it as a truth **or** you try and prove to others how perfect you are in every way. In both instances, you need to engage those around you to get proof that your self-belief is realized. If passive you will create situations where you find evidence that others are better than you but if you are aggressive in nature it will be your intent to try and prove that you are better than others. In both instances you surrender your personal power to others by depending on them to provide you with the emotional evidence you need to confirm the negative beliefs you hold.

Master of Your Intent

Obviously being aware of what your intent is does not bring immediate change but is a definitive step towards it. Awareness of your intent can provide you with a new insight into the nature of the intents contained in your belief systems. Negative intent can only change if you release the belief systems that they are a part of. Knowledge of the nature of your inner-self and understanding the process by which you create your reality are essential for you to do this.

The power and influence of intent is fundamental to everything we experience as reality. Nothing exists without intent being fulfilled as it underpins the very essence of creation and manifestation. Yet, we are mostly blind to the capacity of beliefs held by our consciousness as a device to create focussed intent, which would endow us with the ability to create the reality of our choice.

You might say that "Intent" has no judgement about its nature, whether it is Fear or Unconditional Love, Acceptance and Trust.
Driven by the innate desire of your consciousness to create, its only objective is to manifest "The Program" held by your beliefs.

If the program is one of fear than your experience of life will reflect this. The many different faces of our fears will determine the kind of life experience we manifest for our selves. Naturally, intent from unconditional love, acceptance and trust will manifest a very different and positive experience.

Chapter 8

The Relentless Needs

Our needs play a major role in our life but not all needs are the same. Just like the need to eat and breath are essential to the survival of our physical self, our innate need to exist in unconditional love, acceptance and trust is essential to the emotional survival of our consciousness. These needs are a powerful persuasive force that can dominate our behaviour and result in positive or negative outcomes in our lives. If the animation of the negative aspects of our sense-of-self will ultimately create undesirable experiences in our life, why do we repeat the same behaviours, reactions and responses? Are we masochists at heart?

The conditions our parents unwittingly set to qualify for their love, acceptance and trust do not just define who we believe we are. They also separate us from who we were meant to be – our authentic self. Besides the unique nature of our authentic self we also start life with the sense that we are wanted, significant, lovable, acceptable, desirable, trustworthy, valued and so on until we become convinced that we are not by the way we are treated. This creates needs that we feel are now unfulfilled in us. If we are made to feel unacceptable through criticism and judgment we will feel the need to be accepted. If made to feel worthless and insignificant we will develop the need to be special, significant and admired. If we are rejected and excluded, we will have a deep need to be loved, wanted and included.

The control that fear driven needs have over our minds parallels that of our negative belief systems. To deny them will cause the intense experience that is a product of their absence. The needs we feel have to be satisfied because we have the sensation that our very emotional survival depends on their fulfilment. Our needs will be activated by specific circumstances, environment or types of personalities that were a part of the inception of these issues in childhood. The negative feelings these encounters generate will fuel our sense of urgency to respond to fulfil our emotional needs.

In any of these moments, we are presented with two choices — to act to fulfil our need or to do nothing instead. We always have the choice to respond differently to our fear based needs even though our feelings have convinced us that there are emotional consequences if we do not. For some of us, the threat of not having our need fulfilled can instigate aggressive strategic behaviour to ensure we do not suffer the perceived consequences. Others can be so convinced that they are powerless to have their needs met that it stops them from even trying. Their response will be passive or sometimes manipulative but hardly ever direct in engaging a process of need fulfilment. Either behaviour will create its own emotional issues which negative effect will be felt over time. For both, the fear of not being able to fulfil their threatens to return them to feel the consequences experienced in childhood.

The exclusion from unconditional love, acceptance and trust remains our deepest and greatest fear affecting our emotional and physical survival.

Much of our effort and time in life goes into the pursuit of satisfying our needs — the need to be loved - accepted - trusted - believed - wanted - trusted – acknowledged – appreciated – praised - listened to – heard - significant - special - recognized - successful and so on.
Dysfunctional needs are driven by fears — the fear of being rejected – abandoned - disbelieved – doubted – ignored - dismissed - invalidated- demeaned- belittled- worthless- insignificant- a failure- powerless and so on.
The emotional pressure created by our need to survive drove us to find strategies to meet the conditions we were presented with in order to avoid the consequences. These conditions we are expected to meet also created the need to be loved, accepted, for attention, validation and so on. Once we accept that we cannot just expect to be loved and accepted without fulfilling certain requirements, we are in contradiction with our innate entitlement to receive and experience love and acceptance and so on unconditionally.

Our reliance on our strategic behaviour to satisfy our various needs will cause us to choose, behave and react in ways that not representative of who we really are. Fear is in control and distorts the intent and need for our behaviours. Even if others try to tell us that we are not being rational or reasonable it is unlikely to make much difference to us. We will more than likely justify and defend our behaviour in response to their comments. Once we are in fear of not having what we believe we cannot live without; no explanation, logic or reasoning and no amount of intellectual dissemination of the situation will influence our minds.

In spite of being told why our behaviour, attractions and choices are wrong or cause our pain and suffering, we are likely return to the original behaviour or choice without a moment's hesitation. The truth is that even if we were to deliberately alter our behaviour and choices, we would still suffer duress because it will feel as if we are acting in contradiction to what we should be to doing.

However, fear based needs are not only just the domain of individuals we see as weak and vulnerable. Those, who display aggressive or dominating strategic behaviours and perceive themselves to be powerful and in control of their lives often refuse to acknowledge that they are driven by fear, The fear of being powerless and without control is the source for their need for power and control. The need to prove that they are more significant and better than others is often included in these fears. The process of fulfilling needs does not necessarily suggest a passive, submissive approach. Aggressive and dominating strategies may give the impression of strength and power but they are just as much a product of fear-based beliefs as submissive subservient behaviour.

Our negative beliefs automatically create needs, feelings and behaviours that then form part of our sense-of-self.
- *If* you feel rejected and unwanted you will feel unlovable and unacceptable of yourself and others.

How much love, attention and affection do you think you need to feel loved and wanted?

The Truth: It will never be enough (until you love and accept yourself).
- *If* you have fear of failure you may have the need to prove that you can be successful.

How big does you success have to be before you are satisfied?

The Truth: It will never be enough.
- *If* you are locked into the fear of being poor and destitute you will have the need to have money and wealth.

    How much will be enough to stop your fear?

The Truth: It will never be enough.
- *If* you have been raised to believe you are dumb and stupid and now are fearful that you are intellectually inadequate and an intellectual embarrassment.

How much education do you have to have to prove to everyone how smart you are?

The Truth: It will never be enough.
- *If* you are terrified of confrontation, what will you do to avoid any kind of conflict or aggression?

    How much of life can you avoid before you have no life at all?

    The Truth: You will avoid more and more of life's experiences until your fears become your emotional prison and you have no life at all.

The list is endless because just about anything in our perception can be a fear.

The World to Exploit

Satisfying our fear-based needs by engaging others and the world is an automatic response for us. We try to deal with our fears by either aggressively engaging others or suppressing ourselves (and sometimes both). Our parents unconsciously teach us very early in life by the example that the outside world is to blame for what we feel. When they are upset, angry or dissatisfied with us or others their behaviour and attitude confirms that they are not responsible for what they feel and that others are guilty. Their strategic behaviour makes them appear as the victims and makes us out to be the guilty party for what they feel. Their blame of us will define the nature of who we believe we are— our sense-of-self. Our parents and their fears and insecurities are the mirrors by which we innocently create our inner identity.

The deep affect this fear-based self-perception has on a child can drive it towards either a greater need for self-sufficiency or to greater dependency and powerlessness. The innate drive towards independence still exists but the pathway towards achieving it becomes highly distorted. Children naturally strive to achieve independence in every part of their life by walking and eating on their own for example or by choosing, thinking and reasoning independently. Developing self-confidence and trust in their inner-resources, mental, emotional and physical strength are essential developments for our survival.

The innate drive to realize our independence in order to be self-sufficient creates the desire to acquire all the skills and knowledge we need to achieve this. If we fear that we are a burden and an imposition it can drive us try and be physically and emotionally independent before we have acquired the knowledge and ability to prove that we do not need anyone to support us. On the other hand we may under the same circumstances fall into the deep conviction that we are powerless to be independent because we are too young and become very needy for support instead. It is possible to display both of these qualities dependent on the circumstances that are a part of their origin. Because these behaviours are founded by negative beliefs neither are representative of the true nature of the person who plays them out. In its most ideal state our mind has no fear.

The learned reflex to be externally focused to deal with our fears convinces us that this is the only way we can quiet the negative emotional pressure our needs create. We are convinced that only certain people, situations or things will keep us safe, make us happy *or* are a threat to us. Our emotional and sometimes physical response is evidence of this and cannot be denied. Characteristically, over time our choices will fail to satisfy the needs we try to fulfil through others. We will find reasons to be dissatisfied or criticise what we have manifested in our lives. Once we begin to feel unhappy and disappointed, insecure or dissatisfied, the journey for self-fulfilment starts all over again. We do not see that we consistently return to the same emotional point we started from. We are under the illusion that if we make a different choice the next time everything will change. This should be obvious to us, were we not so completely blinded by the negative beliefs we identify with. We misinterpret the issues life presents us with by making the assumption that the causes are external. Our subsequent choices can therefore never be a permanent solution because we are trying to change others instead of ourselves. **We are dealing with the symptoms of our issues and not addressing the source.** As a result the choices we make will always lead us back to where we started. **We** are stuck in the perspective that our issues are a product of how others and the world behave towards us. **As victims cannot and often do not want to see that we are the creators of our own problems.**

Partners in Conflict

Our choice of partner is not only determined by physical and emotional attractions but also by our emotional issues — fears. This should be obvious when we keep choosing the same kind of partner even though these relationships continue to fail or cause us stress and unhappiness. Unsuccessful relationships can take on an obsessive quality and are often hard to close down and linger for months or even years. Love that is unconditional is not painful and does not require us to suppress and compromise ourselves. Reality is that **we are not aware that our concept of love can also be an expression of fear based neediness.** It is dangerous to believe that there is only one person that can fulfil us in life because the form this also includes all your fear-based beliefs. You need to realize that the partner of your choice will, just like you, bring his or her issues into the relationship.

Attractions based on the compatibility between two people are complex but follows certain principles. The match between partners is not only based on positive elements like love, sexual attraction and shared interests but also includes their fears and insecurities. If your 'perfect' relationship turns conflictual, you cannot come to any other conclusion that from the beginning you had a distorted perception of your partner. However, your choice to be with them, according to your attractions, you must also makes you responsible for the consequences. Understanding that you are the instigator of your relationships is a major step in finding resolution for your issues.

Part of the problem in our attraction to a potential partner is our tendency to turn them into something we want them to be for us. Even though we can see some flaws we think we will be able to change them for the better. Sometimes we can sense the potential of what someone could be and convince ourselves that this is who they are. We then dismiss their issues as unimportant because our need to be in a relationship in order to be loved and accepted distorts the perception we have of them.

The assumption that happiness will be assured if we can find the 'perfect' partner is a major error of judgment. On the surface this appears like the most logical thing to aim for but closer inspection of the conditions we place on this expectation will reveal something very different. The reality is that the conditions that our potential partner has to meet actually reveal more about us then them. Analysis of what we expect our partner to be spells out many of our own fears, perceived shortcomings and insecurities. The conditions we set are our subconscious way of dealing our fear based needs through a relationship. Our search for the perfect partner ignores the existence of our own fears and insecurities and as a result we are attracted to personalities whose issues dovetail neatly ours. Instead of finding our perfect match we set ourselves up for a difficult relationship.

If, for example, you believe you are unlovable and unacceptable and unwanted you are likely to believe that you are undesirable unattractive. You will be self-critical and judgemental of your appearance and expect others not to want you. Your ideal partner will be someone who sweeps you of your feet and obsesses over you in order to convince you that you are really special and desirable. You have the need to feel that you are the only one they want to be with, the absolute centre of their attention. Any change in this could bring your fear of being unlovable and unacceptable back to the surface.

If you are fearful of unpredictable changes and emotional confrontation, your need will be to be with someone who is emotionally stable and protective but also non-confrontational. The person you attract has to be in many ways similar to you in respect to confrontation and change. The primary difference between you is that they will appear to be in control of things through their pro-active behaviour in dealing with their fears while you have the tendency to avoid in order to avoid confrontation with your fears or vice versa. Even though both of you are controlled by similar fears, eventually one of you will realize that the other cannot meet expectations.

Parents who have a history of being denied and forced to have to go without having their innate needs met often have issues of being emotionally or/and physically responsible for the innate needs and expectations of their children. This will show thorough their behaviour in their relationship with each other and with their family. It can be that both parents are so focussed on their needs with their fear of being denied that their children come very last. Off course they have no choice but accept this and will grow up feeling un-entitled and denied just like their parents. These children are often made to feel guilty were they to receive what their parents feel denied. Their fear of upsetting their parents in this way creates guilt and makes them oversensitive and responsible for how others feel. They may begin to deny their own entitlement to what they need, want or desire and show this by putting the needs of other before their own. Their sense of guilt causes them to live in constant fear that satisfying their own needs will be the cause for someone being disappointed or discontented.

Parents who constantly act as victims of their family history, life, others and circumstances will unwittingly cause their children to believe that they are some how responsible. Their children will feel that the expression of their authentic self and innate needs and expectations are somehow to blame for their parent's negative emotions and life experiences. The growing belief that they must be responsible creates guilt for what their parents and in time others feel. The reality is that the parents are controlled by the negative beliefs they acquired in childhood and are unaware of the consequences of their behaviour — for themselves and their offspring. In adulthood their children will either be like their parents and feel the victim of life or avoid any kind of relationship where they may be responsible for the feelings of others It is no surprise that the partner they will either attract is someone who feels guilty and over-responsible or someone who is unwilling to accept responsibility or be held accountable.

There are obviously an endless number of examples that can be given, not the least of which is emotional distrusts of your opposite gender. Often the party with the aggressive or passive aggressive in behaviour is very controlling as a consequence can make life for their more passive partner extremely difficult. Eventually this suppression will be intolerable for the passive partner and conflict will ensue. What initially looked like security and stability now begins to looks like an emotional jail where nothing is your own choice and everything you do has to be justified and explained. Even though you know that the relationship is not what it should be, you may feel incapable of confrontation. Your lack of trust and self-confidence in who you are and what you are entitled to and deserve make you feel powerless against your partner.

For the other party the issues are based on loss of control, a heightening of distrust and fear of abandonment. Despite their intimidating behaviour, they will drop their aggressive controlling behaviour as soon as they are threatened with being abandoned by their partner. At this point, their actual neediness and vulnerability will make them say and promise anything to avoid being left. To ensure the door is not closed on them, they will agree to anything to ensure there is a way back into the relationship. Usually they will change their behaviour and attitude and become attentive and caring until they feel safe again. This can cause breakups to drag on for a long time. Their incessant need for company of the opposite gender however ensures that even if you were to leave them they would never be alone for very long. They do not only behave this way with you, they make sure that they always have a few relationship options available to them — just in case.

Conditional Relationships

We will delve into the complexities of relationships in much greater detail further on. For now, we should realise that fear driven needs will in time create issues and conflict in relationships. Generally, each partner has subconscious expectation that the emotional issues they bring into the relationship become the responsibility for the other to fulfil. Just by reading this you already know that this will never work in the long term.

Fear gives our needs urgency because if they are not met we will be subject to negative consequences. We learn very early in life to be in fear of rejection and criticism, guilt and being a disappointment for many different reasons. As a result fear is often the driving force behind our choices and decisions, feelings and behaviour. We channel our fears into every aspect of our life particularly into intimate relationships. They are the force behind many of our illogical and irrational choices, decisions and attractions that we tend to repeat over and over again. They are also the reason and motivation for many of our socially unacceptable behaviours and mannerisms, which in many instances will determine how others perceive and judge us.

The question you need to answer for yourself is a simple one: Am I prepared to examine who I believe I am and the fears I hold in order to ultimately release negative beliefs. What do you imagine your life would be like without your fears? What if you ceased to be a contributor to the fears that drive your relationships and the world?

A world populated by people who live without fear would be nothing like the world you know now. It may be hard to imagine what it would be like but try to think of a world where trust and truth dominate rather than fear, suspicion and secrecy. Think of a world where invention and creation are mindful of consequence, where governments serve the people with wisdom and insight for the future rather than serving short-term self-interest through fear. Imagine a world society intent on achieving a higher sense being for its people, instead of being dominated by economic processes based on fear — power, control and material gain. That kind of world can exist just as easily as the world you live in right now. All it needs is for a large portion of the total population to release their fears and hold positive intent through beliefs that support these values. The capacity to manifest this lies in the individual, not in governments or corporations.

We need to decide what kind of world we want to live in by choosing WHO we want to be. We can start by releasing the fears within us and thereby not confer them on our children. ***The reality is that it all begins with you and your relationship with yourself.***

Chapter 9

The Illusion of Being Free

We adopt our strategic behaviours in response to our fears, as a means to fulfil the needs created by the conditions we believe have to meet. Spontaneous behaviour has no preconceived agenda and does not look for reciprocation or approval. When we use behaviours as instruments to overcome our fear of not meeting the conditions we are convinced exist, they have a definitive intent and are therefore strategic. We develop strategic behaviours when we are subject to the issues our parents play out to meet the expectations they have of us. We use them to meet conditions in our relationship with parents and others or to avoid the consequences we believe would follow should we fail to meet them. They become an essential part of our survival mechanism throughout our life. Strategic behaviours are never random and always have very specific intent and purpose.

Spontaneous behaviour is the mind's uncensored expression of qualities and attractions innate to our spiritual consciousness. They can be involved in creating experiences that have the potential to evolve the awareness and growth of our spirit, mind and body. It can also be a response to our innate awareness to be safe from negative influences. The incessant intent to create and manifest, the desire to learn and know itself in relation to everything our consciousness encounters are innate in us. Their spontaneous expression does not require conscious contemplation to activate choices. Spontaneity trusts the innate knowing of its positive being to support its self-expression.

We generally have difficulty distinguishing ***impulsive behaviour*** from spontaneous behaviour because they appear so very similar. Impulsive behaviour is usually driven fear-based reasons and fulfils specific emotional goals; like getting attention or standing out from the crowd. In this respect impulsive behaviour is totally strategic.

When we orchestrate a particular intent to achieve a specific goal we tend to engage in ***consciously strategized behaviour***. This approach is practiced in a very deliberate and contrived manner in business environments. For some this is the only way they can get through life. They feel the need to plan everything in great detail to remove any potential risk that they believe exists for failure or confrontation. This is generally sensible and logical unless you engage in this kind of approach out of fear. Trying to anticipate any possible negative outcome and controlling the behaviour and choices of others is one way to avoid the potential of their fears being realized. In fear of not being in control of their day-to-day relationships and as a result having to face conflict, which could result in blame and perhaps rejection. Their intent is to make their work and social environment as predictable as possible through planning every tiny aspect of the process to ensure success. It all sounds sensible and logical until you realize that fear is running the show and they are in preparation for any negative eventuality. The problem they have is that our fears have the habit of realizing themselves through our life processes.

Since the majority of us rely on our strategic behaviours to get through live we would feel powerless without them even though our ***strategic behaviours*** are damaging to us. We often totally rely on the success of our behaviour for our emotional survival — to be loved, to be accepted, and to be wanted, to avoid criticism and be powerless and so on. We are blind to the fact that the negative beliefs and their intent stop us from seeing the consequences of our strategic behaviours in our lives and also in the lives of others. Our strategic behaviours are always the result of conditions rooted in fear that we perceive exist. This conviction causes us to transform conditional love and acceptance into a negative belief that then forms our inner-identity and simultaneously adopt behaviours to overcome the consequences we fear.

The beliefs we create and accept as a result disguise all manner of fears and insecurities with logical justifications. Not surprisingly, considering the power that fear exercises over us, strategic behaviour is ever present in much of our self-expression. One of the reasons we so easily persist with our strategic behaviours is that they promise to save us from our fears by creating a positive response in others or avoid manifesting our fears altogether.

Even though we do not choose these behaviours consciously, once learned, they become a typical aspect of our personality and a significant part of our life. From childhood we already begin to learn how to behave to avoid becoming the victims of the conditions our parents set for their love and acceptance of us. If successful they become our preferred way to get us out of emotional conflict and discord — initially with our parents and later with others.

Becoming Strategic

All behaviour has intent but of particular concern is the intent that is subconsciously driven by fear. Behaviour without fear originates from unconditional love, acceptance and trust and will intuitively lead you in the direction of growth and development through the experiences you will create with them. It will be directly motivated by unconditional love, acceptance, trust, creativity, curiosity, desire to learn and understand and so on. Expressed with unconditional love as its core value, the intent within your activities will steer your life into a positive direction. This changes when fear takes control. The primary purpose of your behaviour will then become strategic in order to prevent your fears becoming reality.

Even though it may appear to be in contradiction of what went before, strategic behaviours have the potential to lead you to a path of personal growth and development. This only seems to happen when these same strategies fail to support us and we find our selves in depression, constant anger, anxiety or even physical illness etc. Even though this puts us under enormous emotional pressure it is also a reality check of where we are with ourselves in life. When the situations this creates in our life defines who we are to ourselves and others, we have lost our grip on what is real and what is not. Often for the first time in our lives, the difficult emotional state we are in can force us to look at ourselves for the reasons for the negative state we are in. If we begin to recognize that these negative experiences are an indication that fear is driving our feelings, behaviour and choices, we are potentially making the first step towards real change. Accepting responsibility for the fears or issues you are aware of creates the opportunity for self-analysis and understanding the nature and intent within your behaviours and the causes for your feelings.

A child that spontaneous seeks to satisfy its curiosity is not driven by fear but engages in the act of exploring the nature of its own being in relation to the emotional and physical world it encounters. Significantly, it does this initially in the ***total absence of fear***. This shows that being without fear is possible and likely a natural potential of our consciousness. Unfortunately, a child's lack of awareness of itself and the nature of its being together with its dependence on support, care and protection makes it also extremely vulnerable. It is obviously unaware of many physical dangers but negative emotional influences are its greatest vulnerability. As an emotional influence, parents may act with the best of intent to love and accept their child but if they have emotional fears and insecurities they will supress spontaneity in their children.

The sense-of-self forms progressively in the first 7 to 10 years of life and becomes the foundation for everything we are and express. What part and how much of our sense-of-self is in harmony with unconditional love and how much has fear at its core, shows itself in the way we behave, react and respond. The truth is that you cannot hide the nature of your sense-of-self from someone who has the awareness and clarity to see that fear drives you. Should you act very confident while in reality you are terrified, your lack of emotional balance will expose your fear to those who are aware. Your sense of yourself demonstrates its nature by the way you speak and use language, in your behaviour, the way you move, your gestures and your posture. Even the nature of your health issues will expose the state of your sense-of-self over a lifetime. There are definitive associations between the negative disharmonious aspects of your sense-of-self, your behaviours and your body.

The first strategic behaviours we experience are those of the mother followed commonly by those of the father. Your mother's state of mind plays a significant part in how you will see and relate to yourself and others in the future. If she is stressed, worried, unduly concerned and cannot cope, feels powerless and unhappy — even if she has the desire to be the perfect mother — she will have a negative impact on the development of ***your sense-of-self***. Your mother' worries and concerns will feel as if they are focused on you, making you the centre of all of her fear driven attention. Unable to separate your self from the emotional experience with your mother, you begin to believe and accept you are the cause. You feel that it is ***about you and for you*** and without knowing any better, you will assume that you are responsible for all of your mother's stress or unhappiness and so on.

The expression of your authentic self, your innate needs and expectations are initially spontaneous until you sense your mother's stress and anxiety, unhappiness or disappointment, fear and insecurity. With each new encounter you become more aware of your mother's negative state and it begins to influence your relationship with her. Your inner-harmonious state with unconditional love and your innate expectation to continue to feel and experience this with your mother is challenged by her behaviour and display of negative emotions. Each exposure confirms your conclusion that somehow ***you must be the source*** and therefore responsible for her stressed and unhappy state of mind. You will then unconsciously begin to associate the spontaneous expression of your needs and expectations to the stressed negative response of your parent. You will gradually suppress your needs and expectation to avoid being the cause for your mother's distress as you are accepting responsibility for her emotions. You will also learn quickly that a change in the way you present yourself can lead to a different response from her.

The obvious conclusions your innocent and naïve mind arrives at represent a child's interpretation to ensure its emotional and physical survival. Every fear driven behaviour and intent by the parent also imply the response required to avoid the threat of the negative consequences they hold.

- If your parent is annoyed by your presence, it implies that you should do your best to be invisible in every way to avoid attracting their attention and become vulnerable to being blamed or criticised.
- If your parent is upset or angry because you ask for what you want, it implies that you should not have the expectation to get what you want or the right ask for it. You will feel compelled to suppress your needs and expectations
- If your parent becomes angry or abusive because you do not follow their rules and expectations it is implied that you should be obey without question, be submissive and compliant. You will suppress your ideas, judgments and beliefs to avoid attracting criticism and abuse.

There are an endless number of examples that can be given but each will show that we adopt specific behaviours in order to deal with an emotional environment that does not accept us for who we feel we are. We then believe that it is unacceptable to be who we really are and thus become convinced that there is something wrong with us.

You also begin to realize that certain behaviours and expressions please your mother or father and will get you positive attention from them. In this case suppressing your normal needs and expectations may get you a favourable response. Whenever your behaviour gets a positive response from either mother or father your mind will recognize the pattern. This serves to teach you to adopt appropriate behaviours as a means to get a response that gets you to be loved and accepted — even if it is conditional. This process gives birth to your perception that your authentic self is unacceptable and that strategic behaviours will make you accepted, loved and get you what you want.

Every response of a child to its mother's fears is to ensure the love and acceptance, trust and the sense being wanted are maintained. A passive compliant child that pleases the parents in order to be loved and accepted will usually get endorsement and approval. A parent will judge a child to be difficult and challenging should it be aggressive in its response to the threat of being separated from unconditional love and acceptance. The reason for the behaviours of both children is the same but the contrast in their behaviour puts them at polar opposites in the perception of their parents. Neither child would be aware that it severely compromises its own emotional and mental wellbeing. In their fear of being abandoned or rejected, one feels compelled to suppress itself to meet the parent's conditions and the other by aggressively demanding an unconditional response.

The strategic behaviours children employ are a direct reflection of the conditions encountered through the relationship dynamic with their parents. This will determine the nature of the belief systems that will ultimately determine their sense-of-self — in context, intent and consequence (more about these aspects further on). They will be in of fear stepping outside the parameters defined by these new beliefs in order to avoid rejection and judgment, guilt and abandonment and so on. It may seem that an aggressively responding child is not fearful but it is just acting in defiance of the consequences of its behaviour. Fear is still the emotion that underpins the belief system that promotes its behaviour.

Conflict with Your Self

Once a child begins to experience that it will not be loved and accepted for being its spontaneous, authentic and unique self instead it feels it has no choice but to suppress and hide it to be accepted. This is a gradual process that causes a child to feel fearful of its true nature and its spontaneous impulses because of the negative response that their expression elicits. It is highly unlikely that a mother realizes that her issues have this effect on her child. She will believe as long as her interactions with her child are motivated by her conscious positive intent, she is doing the right thing by it. In her general perception, the child should feel loved and accepted because that is her intent.

The truth is that the impact on her child, is much greater than she could ever imagine. Her issues, however block her capacity to be objective of her own feelings and actions just as it is for any other adult. She may not cope well with her new role as a mother, unexpected issues or with the responsibilities and demands that the child and others place on her. It was probably just like that for her mother. Even though she wanted to have a child, she may not have realized how its needs and expectations would challenge and impose themselves on her. She begins to feel that everything in her life has become about her child and there is nothing left for her. This can create deep resentfulness in her because it causes her to relive the same experience she had with her mother when she was a child — it was always about her mother and never about her. She would like it better if the baby did not depend on her so much and did not require this much care and attention. She is not aware that her child senses and knows it, just like she did with her mother.

Even though she feels guilty about her selfish feelings, she cannot help putting her needs before those of the child and does so more and more as it matures. She does not realise it but her child is growing up in the same way as she did and is likely to have the same issues. It will come to the realisation that its life, needs and expectation are a burden on its mother. It will innocently take full responsibility by accepting beliefs that its existence is a burden and an unwanted responsibility. In an attempt to win its mother's love and affections, it has learned put its mother needs before its own. It will mean however that its own needs and expectation are now unlikely to be met.

The belief systems it will adopt out of its sense of guilt will effectively stop it from expressing its innate needs and expectations for support, care, love and protection. It has learned that it is responsible for its mother's inability to cope and feels guilt when its mother is stressed or upset. The mother's unfulfilled needs and her discontent for feeling denied will also begin to feature as the child's responsibility in its sense-of-self. Part of its strategy is to be in constant awareness of its mother's emotions and feelings and remain sensitive to her fear-based needs and expectations to avoid being rejected by her or causing her pain. Learning how to read her parents emotional state and knowing how to respond to it becomes and essential part of strategic behaviour. It fears that the expression of what it innately depends on to fulfil its needs, expectation and potential will cause conflict with its mother or father. In order to maintain a "positive" relationship with its parents it has no choice than to suppress or be cautious in voicing what it wants. The process of integrating negative beliefs is gradual in most situations but extremely powerful and complete once incorporated in a child's sense-of-self.

The experience a child has of itself in depends on the emotional dynamic created by its family. The actual nature of its sense-of-self will depend on the issues, fears and insecurities of its mother and father, who unknowingly act as psychological mirrors for their child. If the parent's sense-of-self were in harmony with their own innate nature and therefore unconditional, they would automatically be in harmony with the innate nature of their child. If the parent's behaviours and attitudes are disharmonious because of their fears and insecurities, their child will feel that its authentic and spontaneous self is unacceptable and disapproved of by them.

Once these children reach adulthood they still feel the lack of entitlement to have attention, ask for what they want and have their needs fulfilled. These beliefs can make them either become pleasers in order to get attention without asking for it or become extremely selfish by putting themselves before all others for fear of missing out. Their need for love and acceptance will be intense and they may not cope well with the prospect of rejection or the expectation to be there for others.

They will have the tendency to edit themselves before they speak to avoid being responsible for others being upset in some way. If aggressive they may act as if they do not care about the feelings of others because they see themselves as the victim in most situations. Others will never know what really goes on in their minds because they keep their true feelings, thoughts and intents to themselves to avoid confrontation or conflict All or any of these negative qualities will be reflected in their behaviour and self-expression should he or she becomes a parent and inevitably be passed on to the next generation.

Lost in Behaviour

Achieving our emotional and physical independence through adulthood is a significant milestone in our life because it is both the innate intent of our consciousness and a necessary part of our emotional and physical survival. By defining ourselves as mature adults, we usually believe we have moved ourselves into a realm of intellectual, emotional and physical independence and freedom and self-responsibility. We generally have the expectation that mature adulthood is the stage in our lives that allows us to be the master of our own universe and create our own destiny; at least, that is how we would like it to be.

For many, this idealised vision already begins to crumble before adulthood has even been reached. After experiencing intense emotional difficulties getting though their child and teenage hood, they struggle to create an optimistic vision of what their future might be like. Frequently their emotional issues have already spoiled their education, which can act as a restriction on their opportunities in life.

Those, who had a childhood without obvious abusive or violent incidents, often view their childhood as normal. They do not realize that fears and issues do not necessarily have to be played our aggressively or abusively. Even though their parent's emotional limitations and fears might have been passively expressed, they will still be a negative influence on their sense-of-self. Many do not realize their issues until they are adults and engage in serious intimate relationships but they are present in every part of life.

The undeniable truth is that fears and insecurities will always manifest themselves in our lives; there is no escape from a fearful sense-of-self.

The notion of a perfect childhood will be a handicap if you want to resolve your issues because you are likely to look in all the wrong places for what the causes are. Unless your parents live their life absolutely without fear — which is highly unlikely — the fears and insecurities they have will make their relationship with you conditional. Assuming that your parents have fears regardless how well intended and passive they may be, will give you greater scope when you are trying to understand the causes for your own issues. Always remember that they are the victims of their childhood experiences and so being angry or critical of them is not justified.

Do not think you are the only one with problems in life. Everyone has to face their fears in the process of living. Our issues appear in relationships and work, social activities and sport but the most importantly in our relationship with our self. Our fears may appear to be entirely different in each of these areas but often they are a product of the same negative belief systems within our sense-of-self. For example, the issue of being unacceptable may appear differently at work than it does in relationships or say sport yet the basic reason can cross all of these.

When you find yourself back in situations with characters that mimic the original emotional conditions under which you accepted your negative beliefs, they will act as triggers that will cause you to re-experience your childhood fears. The feelings this will bring up in you will act as a springboard for strategic behaviour. As you mature your behaviour will become more sophisticated but it will still have the same basis and intent that it had when you were a child. Part of growing into an adult is to learn to socialize and know how to interact and behave in a manner acceptable to others. So when your initial behaviour in childhood became unacceptable, you would have evolved new behaviours that saved you from being judged or criticised — passive-aggressive, assertive or manipulative behaviours for example. Alternatively, you may use guilt by playing the victim thereby making others responsible for what you feel you miss out on or denied. You might get away with it in friendships but in personal relationships these behaviours commonly lead to problems and eventually conflict. Not so strangely, in the corporate style environments or workplaces, aggressive or manipulative behaviours that get financial results for the company are often rewarded instead of being judged as morally inappropriate.

Someone who is an aggressive perfectionist will find life similarly challenging. Their perfectionist expectations convert into criticism and judgment of them selves and with others, which makes them appear demanding and hard to please. The same behaviour in their job however, can create a very different outcome. These personalities are usually very controlling as well as high achievers and hard workers. Perfectionists typically want their achievements to be based on their own values and ideas of perfection and need to be in control of every aspect of the process they engage. Their need for recognition and approval to have their idea of perfection validated makes them vulnerable to being taken advantage of in working environments.

Often unable to refuse any demand made on them, for fear of being judged as inadequate, they will strive to meet expectations. Always in fear of not doing anything well enough and always elf-critical and dissatisfied with their own work, they toil long hours to meet the demands of their superiors. They tend to achieve in excess of what is required but commonly sacrifice their emotional and physical health and everything else in their life in their quest for perfection and approval.

Their strategic behaviours are highly sophisticated but always find justification and purpose in the environments in which they seek to be recognized. It is difficult to see that behaviours that appear to get what you believe you want — recognition, reward and celebration — could represent something negative within your self.

In fact, the prospect of giving up strategic behaviours that will bring positive results in the moment can be difficult and create intense fear. This fear can paralyse your intent to confront your issues and negative beliefs that underpin them. This is no exception for the perfectionist whose strategies bring a positive response at work but who will have issues in personal relationships because of the fears that drive their perfectionist behaviour. They will naturally resist losing the emotional tools that they depend on to get what they believe you want and need. Just like others who resist confronting their issues, perfectionists will always find justification for their behaviour and the beliefs that drive them. After all, they depend on them to avoid failure, rejection or judgement and so on and at the same time it gets them success and recognition. The fear of living without strategic behaviours will make personal change a difficult challenge.

We have a conflicting appreciation of our behaviours because their success depends on how they are expressed in any situation. Much of our understanding of how world functions psychologically is a result of the behaviour and attitudes our family imposed on us. The emotional history of our family also reflects social influences and concepts supported by society at that time. The stories that appear in books, film and other media, advertising and 'official scientific understandings' act as confirmation of popular 'truths'. These popular beliefs and notions can also suppress our motivation to question our emotional understanding of reality.

Just about everything we are presented with in the media contains to one extent or another the implication that others or the world in general are responsible for the life we or others experience. It is present as a general context within the material studied in schools and continues to influence us in adulthood. Every time we are exposed to this perspective, it acts as evidence that our self-power and control in life is extremely limited or non-existent. This has become so deeply ingrained in our psyche that to hold someone responsible for their own unhappy or negative experiences in their life will usually elicit strong reaction of denial. Most are convinced that they would not or could not have possibly created the negative events they experienced — "Why would I deliberately do something that causes me pain and suffering?"

The concept that we are the creators of our personal and shared life experience is absent in almost every aspect of our culture.

The truth is that no one would consciously choose a life of unhappiness, pain and suffering. It is also true that we can only understand the reasons and causes for our negative emotions and life experiences *if we accept that we the source.*

Regardless of the unique and different life situations, relationships and events we experience, we are the only consistent presence in all of them. From that fact alone, we can assume that we are highly involved contributors to our own lives. Add to this that every event and evolvement is a product of our own choices and decisions, than there is positive proof that we are the originators of our own life experience. If, further to this, you consider that each person has an individual experience of the same event and it becomes clear that we seamlessly create our own reality. ***The truth is that individually and collectively, we are always the creators of our experience of life.***

When we say that we are not involved and responsible, it is because we do not know nor recognise the effect that the negative beliefs of our sense-of-self have on us and in the world. Consequently, we do not take into account the subconscious negative intent of our fear-based beliefs, needs, feelings and strategic behaviour. If we did, we would know how we are involved in every one of our life-experiences and we would be able to accept the emotional responsibility that can lead us to self-change. Gaining self-awareness and self-realisation of what is subconscious in you is the first step towards the transformation of your sense-of-self.

Depending on Strategies

Once the illusions created by negative beliefs become the truth of who we are and determine our needs and behaviour they will also control how we express ourselves. They also become the framework that we depend on for our emotional survival and they have become, however flawed, our fundamental connection with love, acceptance and trust. As long as we meet the perceived conditions through our aggressive, passive or defensive strategic behaviours, we live with the promise that we will be loved and accepted even if we do not recognize it is conditional.

Behaviour represents our most obvious and recognisable psychological aspect for others and is commonly seen to be representative of who we are. The primary reason for this is that they — just like you — identify themselves by their behaviour, likes and dislikes. Unaware of our own negative subconscious beliefs we do not recognise that our strategic behaviours complement the negative beliefs and behaviour of others. We assume, just like they do, that we are truly being our selves while in fact we are responding to negative beliefs ruled by fear. It should be obvious that when fear is in control it is not possible to give a voice to our authentic self. Especially when you have learned to expect that giving expression to your authentic self will provoke criticism and rejection. It is not likely that you will see that these fear-based beliefs are actually illusions.

Even when we deliberately adopt new behaviours because we believe that these will be more effective in getting what we want, we are responding to the negative consequences of our old strategic behaviours. We hope our new form of expression will serve us better and usually it will for a while. However, in the short or long term they will eventually fail and the fears that drive them will find realization. You will experience the consequences of the intents of fear present in your negative belief systems until you release them.

For example, learning behaviours and strategies so that you can confront and be assertive in negotiations or in conflict can be helpful and provide insight into the personal dynamics that take place in these conditions. Without understanding and dealing with the origin of the fear-based reasons why you could not face potentially conflicting or aggressive confrontations in the first place, your fears remain. You will just be a little better at managing them because of your newfound confidence in your newly learned strategies. The intent within your fear will not disappear nor rest. If not dealt with, they will always be lurking in the background of your mind; ready to overwhelm you at a critical moment your strategies did not prepare you for. The point that is missed is that in the absence of your fear of confrontation you would deal with negotiations with a different mind set to begin with. You would learn the complexities of the dynamic of negotiations with confidence in your capacity to handle any situation.

Our inability to see who we are beyond our behaviours prevents us from understanding how they are a part of us. Were we were to take an objective view of what the effect of our behaviour has on others and theirs on us, we would be more likely to make a step towards emotional self-responsibility. Unfortunately the prospect of accepting that we are the source of your life experience usually triggers the fear of admitting that we have faults, weaknesses and failings. We would expose shortcomings we do not want others to know or see and therefore resist acknowledging our fears. However by accepting our fears — without judgment — we take ownership of the source for our life issues and thereby put ourselves in a position of control. As the owners of our fears and the creators of our lives we are also capable of personal change because we cease to be victims of our fears.

***Our biggest disappointment is not that we let others down,
but how we are a disappointment to ourselves.***

Self-acknowledgement of the reasons for your issues moves you towards self-realisation and awareness. The next step is to look within your self, at the nature of your own sense of being **by taking ownership of who you believe yourself to be — your sense-of-self**. Your choice to accept responsibility for what you manifest in your life will be your first act of true self-empowerment. Possibly for the first time, you would be claiming back the power you gave to others and the world and take control over your life — past, present and future.

Chapter 10

Our Greatest Fear

Probably one of the greatest crimes ever committed against human consciousness is the separation of spirit, mind and body as distinct entities through centuries of empirical influences — laws, religion, commerce and science. The ongoing negation of the significance of the intent, validity and purpose and meaning of consciousness denies humanity as a whole an integrated understanding of the nature of our spiritual, mental, emotional and physical being. In absence of this understanding we exist in a general state of fear and as a consequence live our emotional illusions as if they are reality. Our distorted perception causes us to be lost in the material reality of the world because we have learned to rely on it to provide solutions for the emotional vacuum created by our fears.

Unaware that we are the originators of our life, we believe the reasons for our fears are caused the events we experience and the people confronting us. They are present when you feel you cannot speak your truth or confront your partner or your boss with your opinions or feelings, needs or expectations and so on. It is present in your anticipation of failure or when you feel embarrassed or ashamed. It is felt when you expect to get something wrong and make mistakes or in your hesitation when making new choices. It can take a grip on your mind when sudden and unexpected changes or new events storm into your life. Its destructive force is active when you judge yourself and put your self down. It drives you when you want to prove yourself better or superior to others. It is your motivation when you try to be the centre of attention or get others to like you and be your friend. It controls your behaviour and self-expression when your greatest concern is that what you say or do will upset, offend or anger others. The reality is that in all of us, fear rears its emotional presence in too many ways to ignore it.

In Fear of Love

Our fears may appear wide and varied but there is a core fear at the basis of all of our fears. This, our greatest fear and it is acquired at the very beginning of life. The influence and control it will have over our lives is enormous. The extent of its negative effect on our consciousness and lives depends the intensity and quality of the negative influences of our childhood experience. Its capacity to influence our minds also relies on our suppression of the original nature of our unique consciousness.

Once we have been forced to distrust and therefore reject much of our authentic self we have no choice but to accept conditional love, acceptance and trust as the only love we are entitled. Our naïve choices, which are now motivated by our innate fear for our emotional and physical survival, also cause us to distrust and dismiss unconditional love and so on. This separation creates a division in our sense-of-self. Where first only unconditional love and acceptance resided there are now conditions to be met and with it the fear of failing this expectation. **Conditional love and acceptance** etc. become the reasons and cause for our greatest fear because on every level of our consciousness **we cannot accept an existence bereft of unconditional love acceptance and trust**. It creates a state of internal separation which represents disconnection and exclusion from our Spiritual Origin without which consciousness cannot maintain a harmonious sense of being.

We become like rudderless ships on the sea of our own consciousness without any idea of who we truly are, lacking both purpose and direction. Without knowing and understanding the nature of our unique being we are without direction in our lives. Our lack of drive and motivation or aggression and domination exposes our sense of insignificance and the feeling that our lives do not matter. This is then reflected in our negative behaviours and attitudes and the consequences these have on our existence, which in turn impacts onto on others and the environment. Our deepest fear becomes an indistinguishable part of our sense-of-self and is then expressed through feelings and needs. These are translated into strategic behaviours, actions and choices that have consequences, which become the experiences that shape the current state of our lives.

We all innately sense that the fulfilment of the potential of our consciousness depends on being in harmony with our Origin and through this we will know the eternity of our spirit.
By living our lives in unconditional love — in the absence of fear — we can become aware and feel this harmonious connection with the essence of our spirit.

The need, desire and innate expectation for unconditional love, acceptance and trust are incessant in every human consciousness. It is the core driving force in our life and underpins the creation of our issues. The moment we are in a life situation where we will experience separation from unconditional love we are in the emotional state that we call fear. Our subconscious awareness senses innately that we cannot exist without it and we therefore fear not meeting the conditions we believe exist in order to receive it. In that sense our fear of existing in the absence of our essence acts as a constant emotional compass for our highest state of being and represents an irresistible force in our consciousness.

When we believe we are excluded from unconditional love, our mind is in emotional disharmony and contradiction with the core of our being. The childhood influences that caused us to have to dismiss our expectation of unconditional love within the context of our authentic self convinced us that the only way to fulfil our emotional needs and expectations is through others and the world. As a result we try and satisfy our fear driven needs and issues, by depending on our strategic behaviours to receive love, acceptance and trust from others.

The apparent positive outcome from the use of strategies fools us into believing that we are getting to what we are entitled. Nothing could be further from the truth. You will have to repeat your behaviour over and over again to try and create the same result always in fear that your strategies will fail you. In spite of your faith in your strategies, your fears will always be in contradiction to the essence of your being and your authentic self. Ultimately this puts you in a disharmonious state with your core values, with others and the world.

Trapped in Conditional Love

Our negative personal beliefs separate us from unconditional love and do not support our authentic self and yet we cling to them without apparent rational reasons. All the unhappiness, pain and suffering in the world does not appear to be enough motivation to make us let go of the negativity that drives them. It seems that the emotional force that keeps us from releasing them must be greater and more influential than our desire and conscious intent to dismiss them from our mind.

If we are to understand the reason for our attachment to our fear based convictions, we need to appreciate the nature and power that it has over us. It is clear that all of us have great difficulty changing our behaviours, feelings and perception or pessimistic thoughts. You can try and alter any of these by telling yourself that you should not behave, feel or think a certain way but that will not stop it. You can use various methods or distractions to make yourself feel different by but usually this is of little or no help in the long term. It has the potential to add to your problems by creating a self-critical mentality that reinforces your awareness of the issues in question or cause you to go into denial or greater avoidance.

Avoiding your negative feelings and thoughts does not allow you to develop an understanding why and how you came to have them in the first place. Most people are so controlled by their negative beliefs that conscious analysis only leads to justifications or blame for how they came to feel the way they do. Even if they attempt to create changes in their feelings, thoughts or behaviour is likely they will soon return to their original state. It is obvious that logic and reasoning based on our current understanding of the expression of human consciousness cannot provide an emotionally acceptable answer for the reasons we cling to our issues.

To illustrate this dilemma, imagine for a moment that you are going on a long journey by boat, innocently trusting that it cannot sink no matter what kind of calamity it will be exposed to. A big storm comes and you get washed over board without anyone noticing. Even though the boat is not far from shore, you cling to a piece of flotsam as you see your boat sail away. What if you are convinced that you do not have the strength to swim and reach the shore? How important do you think that piece of flotsam will be to you if you believe it is the only thing that will save you?

When unconditional love is denied, the conditions you will feel forced to accept are an emotional trap. Acceptance of your parent's conditions makes you doubt, distrust your innate inner qualities and ultimately reject your unique authentic self, little by little. The unconscious rejection of your innate core values and unique authentic self and subsequent adoption of strategic behaviours is your attempt to grasp for a means to make you loveable and acceptable to your parents. This inevitable choice will not be without substantial cost to you state of being. Your fear-based beliefs are like the flotsam you desperately cling to for your survival. It may appear like a good choice but your absolute emotional and physical dependence on it will negate any apparent benefits.

As a result, you will develop an inner-identity that has very little in common with who you authentically are. Your newly acquired sense-of-self will now and in the future determine whether you are worthy and deserving of love, acceptance and trust or not, whether you matter or not and are of value or not. The acceptance of conditional love will redefine the nature of your being by distorting your inner-perspective of who you believe your self to be. This will also affect the expression of your innate resources and capacities, talents and abilities and so on.

Growing up with the emotional conditions set by your parents, you do not realise that your parents are two people out of billons on the planet and that their state of mind is unique to them and a product of their family upbringing. By accepting their version of reality, as your truth, you have unconsciously accepted illusions as if they are reality. Their negative beliefs are as much a distortion and an illusion for them as they will become for you through your dependence and trust in them.

Once negative beliefs have become the only thing that you trust will support you they represent your only resource for love, acceptance and trust. As a result the only love you have learned to accept as real has to match the conditions held by your negative beliefs. If you were offered unconditional love you would probably not recognise it for what it represents and reject it. The conditional love you have learned to accept in childhood is the only love that you will recognise and trust **because** it is in congruence with your conditional belief systems.

Fear, Illusions and Unhappiness

Fixated by a distorted sense of yourself, your altered perception will unconsciously create evidence that your fears and insecurities are true. You provide your own proof through outcomes you create in your life with your intent, choices and decisions. You are not aware that your negative belief systems determine the type of decisions you will make, that it shapes your attractions and resentments, thoughts and feelings. To you, it will feel normal to be the way you are. Your mind, distorted by fears, draws you into situations and brings you in contact with people that are a reflection of your sense-of-self — your negative or harmonious belief systems. If you fears influence your relationships than you will be attracted to and attract those who have fears and insecurities that complement your own. By involving yourself with them your fears and issues will begin to play out in their presence.

Believing you are not good enough, not what you think others expect you to be or not performing to expectations and so on will generate stressful and anxious emotions. In this state of mind you will depend entirely on the success of your strategic behaviours for your sense of security and happiness. However, your fear of failure, embarrassment and criticism for instance, will always be lurking in the shadows of your mind because you can never be sure that your strategic behaviour will succeed. If, for example, you believe you do not matter, you will be drawn to be part events and with people that can provide proof that you are significant and special. You may be convinced you need to associate with wealthy successful people who make you feel special by association. But since you live with the belief that you are insignificant and therefore need to prove that you are significant, the experience you create is nothing but a lie to your self. It is an illusion to believe that mixing with significant people makes you special. Nobody can make you feel special but you. In one form or another we are all guilty of this because we all have fears that are represented by our negative beliefs. Should you believe you are unlovable or powerless, insignificant or unworthy and so on you will create or attract people, events and situations that you will try and use to prove the opposite to your self. If you are passive you will react to these situations by trying to avoid them or by seeing your self as a victim of them.

One of the most difficult things to hold in your mind is that every person around you is living with their own version of negative belief systems. Reality is that everyone has issues and fears and therefore everyone employs strategic behaviours to survive emotionally in the process of living their lives. The seamless attraction between our selves and those with complementary issues stops us from recognizing that we are controlled by our fears. Our lack of inner awareness of our illusions as well as the seemingly natural way our strategic behaviours are a part of us, make the truth invisible to our consciousness. We literally do not see the wood for the trees. Our minds are skewed to see life and living in the context of the beliefs we hold in our sense-of-self because they shape our perception and reinforce their own truth in us. If you cannot see the deeper emotional forces at work within your own mind it is easy to judge life situations by applying simple cause and effect principles. It likely that by doing so you will blame others and see yourself as innocent or the victim and you would probably be wrong either way.

The most common example for this happens everyday in virtually everyone's life. For example, if person A were to say something to person B that B became emotionally upset about, others observing this would likely blame A for causing B to be upset. We are taught to believe that we are responsible and to blame for what others feel, as if we have the power to create feelings in others. People, who have negative beliefs that make them emotionally vulnerable and fragile will be easily upset a variety of things. Does that mean that those who have done or said something over which they became upset are responsible? Or, could it be that *the negative fearful beliefs they hold themselves are the cause for what they feel*? It should now be obvious that the latter is true *but that is not how we generally see it in the world*.

Once you have learned that you are responsible for what your parents feel you will conduct relationships burdened by guilt. Fearful of being blamed should someone feel upset by what you express, you edit everything you say to protect others from their fears. This is actually not helpful to them and serves to compounds your own issues. It is wrong to believe that you are being caring and protective by accommodating their fears, accepting guilt and taking responsibility for their emotional reactions. By protecting them from their issues you are creating an environment in which they will not have to confront their fears and insecurities. Your guilt issues around being blamed and held responsible for their disappointment or feeling disrespected, feeling unacceptable or anger and so on in others will control your behaviour in all of your relationships. You may justify your behaviour as 'protective and caring' but guilt and fear of being blamed are the real reasons. Your effort to avoid being held responsible for the negative feelings in others — avoiding guilt causes you to suppress your authentic self. You do not allow yourself to be who you really are because you believe it is the original reason for your guilt. As a result of your guilt and consequential behaviour the vulnerable and fragile belief systems of others are never confronted. They will never have a reason to change as long as you accommodate their issues and likely spend the rest of their life with their fears. If you do not wish this for yourself then why would you let this happen to others?

You may have always thought that the events and encounters in your life were created by coincidence, random people or by misfortune. In actuality, they are all experiences that you manifest in concert with others through the power of the intents each of you hold in your belief systems. Your sense of yourself, positive or negative, will always exert its intent through the beliefs it holds. All your intents will drive you into passive or aggressive action through the feelings they generate. Illusionary or not, they are the central emotional forces that control every aspect of your perception, emotions and self-expression and thereby create our life experience. **Your life and the people in it are always a reflection of who you believe yourself to be.**

Whether we are aware of it or not, the innate intent and desire to be in harmony with unconditional love, acceptance and trust is the infinite force at the core of our consciousness. **This creates an inevitable bias within our being that views any deviation from its unconditional and authentic nature as an unbalanced state in reference to the essence of our spirit or consciousness.** Were we not to have this state within us we would not know the difference between unconditional love and fear, good or bad and negative or positive emotions. We would act out and experience their consequences or influence without recognizing whether are of a positive or negative nature for us or others. There would be no reference point for our state of being and we would therefore have nothing to measure the nature of our consciousness by. The fact that we experience good and bad, negative or positive emotions is evidence that ***this reference point — unconditional love, acceptance and trust — is an innate and indivisible inclusion in our consciousness.***

Chapter 11

Your Emotional Body

Were we in perfect harmony with our essence we could expect to live life without fear and our Spirit, Mind and Body would operate in perfect harmonious synchronicity and make life a positive experience. Our positive state of mind would not only bring emotional and psychological benefits, but it will also promote a high level of physical health and wellbeing. For many of us, this ideal is unlikely to be a reality because we are wedded to tightly to fear-based beliefs. Most do not realize that their negative emotional states are detrimental to their emotional and physical health and that they are the only ones that can change this.

We are not only a product of our family upbringing but also of the culture and history of our race and nationality. Specifically, our bodies are a product of the genetic composition of that of our parents and the generations that went before. The past generational, environmental and psychological influences have profound impact on our mind and our bodies. These fears and illusions are passed on in an incessant cycle by one family-member to the next, from parents to children. Right now your mind and your body are at the end of the generational chain of your family but once you have children you will pass on both your physical as well as your emotional "genes to them".

How the Body Meets Your Spirit

Our bodies are inter-active with our minds because of the relationships that exist between the mind and body. The built in resilience of your body is a property of its innate intent to exist and express itself at the highest possible level of health. Your immune system and the capacity of many organs to regulate their biochemical and hormonal state are employed to assure the body's highest possible functionality. Dependent on what the body is exposed to emotionally and physically this will be positive or negative. When the body is exposed to negative influences, our capacity to feel physical disharmony and pain causes our immune system to spring in to action to heal the issue. This innate reaction to anything disharmonious or toxic ensures that your body is always driven towards greater health.

The body's approach to maintain optimum health is very similar to that of the mind. It seeks the highest possible state of being by creating an existence without fear. Even though the order of influence is spirit over mind and mind than over body, our physical self has its own internal reference points. Should there be a deviation from these our consciousness will alert us that something is amiss. The body will always be entangled in the emotions of the mind whenever negative life experiences cause fear based emotions — powerlessness, anxiety or stress and so on.

The idea that body and mind are separate entities is so deeply ingrained in our psyche that we have difficulty recognizing the connection between them. We generally prepared to accept that our headaches, stomach aches and back pain can come from the stress and worry of our life situations but we seek to address the causes as a resolution. Our skin — the largest feeling organ — has probably the most obvious metaphorical relationship with the emotional mind. One of the main functions of the skin is to provide the capacity for feeling in a material world. Our capacity to touch and feel things gives us the means to be physically aware of the three dimensional reality we live in.

Our feelings and emotions give us the capacity to be aware of the psychological environment we are in. The sensory function of both our skin and emotional sensitivity are similar in their intent — they make us aware of how we relate to either a physical or emotional environment we occupy. Energetically, the vibration or resonance of their intent is therefore very similar and this forms a metaphorical relationship between them. The emotional intent of our inner-senses is mimicked by our physical senses. This also provides a semi-specific pathway for emotional issues to become physical in the form of a disease. It is therefore not a surprise then that many pathologies of the skin are a direct result of emotional trauma, stress and fear and often appear when any of these emotions are triggered.

Many of our chronic illnesses can be traced back to stress and fear related emotional states — cancer, kidney, liver, stomach and gallbladder issues for example. Even then, it is likely the focus for treatment will only deal with the physical side of the problem. This is understakable in the initial phases of treatment because of the urgent physical attention it may require but that is usually as far as it will ever go. Generally the emotional aspect of our physical diseases are ignored and therefore hardly ever dealt with.

Considering that the onset of most diseases is not well understood, the exclusion of the emotional mind as a considerable influence on our health does not make a lot of sense. Acute observation of known physical responses to fear related emotional states should make it obvious that our bodies do not exist in isolation of our mind or for that matter our spirit. In our desire to understand the nature of our whole being we have separated them into discrete elements, which have over time become so partitioned by science and religious influences that they are now generally viewed as different entities. As a result we do not recognize that every part of us functions as an integrated and interrelated whole. There is however, a hierarchy in the how our total conscious being expresses itself into three-dimensional reality.

Our spirit is the seat of our unique consciousness and holds the essence of our being— unconditional love acceptance and trust. It also holds the innate capacities and drive that support its growth and survival — to create and manifest, to learn and evolve, for change and experiences.
Spirit determines the unique nature and qualities of our mind — our unique talents and abilities, passions and desires, fantasy and imagination, attractions and fascinations.
The innate capacities of consciousness defined as our intellect, creativity, instinct, intuition, emotions feelings, beliefs, inspirations, potential, aspirations, curiosity, inventiveness, imagination, fantasies, talents and abilities, learning, memory, logic and reasoning. Our sense-of-self or ego is the container if you like of all of this and its shape is defined by the belief systems that form it. It contains our self-beliefs, both positive and negative, which play a determining role in how we will see, feel and express who and what we believe we are.

When the Body Speaks

The voice with which our emotional mind speaks through our body is not random in its effect but follows pre-determined pathways that represent metaphorical connections between body and mind. Each part of our body has one or more functions whether it is an organ, a joint or a system of organs. In fact since there is no part of us without a function every part of our body relates back to our emotional mind. If something has a function then it also has intent and its own resonance, emotionally and physically. The nature of the intent of a belief system has its own resonance just like the functional intent of any part of our body. When expressing a belief that is harmonious in its emotional intent, its resonance acts as a positive influence on those parts of the body which functional resonance is closely related. The positive emotions will then promote greater health and wellbeing because it acts as an enhancement on the functional capacity of that part of the body. If a belief has negative intent it will resonate out of phase with our core essence and therefore also with those parts of the body that match its resonance. The positive functional intent of those parts of the body will than be inhibited and this can over time result in disease affecting our physical health.

For example, if your mind were in emotional conflict about issues related to powerlessness, this would create disharmony, which is felt as a negative emotion such as stress, which in turn interacts with your body. That part of the body metaphorically representative of power is our sacrum (the triangular bone between your hipbones that supports your spine). Your body depends on the sacrum as a central support system that sits between your hips and is the seat for your spine. Without it you would literally fall apart and be physically powerless and immobilised. It provides your body with a platform for stable anchoring points for your muscles, which in turn allows your body to be strong and powerful in its actions. The sacrum is also the location of your power — "chi" — in Chinese medicine and martial arts. Strong feelings of powerlessness have the effect of weakening the core strength of our bodies in this very important location, which then can lead to hip and lower back issues. In women this emotional state can lead to issues in relation to the uterus and ovaries particularly when there are also issues with creative and free self-expression.

Each emotional state such as powerlessness, indecisiveness and fear of free expression create their own unique emotional disharmony within our bodies. Depending on the emotional state it can affect our lower back, jaw — teeth grinding, throat, the kidney adrenals and so on. Each body part effected represents a physical metaphor with an emotional issue consistent with negative belief systems. Due to the complexity of the intents of our negative belief systems and how these relate to our body, an issue will commonly affect various parts of our body. If fear based issues are constantly active they create an incessant negative pressure on the metaphorically related aspects of the body. These can be organs, body structure or different systems such as the endocrine system. Should we persist in ignoring the emotional signals generated by our psychological disharmony then our bodies will be the final place where the conflict between unconditional love and fear is manifested. The result of not dealing with your emotional issues can eventually show up as critical issues with your health or in the wellbeing of your mind. How and when this vulnerability to our emotional issues will physically depends on the inbuilt resilience of your mind and body. This can due to the innate strengths or weaknesses of your physical genetic make-up and those of your authentic self.

The neck is a vulnerable but significant part of our bodies because it is **physically responsible** for carrying and supporting our head, which contains organs *critical to our survival* —our brain, eyes, ears, mouth, tongue etc. (thinking, seeing, hearing, speaking, tasting etc.)

Have you ever said to someone: " You are a pain in the neck"? Or that something in your life is a: 'Pain in the neck". The reason for saying this is that you experience them as source of stress. When you actually suffer from neck or shoulder pain you may not realize that your mind's perception of others or certain responsibilities or demands are at the source. Not the actual task or responsibility but your perception of them. Certain fear-defined beliefs may cause resentment or even anger with what is expected of you and this will determine how you view others or your responsibilities. You experience this emotionally as stress or anxiety because feel that you have to force yourself to do something you resent and but feel powerless to refuse. This inner-conflict can than manifest itself, often immediately, as a contraction of muscles in the neck, compressing vertebrae and restricting blood supply. We feel pain in the neck and often shoulders, frequently together with headaches.

Stress does not affect everyone on the same way even if there are some forms of physical expression of certain emotional issues more common than others. How you give a physical voice to your emotional issues depends on your perception of yourself in respect to your fears and insecurities. The level of fear you feel for having to be responsible for something of critical importance is proportional to your belief in your powerlessness, incompetence and inadequacy and so on to live up to these expectations. This usually mirrors a childhood in which you were not trusted with any responsibility and therefore could not develop trust in your innate capacities and abilities. Exposed to criticism for being a disappointment or to distrust in your capacity to be independent, you will have learned to doubt and distrust yourself. Having to face responsibilities with these insecurities will logically create stress and fear. The solution for this does not lie in reducing or eliminating responsibility or the expectations of others from your life or by employing better strategies. Permanent resolution lies in **changing who you believe yourself to be in relation to these responsibilities.** You need to release your negative beliefs in order to rediscover your innate trust in your own consciousness.

In the hierarchy of cause and affect, the emotional issues are responsible for driving the body into physical problems. If you release the emotional causes responsible for the stress you create, you are likely to spontaneously release their physical affects if they have not caused any permanent damage over time.

Mind Rules the Body

There are many more examples of how our bodies respond to our emotional state. Most common is the queasy and often nauseating feeling we have in our stomach when we are confronted by stressful events that overload our senses. Embarrassment or shame causes us to want to be invisible but hyper awareness of our predicament causes us to think that everyone can see our shameful state. As a result the skin of our cheeks and ears flush with blood turning our faces bright red. Instead of being invisible we have become highly noticeable to others thereby increasing our sense of shame.

When we are afraid to give expression to our truth, feelings or point of view, our throats can become dry and tight. There are many more examples of how our bodies respond directly to our emotional state but we need to realise that the metaphorical connection between body and mind operates on every emotional and physical level. That is not to say that there are no environmental biological or biochemical influences or that we cannot inherit certain genetic predispositions. These effects are recognized as epigenetic influences on our genes and can vary depending on the emotional state of the mind and the inherited strengths or vulnerabilities of our bodies.

If the human body is seen from the perspective of oneness of spirit, mind and body then health or illness should be taken as a breakdown in the harmonious relationship between each of these elements. Commonly, we start life without emotional issues and with healthy bodies and at that time the mind is essentially in harmony with its essence. Our state of consciousness already acts as the primary reference point for the body's propensity towards its greatest possible health. The emotional compromises we make to meet the emotional conditions set by our parents result in a contradiction between our sense-of-self and the essence our consciousness upsetting the original balance between spirit, mind and body. The innate need to be loved and accepted makes us accept these conditions. The compromises that result from them become negative disharmonious influences on our bodies.

Chapter 12

Creator of Your Own Reality

The belief that we are creators of our own reality is not an entirely new concept. Even though we have an intrinsic awareness of this, our conditioned interpretation of our relationship with physical reality prevents us from understanding how we actually do this. What follows is an explanation of how we use our emotional minds and energetic being to bring about our personal own life experiences — individually and collectively. It will show how and why we attract specific personalities and manifest certain events in our lives. This understanding will empower you to recognize your role in your experience of life.

Our intense aversion to being blamed, held accountable or feeling guilty and other fears are largely responsible for our resistance to accepting responsibility for creating our own life experiences. We protect ourselves from this by manufacturing endless reasons and justifications to provide proof that ***we*** are not responsible for negative outcomes in our lives. Instead of taking responsibility, we try to prove that we are the victim of others or circumstances. When others want to link us to a negative event or outcome we are quick to come up with excuses and explanations that absolve us from any responsibility. ***Our explanations usually exclude us and involve others, bad luck or inexplicable circumstances over which we have no control.*** Rarely do we put ourselves forward as the responsible party because our fear of being held accountable and being judged. The beliefs that support this perspective, blind us from seeing how we are directly or indirectly the creators of every experience in our lives.

Proving our innocence becomes our main priority, particularly if it directly involves the core values of our spirit — love and acceptance, trust and being wanted and included. Relationships in conflict can generate fear and guilt, pain and anger and raises the stakes to emotionally intense levels. The fear of being rejected or abandoned because we do not meet expectations is often at the core of our fear taking responsibility. Our fears go back to childhood situations that were discussed earlier. We believe that the only way to retain love and acceptance from others is by assuring others that the negative outcome was not our fault. We do not realise that our responses and reactions are still those of the little girl or boy we once were — still in fear of judgment, criticism, rejection, failure, being a disappointment and guilt. In some respect it is as if we have never grown up and time has stood still.

We also learn very early in life that guilt is followed by some form punishment or blame and potentially rejection and we still respond to these fears as adults. Convincing yourself of your own innocence also releases you from the guilt that you may have been responsible for pain and suffering in others. The other reason children acquire these beliefs stems from the avoidance of responsibility by their parents. By blaming others for their fears or any negative outcomes they have unintentionally taught their children to do the same. Their behaviour teaches their children *who is responsible for what and demonstrates how to behave if confronted and held accountable.* There is no doubt that children will always mirror back what their parents show them — good or bad.

We have great difficulty recognizing how a negative event or outcome is linked to the actions and choices that brought it about and how this relates to who we believe ourselves to be. Should the outcome be positive, we often try and convince others that we are responsible in the hope we will be celebrated and praised. Most are willing to accept the view that we are only responsible for our life under certain and specific circumstances but believe that in all other cases we are the victims of others, circumstance or even bad luck. This perception is highly inconsistent but convenient because it allows you to pick and choose the responsibility or circumstance that suits your purpose. If the process by which we create and manifest our lives were understood, we would realize that there has to be a connection that leads back to us, whether it is obvious or not. Which proves, that *it is not possible to be innocent bystander in the manifestation of your life.*

Our negative belief systems — emotional issues — have the property of altering our perception and creating strategic behaviours with the aim of getting from others what is missing within us. In other words, we have learned and are convinced that the emotional void that our issues create in us can only be filled by what we can get from outside of us. If for example we believe we are unacceptable, we will engage strategic behaviour to convince others we are acceptable. If our strategy is successful and they accept us we have created proof for ourselves that we are acceptable by convincing others. Should they reject or criticise us instead, we will be convinced that it proves that we are unacceptable. In this way our dependence on others holds us in constant emotional vigilance with others in fear that anything we do or say will cause judgement and rejection because we will prove to be unacceptable. No matter how dysfunctional this appears to be; from the perspective of our need for emotional survival from a distorted sense-of-self, it is perfectly logical to behave this way.

Deceived by Conditional Reality

Everything in existence moves and changes in synchronicity with everything else and thus all elements, including all consciousness are connected to each other in the process we call life. We manifest every experience in our life individually and collectively every moment of our existence in concert with everything that exists. Our contribution to our own existence and the experience of it through its relationship with self, to the environment and all that exists comes from conscious, subconscious and innate intent.

Generally, the influence of fear will attract people and events into your life that will cause you to experience the original reasons for its existence within your sense-of-self. Positive or harmonious intent will also attract its mirror image not only through events and people but also through creativity and free association with others and the world. This inevitable process of manifesting our own reality causes us create life situations and encounters that will confront us with our childhood issues if they are negative or fear based. Our negative feelings are there to prompt us into realization that we are creating our life experiences from a disharmonious aspect of our sense-of-self. This creates the opportunity to address the illusions by which we make our choices and decisions. Unfortunately our immediate reaction to negative feelings is to reject or suppress them. We judge them as being the messengers of truth in relation to the experience that generates them because our negative feelings colour it as a negative event. The mind has learned and is convinced that if it gets rid of these negative feelings than the events they are associated with are no longer an issue. This misconception leads us to suppress or avoid negative feelings in order to avoid having to deal with related negative events or confrontations. Unfortunately this will never work.

Our reaction to our feelings is not chosen consciously. The reasons for how we respond to what we feel are generally subconscious and dependent on the underlying intent within our sense-of-self. What we feel is an emotional description of the nature of the beliefs are the source for them but usually invisible to our awareness. Unfortunately, from this lack of awareness comes the general view that we cannot be in control of our feelings. When expected outcomes do not manifest in the way we believe they should, it is our feelings that are the informant of the actual outcome. What we feel will take us into behaviour and reasoning that can cause us to be defensive of our actions, go into denial or total guilt. It all depends on the nature of your negative beliefs. Rarely do we look deep inside of our self for the real reasons why our relationships or enterprises are unsuccessful.

The mind, controlled by illusions created by negative beliefs, seeks to avoid responsibility by finding cause and reason outside of itself to prove its innocence through victimhood. Should this prove to be difficult, we often try and grasp at universal paradigms as an explanation for the issues life presents us with. Statements such as: "Everyone has issues" or "It is normal to get angry", "No-one is perfect" or "Everyone needs love" are used to justify our neediness or lack of success. Were we to put our blame, justifications and general excuses under close and critical scrutiny however, we would realise that they have no real validity and we would have to accept that the real causes lie within us.

Our perception of whom and what is responsible for our life experience also determines how we view ourselves and the world and this plays a central role in how we will choose to live life. It follows that if our perception is distorted by fear-based beliefs, we are guided by illusions in our decision-making, judgments and conclusions. It is difficult to let go of what you believe to be true if for most of your life you have depended on it for your security and emotional survival.

Questioning your negative life experiences from a position of self-responsibility will initiate a process of self-reflection that can lead to answers that can give you an insight into the beliefs your mind holds. The answer lies in seeking awareness, acknowledging what you find as your own and then engaging in the process of releasing the negative beliefs at the source of your issues. A new insight into our sense-of-self will give us the fundamental clarity to recognize what is real and true and what is not.

Because we cannot imagine that we would consciously choose or do anything that would make our lives miserable or painful, we resist any implication that will prove us to be the responsible party. This is correct in so far that we would rarely make deliberate choices that would create suffering, unhappiness and pain. The trouble with this idea is that you cannot be aware of something that is hidden from your conscious mind. Without critical knowledge of your sense-of-self, you are limited by what you are aware of and can see. This may give the impression that all of us have an inner-reality that cannot accessed and therefore remains unknown but that is not so. Even though our fears can separate us from knowing who and what we really are, we an innately capable of living in the awareness of our sense-of-self.

Just like we may not be aware of the origin of the wind, we know its presence by the way it touches our face and moves the leaves in the trees. Were we to trace the wind to its origin and measure the conditions we would know how and why it came into being. Similarly, our negative belief systems and their intent leave their impact on our lives in the form of negative and positive emotional experiences. We can find out their origin by understanding the process by which they came to be a part of us.

Our negative feelings, fear driven needs and compensating strategies are all part of any life experience that cause suffering, anxiety, fear, insecurity, stress and emotional pain. We need to recognise that even though these are not desirable sensations, all feelings represent signposts that mark out whether our lives are founded in fear and illusion or unconditional love. That is not to say that our negative feelings are not a real sensation, it is just that the causes and reasons for their presence have no actual reality outside of us. Fear has the capacity to fool the mind through our emotions into believing that we need to respond to the negative sensations it creates for our emotional survival. We have grown up to find it normal to identify completely with negative feelings so that we will engage our fear based needs without a thought. We respond by automatically applying our learned strategies to meet conditions that we are convinced exist.

Like actors playing out a well-rehearsed script, we react and act automatically to a situation that reflects our negative past. The trouble is that we, the actors, are so lost in the character we play as a part of the story that we are no longer aware that we are acting. In the same way, we accept 'the script' written by the mindset of our parents and the family paradigm as the truth of who we are. Once we internalize it as our identity, we have become what has been psychologically imposed on us. Our state of being — our sense-of-self — than determines how we will manifest our lives. We will unconsciously live our life by our parent's fears, beliefs, conditions, values and standards. You will be so convinced that your "script" represents the truth of who you are that if challenged, you will even fight to defend the role you play and the illusions you live by.

In living out a distortion of your truth you will find that you will attract and are attracted to others who are your emotional counterparts. Their presence in your life serves to give a sense of reality to your illusions, as you will in theirs. You share or compliment each other's fears and similar perception. Their issues and behaviour promises to fulfil your fear driven needs and expectations and vice versa. A relationship can feel like a perfect match until issues start to surface and then you begin to realize what you thought was perfect is severely flawed. You will not necessarily see that this relationship is in likelihood the emotional equivalent of the dynamic that existed between you and one or both your parents. The danger is that because you care not aware of this, you will blame your partner or others for the relationship going wrong. If you your partner separate without this understanding neither of you will have learned a thing. Potentially both of you will repeat the same experience with someone else because you have not understood your role in the demise of your relationship.

We keep on recreating life according to our individual scripts and by our acceptance of common consensus of what is true or false. No matter how painful the experiences we create with one another, our convictions expressed through our choices confirm our version of ourselves and reality we believe to be true.
As long as our mutually agreed version of reality keeps us blind of our responsibility for the life experiences we create the difficulties and conflicts that arise will ultimately be blamed on one another.
Others, just like you, do not realise that their 'script' has altered their judgement and perception and has come to define who and who they believe they are. The result is that even though we may be in conflict, we share the illusion that our distorted version of reality is the correct one.

The Habit of Victimhood

Life is full of examples of apparently inexplicable or unfair situations that we cannot see ourselves be responsible for:
- Take for example the girl who has always has had issues with her father; as an adult she may find a boss, or co-worker or a partner who will be an emotional copy of her father. She is likely to relive her father issues with many of the men she becomes involved with.
- Or the boy who as second child in his family was always blamed for everything that went wrong or any conflict with his siblings. Even as an adult he is still living in guilt and in constant fear that at work or in his relationships, others will blame him whenever something goes wrong or someone gets upset.
- A man who as a child experienced constant dismissal and invalidation of anything he said or wanted now keeps on failing in all of his enterprises. He has learned to believe every thing he thinks or chooses is flawed or wrong because his parents never trusted his intellect, talents and abilities.
- The woman who was demeaned and abused as a child because both her mother and father prized her brothers over her is still being abused and made insignificant as an adult because she is attracted to and attracts chauvinist males.

Our normal reaction to the story of the girl and her abusive dominating and critical boss would be to blame him for abusing her. We would see him as the aggressor and her as the victim. In reality however, she unconsciously "chose" him to be in her life as much as he attracted her through his business. In accepting work with a man who will confront her with the issues she inherited from her father, she is presented with an opportunity to resolve them. However, this will only be the case if she recognizes that she is the instigator of her own experience of this. If she blames him, convinced that she is the victim, she will totally miss the reasons for her emotional confrontation with her past. Transferring the responsibility for her negative experiences renders her powerless and surrenders the power over her life to him and men like him.

Her aggressive dominant boss will have unconsciously attracted her in his life because she may be representative of the childhood relationship he had with his needy and demanding mother. She controlled him through guilt making him feel powerless to refuse or disagree with her. He too is in a potential learning experience. Although he may seem powerful to her, his aggression is nothing more than an emotional strategy to keep him safe from his fear of being made responsible for the feelings, needs and expectations of his mother — women.

The man who fears and believes that he is guilty for the negative emotions and reactions of others may get our sympathy but we will often judge him to be oversensitive and weak. His fears paralyses his self-expression and decision making because he lives in constant fear of getting it wrong and thereby attract criticism and blame. He will therefore avoid change and initiating new ideas for the same reasons. He needs to get general consensus from others before he makes a decision. He is unlikely to progress to positions of responsibility because his need to avoid blame and feel guilty dominate his mind. No one, especially the man himself, will understand that his behaviours are a product of negative beliefs integrated in childhood. As long as he is still controlled by his emotional issues, he will show himself to be very different from his authentic self and actual potential.

Were we to listen to the man with his failed enterprises, we would try and solve his issues by determining where he went wrong in his decisions and judgments and then proceed to give him advice on ***how to do it differently***. In hindsight it is easy to recognise what he may have done well or badly. In only paying attention to the business process that led to a negative outcome we fail to see that his inadequate judgment or bad decisions are not the core of his problems.

The reality is that his fear-based sense-of-self and the negative beliefs that underpin them are central to his business failures. Potentially the lack of trust he has in himself gives rise to his need to prove to others that he knows and is competent.

His fear of being perceived as being inadequate, insignificant or incompetent stops him from seeing the flaws in his own perception and reasoning. He will not even realize that his effort to prove himself by perhaps becoming wealthy, powerful and successful is a reaction to his parent's lack of belief and trust in him. His need to try and prove to others —his parents — and especially himself that he is intelligent, capable and competent is his strategic response to the negative beliefs which have come to define his sense-of-self. The same need of having to prove his capacity for success to others also may incite him to take grandiose risks that could eventually cause his downfall.

The girl who is discriminated against because of her femininity will be judged to be inferior to her brother. Both her mother and father place all their hope and pride in him, unaware that by doing so both their son and daughter will suffer life long consequences. Exposed to the preferential way her parents treat her brother, the girl may respond by instinctively suppressing her femininity and adopt masculine traits in order to become acceptable to her parents. She is now unconsciously in competition with her brother to get positive attention from her parents. She may try and be everything her parents expect her brother to be and often try and exceed expectations. Proving she is academically superior or excels in sport she tries to prove that she is worthy of love, acceptance and praise. All of her efforts will be to no avail if her parents are lost in the worship of their son. He can make a mess of his life and be a total failure and still receive support and adulation because in their eyes he can do no wrong. By the same token, their daughter can achieve great success in her business or profession without attracting any praise, validation or acknowledgment for it. Instead, they might make her successes and achievements responsible for making her brother feel like a failure.

These examples each show just one possible scenario that can come from the circumstances described. Each shows how being ignorant of your inner processes does not only cause you to unconsciously sabotage your own life but it also makes you blind to any real solution. Relegating the reason for your problems to your environment does nothing but put the power over your life in the hands of others thereby leaving you to be the victim. The reality is that you cannot really control people and events in your life through strategic behaviours, by force or manipulation. At best it will keep the consequences of your fear and insecurities at bay in the moment. The only way to be in control of your life is by examining the negative beliefs that define your sense-of-self. Once you recognize *"who you believe yourself to be"*, you will also become aware of the origin for your life experiences.

Each individual in these examples does not feel they have any real control over the situations they have created and have to confront. They are under constant stress of fear of failure of their strategic behaviour with only one thing on their mind: to gain acceptance, love and trust. As long as they are in need of this from their parents or later from others it will does not matter whether the end result is conditional or not.

To begin their journey of self-change they need to make a fundamental choice: *To take ownership of their life by accepting responsibility for the life experiences they manifest — or to live believing that they are powerless in life and the victim of others.*

Life Without Fear

An intellectual understanding of how you create your reality does not automatically give you power over your life but your awareness will promote a new way of thinking that is an essential step in the right direction. If you are to have influence over your negative life experiences you need to change the illusionary negative beliefs that make your life and relationships what they are right now.

- *Releasing your negative beliefs (fears) will change who you are and start the process of revealing your authentic nature.*
- *Changing your sense of self will automatically alter your feelings, perception, thoughts, behaviour and choices.*
- *Your renewed realization of your authentic self will create, attract and manifest a brand new life experience.*

Achieving this is a gradual process but as each illusionary part of your sense-of-self is released, more of your authentic self will be realized in your life with obvious positive consequences.

Chapter 13

Responsibility Without Blame

Guilt is one of our most powerful and influential emotions. Once we accept the belief that we are guilty of what others feel, we commit ourselves of being responsible for their emotional state of mind. The reasons for being guilty and feeling guilty can be vey different. If you hurt someone with premeditation, your act of doing so makes you guilty. Should you feel guilty because someone is in pain, sad or upset, your feeling of responsibility for his or her emotions is unjustified. There are people who feel no remorse or guilt for what they have done but there are many more in a constant state of guilt. Should a person dominated by guilt be exposed to people who are in some way suffering, they are likely to feel an undue sense of responsibility for what they witness. Guilt creates the automatic response that they must in some way contributed to it. That type of guilt is something entirely different from being guilty of a planned action to create harm. Guilt incites you to accept responsibility and even the blame for the emotional states of others while in reality these are totally beyond your control.

Extreme guilt has the capacity to keep you in its emotional grip over a lifetime because you do not realize why you feel responsible for the negative emotional states in others. Often, feelings of guilt cause you to respond in ways that makes you appear kind, considerate and caring while that is not the core reason for your behaviour. The underlying truth is that the intent of your behaviour is to avoid your overwhelming sense of guilt by trying to alleviate the suffering in others. The power of guilt is to create the illusion that you must be somehow connected to their pain and suffering while in truth this cannot be the case.

Our feelings of guilt are a powerful force that can act as a control on our relationship with others and the world.
Guilt will cause us try and anticipate and be prepared for what others need and expect from us, what their fears or vulnerabilities are and what will make them angry or upset, critical and judgmental. As a result we suppress who we truly are, in order to become what we believe others expect us to be. In this way we try and avoid conflict, being blamed and held accountable for what they feel.

Guilt will keep us in relationships we do not want to be in because we fear being responsible for the pain and suffering of our partner should we leave.

Guilt will cause you put the needs, wishes and desires of others before your own for fear of disappointing them. Giving them priority and putting yourself last is your strategy to avoid feeling guilt should they feel denied. You have convinced yourself that if you look after them your turn will come but it never will.

Guilt will have us comply with the needs, demands and expectations of others even if it compromises us or comes at the cost of our own wellbeing.

Guilt will have us make choices and give support that benefits others but cause us to sacrifice the fulfilment of our own life potential. Once we feel all opportunity is lost we can develop feelings of resentment or powerlessness and feel victimized by our own sense of guilt.

The many faces of guilt are confusing because they can have the undesirable habit of parading themselves as socially praised or celebrated personality traits. Your responsible and caring behaviour may collect praise and admiration from others but that does not compensate for the long-term effect guilt has on you. If you are unaware of the underlying motivations for your behaviour, you will also not see how it affects your life. The approval you crave to get from others only serves to justify your actions and choices even though you will be denying yourself the fulfilment of your life potential.

It is important to realize that the actual dynamic between the guilt driven person and others involves other elements. So far we have looked at the person with beliefs of guilt — over-responsibility for the negative emotions of others. Their state of mind and attitude is attractive and attracts those who have beliefs that convince them that they are powerless, helpless and often victims of everything and everyone. They have the need for someone to be responsible for them, someone who will never confront them or upset them and put their needs and expectations first. No wonder that the two are attracted to each other because their relationship dynamic is perfectly matched. Each fulfils the belief system needs of the other. As long as the individual with guilt supports the victim and the victim can find someone to take responsibility for them neither of them needs to change. Both will keep on playing out the beliefs that have come to define who they are to themselves and others until one begins to feel unfulfilled in their own needs and the other feels unprotected and denied.

This is not to say that you cannot be giving, caring and sensitive to others but you never have to give away your power or the fulfilment of your potential. You can only be unconditional with others if you are unconditional with yourself.

Usually those who have issues with expressing their own needs, wants and expectations suffer from guilt. They have learned to believe that fulfilling their needs and expectations, wishes and desires will deny others what they want. The natural expression of self-fulfilment and expressions of entitlement is seen as selfishness or unreasonable or unfair. To someone steeped in guilt it would feel selfish and greedy, not to respond to the neediness and expectations of those who see themselves as victims of being denied. Unaware that their behaviour is rooted in guilt they are convinced that to do otherwise would go against their 'principles'. The real intent of their behaviour is to avoid guilt and gain acceptance and praise.

Guilt can drive you to convince others that you have no needs or wants, wishes or desires. In childhood have learned to be grateful for what you are given and asking for more makes you a burden, selfish or demanding. You become convinced that you therefore should never complain or want or need anything. Later in life, you will still deny yourself expression and fulfilment of your wants and needs and still find yourself doing without. You have to convince yourself that there are sound and justifiable reasons for acquiring something before you can let yourself have what you desire.

Your guilt issues are revealed when you feel uncomfortable when you are receiving gift or others do things for you.
If you never need help, support or looking after.
If you never show others you are sick or have issues, or are going through an emotionally difficult time.
If your presence, needs and expectations feel like they are a burden to others
If you never expect, want or need anything from any one.
If you suppress your feelings and emotions to avoid others being negatively effected.

You will find that if you have played out you guilt issues out consistently and convincingly to friends and acquaintances that:
There is never anyone there to help you when you need them and as a result you have to do everything alone.
You get the sense that no one is interested in how you are because you have convinced them that you are always fine.
You find that you are always needed when others have issues but there is never anyone to support you in yours.
You see others having and doing what they want while it feels that you are always watching from the sideline and missing out.

Overcoming guilt begins with learning how to recognise that we are being controlled by our sense of over-responsibility for the fears and insecurities of others. Those who do not take responsibility for their life and feelings usually trigger our feelings of guilt. They often strategically hold others responsible for how they feel and what they experience — passive-aggressively or aggressively.

As observes it appears that those who give are being generous and caring and naturally the recipients are also likely to think so. Looking deeper into the giver's motivations might show that it can be there may be more to this act than the obvious. For example, you may give in order to be liked and accepted or to avoid shame, which makes your gift conditional and your motivation less than altruistic. To be seen to be giving and appearing philanthropic can be a way to gain status or a sense of superiority. Even though the experience for the recipient may be the same, this kind of giving is coloured by the giver's various issues and fears.

Whenever guilt comes into play there are conditions to be met because of the giver's sense of over-responsibility and sensitivity to the emotional plight of others. The need to alleviate the fears, issues and suffering of others is an often product of their own fear of being victims of blame and the fear of not being able to prove their innocence. This causes them to be in empathy with those who carry the similar fears.

To understand the reasons your own guilt it is important to recognize that nature of the beliefs of those who profit and benefit from them. Passive victims are in fear that their inner-resources are not sufficient to help them deal with aggression, confrontation, conflict and so on. Just living life, meeting the expectations of others or at work can feel overwhelming for them. They truly feel powerless and believe they cannot live without support systems provided by others. As children they may have been overprotected or never had the chance for other reasons to develop trust in them selves.

There are individuals who also have also grown up with guilt issues but are fierce in their avoidance of blame and responsibility. They often employ aggressive strategies designed to prove to everyone that they are powerless victims of everything in life. As victims they tend to blame and accuse others for every ill in their life by constantly playing the victim card. At no time will they take responsibility for what they have created in their life as a result of their choices and behaviour. Their circle of friends usually consists of other victim minded empathisers who give support if for no other reason then to justify their own victim mentality. If challenged they will pull together to convince others they are powerlessness in life and victims of the world.

Giving and receiving can also be tainted by guilt. In an ideal world, all giving is unconditional and joyful and devoid of negative attachments for both the giver and the receiver.

Guilt invariably involves others even if your victim thinking happens only in your own mind. Accepting responsibility when an issue concerns others does not have to involve guilt or blame. It is always appropriate that those who are responsible for a negative event are also held accountable. In this case guilt or blame are of no consequence because it should not matter to you whether they are prepared to accept responsibility or not. What truly matters is that you do not accept responsibility for them — their issues and emotions. Their mind-set and the actions, choices and behaviour it initiates are not under your control and therefore completely their responsibility. Re-defining actual responsibility versus perceived guilt is really important for a clear understanding of what emotional guilt is all about.

Some of our beliefs about emotional guilt are so ingrained in our general perception that even our choice of language around it supports it. At one time or another we have all experienced someone getting upset by what you say. The general assumption is if it is a result of what you, you must be the cause for the other party's response. Under these circumstances it is common to be subject to criticism and even aggression from those who observed the situation and feel the need to be protective of the victim. We have noted before that it actually not possible to create feelings in someone but if the basis for it is pre-existent then making reference to it may trigger unpleasant emotions.

Responsibility changes for us as we grow from children into adults. We cannot be responsible for our own emotional and physical survival when we are born and for 8 to 10 years that follow. Children need to gradually learn the concept of responsibility, accountability and self-discipline by becoming aware that their actions and choices have consequences. They are unlikely to have developed these qualities as a part of their sense-of-self if raised by parents who do not take responsibility for their fears and insecurities.

The truth is that no one has the power to create emotions in others unless the reasons for them already pre-exist within a person. We are completely responsible for what we feel. Once beliefs which are the precursors for our emotions are present in our minds we become vulnerable to having them triggered by our surroundings — others. Without the beliefs that support this state of mind, others would not affect us. The question that we are faced with is this; **should we expect others to change to accommodate our fears or should we be responsible for overcoming our own fears?**

Were we to decide ***not to take responsibility for our own feelings, we will transfer the responsibility for our fears to our children by making them responsible for what we create and manifest out of fear.*** In later life you will more than likely attract and be attracted to the counterpart to your issues depending which of the two you are. Your issues subconsciously determine your attractions and that does not allow you to be emotionally neutral when engaging in a relationship where guilt is the central focus between you and your partner. You will play out your guilt in whatever form it is a part of you and so will your partner.

When Guilt Dominates

Reality is that you can only be responsible for those things you truly have control over. It is just as true that if you are not aware that you are be responsible and therefore do not exercise this power you are still accountable. In emotional terms this means that as an adult you are and can be the only one responsible for your own being and intent, feelings, behaviours and choices. Children are the only exception to this because without having developed a sense-of-self they lack the awareness of intent and consequence and for self-responsibility. They still need to depend on adult guidance and support to teach them. When children reach the age of 8 to 11, the foundation of their sense of self is already formed. Who they believe themselves to be and their behaviour now drives their actions and choices and what they want, need and expect. The emotional chasm that often appears between parent and teenagers is a result of the conditional behaviour the parents have unconsciously imposed on their children.

Not that they are aware of it but at the core of their fear and anger is their sense of powerlessness for not being unconditionally loved and accepted for whom they truly are — their authentic and unique self. Therefore they do not believe that they are unconditionally lovable, acceptable or trustworthy.

Both parents and their teenagers are usually not conscious of the deeper reasons for their differences. They do not realize that the conflict is really just a symptom of what lies beneath the surface of their conscious experiences. As they grow towards independence, they feel physically and emotionally more self-confident and then often give expression to their issues. This can take the form of recalcitrance, anger and open defiance and so on. More than often parents are surprised and frightened by the emotional intensity of the reactions from their teenage children and usually cannot fathom why and how this has come about. Their own fears, limitations and insecurities blind them to the fact that they are central to reasons for the conflict they now experience. This lack of awareness to appreciate the characteristics of their own issues and the consequences these have had on their offspring is a typical characteristic when our consciousness is by and large controlled by fear. Our perception will in almost all instances be blind to what we create and manifest as a consequence of expressing our fears and insecurities. **'Emotional blindness' is a by-product of the fear-based beliefs held by our sense-of-self when these construct a perception and experience of reality we hold to be true.** This illusionary reality is so convincing to our senses that we will even fight for it in contradiction to logical argument. This alone can be the cause of intense conflict and disagreement and longstanding arguments.

Dominating and controlling men are usually only attracted to passive compliant women, just as women who feel powerless and insecure feel themselves attracted to superficially masculine strong men. The wife of such a man may have a daughter who adopts her fearful beliefs, mentality and behaviour or one that is the opposite. She may take on her father's dominating strategic behaviour in fear of being powerless like her mother. Adopting many of her father's aggressive strategic behaviours she becomes masculine in order to have the power and control her mother does not. In the same family, a son may have taken the role of protector to save his mother from the aggression of his father. He may unconsciously suppress his assertive masculinity to avoid being a threat to his mother the way he sees his father is. In the future this will cause him to be passive and compliant — a pleaser — of women in order to avoid being guilty for upsetting them or causing them pain. As future mates, he is likely to attract powerless passive women who need to be saved but also potentially domineering and aggressive-victim types who do not want confrontation.

Conditional Parenting

The conflict that appears in families with teenagers commonly referred to, as the 'generation gap' is actually a dynamic of issues that are a product of the conditional love acceptance and trust of parents with their children. When triggered, there will invariably be blame on both sides; parents will blame their children for being noncompliant, disrespectful or ungrateful for what they have done for them and teenagers will blame their parents for whatever the believe the reason for conflict is. It is very unlikely that the parents will admit that they regret unknowingly imposing their fears and insecurities on their teenagers. It is even more unlikely that teenagers will understand why and how they came to be subject to their parents' fears and what the effect on them has been. As confusing the actual experience may be for parents and teenagers, the truth is that each is being an emotional mirror for the other. The parents experience the outcome of their fears and insecurities through the behaviour, reactions and responses of their own children. Unaware that they are the origin for the way their teenagers act and behave they naturally blame them for the conflict while the their children do exactly the same for the same reasons. The process by which universal consciousness manifests never fails to show us what we need to learn.

Real progress would be possible if both parent and child were to take responsibility for their own state of mind and feelings and accept they both contributed to the conflict in their own way. It is important to understand that the parents cannot undo the consequences of having parented with fear no more than their children can make the instant choice of letting go of the emotional impact this made on their sense-of-self. The argument that "I did the best I could do" becomes feeble when your children go off the track and involve themselves in crime, drugs or alcohol. The damage they can do to them selves may last a lifetime. Eventually most children grow up to be parents and unconsciously affect their offspring in the same way they were by their parents.

The reality is however that both parents and teenagers own and are responsible for their own state of mind and the beliefs systems that form it. **Only they have the individual power to choose to change who they are**. Blaming each other or living in guilt or remorse will not make a difference to either party. Real insight and change are only possible if they accept responsibility for who they believe themselves to be. If the parties are locked in conflict, engaging in frank communication, without judgment and blame, might be difficult but is essential to finding permanent resolution. Each, taking ownership of their own feelings and issues would facilitate a new level of communication that can lead to closeness and understanding in their relationship.

Living life in ignorance of the consequences of your behaviour and feelings, choices and intent has to become unacceptable.

This can be difficult to accept but once you begin to live life by your own choices you are not only responsible for the outcome but also for the reasons that caused you to make them in the first place. ***Your sense-of-self is*** the definition for who you believe you are and this makes you ***responsible for the beliefs that create your perception and feelings, choices, behaviours and intent and the outcome they create in life.*** Ultimately, because **no one holds on to these self-beliefs but you,** your state of mind can only be your responsibility. You cannot allow yourself to avoid this responsibility by making excuses, justification or blame others.

As an adult, you are fully responsible for what you manifest in your life despite the fact that your family is at the origin of your issues. This is because ***you are the only one with the power to change your own negative beliefs***. Your fears will not leave by themselves and you cannot magically make them disappear by wishing they would. You cannot control others and the world by making everyone and everything behave and act to suit your personal fears and insecurities. Even if those who are the origin for your issues were to change you would remain the same. It is up to you to take ownership and accept responsibility for the negative beliefs that you accepted and became your inner-identity. Your choice to be responsible for what you believe will have more power in its intent if you do not put any conditions or expectations on your process of self-realization and change.

Any conflict that arises in a relationship is the product of the dynamic between both parties and therefore each carries responsibility for the part they experience and contribute. Commonly one will blame the other for their pain or discontent in an effort to allocate guilt and promote their own innocence or victimhood. Even though both contribute and there are no innocent parties, neither of them may be willing to accept responsibility for their part in the conflict.

A person may have the belief that their needs, expectations or security in the relationship is their partner's responsibility. Their partner may believe that they will only have value and become deserving of love and be accepted if they can meet the expectations of others. Their behaviour is designed by make a partner feel content, safe, loved and wanted. The issues each of them has are complementary in that one is aggressively needy but not responsible for feeling loved and accepted and expects others to create make them feel this way. The other has learned to please and put them self last as a condition to be loved and accepted. Should the needy partner begin to feel insecure or unhappy the other will try and do anything to fix it to avoid feeling guilty for disappointing them. Once the needy partner begins to feel dissatisfied the pleaser will feel that what they do is never enough and will start to feel inadequate and guilty for not fulfilling expectations. As soon the guilty partner starts to give up trying to please, the other will feel neglected, abandoned and angry. They will feel a victim of not receiving the kind of attention they need to feel loved and secure.

They both lack the inner connection that would allow them to love, accept and trust themselves and each other unconditionally. In order to be ready to love unconditionally, one needs to have a strong sense of love and acceptance for one self. Trapped in needs and strategic behaviours born out of conditional love, acceptance and trust, each looks to the other to find what they lack within themselves.

The Source for False Guilt

Children interpret their parent's expression of emotion, attitude and their behaviour very differently to the way an adult would. An adult will draw their conclusions relying on experience and intellect but is usually unaware that they already function through the emotional filters of the beliefs that represent their inner-identity. A child has neither the experience nor the knowledge or an informed sense-of-self to differentiate its own emotional experience from the emotional reaction and behaviour of the parent. As it is as yet not burdened by a host of negative belief systems that would act as filters and determine its perception and behaviour. In the purity of its naïve and innocent consciousness, it is open and unconditionally trusting within the bounds of its instinctive need for emotional and physical survival.

A display of weaknesses, insecurity, worrying, anxiety and unhappiness by one or both parents will bee seen by their child as an inability to cope with its need for love, support, care, nurturing, protection and this has profound consequences. Unconsciously begins to suppress its need for love and support in fear that it is a burden to the parent and therefore lose the parent as an emotional and physical support. Unable to discriminate the parent's behaviour and negative emotions from who it is it believes ***that it must be responsible*** for their stress and unhappiness. In taking on this responsibility, ***a child unwittingly accepts guilt*** for being the cause for the parent's negative emotional state.

A child will sense if a parents are unhappy or resentful with each other even if it is not directed at the child. It will not be able to able to determine whether it is the cause for the unhappy emotional state or not. Even if a parent was aware of their emotional issues and tried by consciously to alter their behaviour to not do what their parents did to them it is still likely to have a negative impact on their child. Even though a parent can consciously change how they act and express themselves, their actual emotional state would be incongruent with how they behave and it will lack integrity, truth and sincerity. A child will be subconsciously aware of this and receive contradictory messages. It will be as if the parent is saying one thing but meaning another. They may tell the child to function and be in the world without certain fears while they do not have the capacity to do so themselves. The parent's unspoken fears still find emotional expression within their behaviour and language. These emotionally mixed messaged will cause a child's to doubt its innate capacities and strengths necessary for confronting life. It will default to using behavioural strategies of avoidance or aggression to ensure its emotional security. There are so many variations on this emotional paradigm that it not possible to cover them all.

As children we feel guilt almost as soon as we begin to interact with our parents and you could say that in some ways it is almost unavoidable. The capacity of our perception to discern is greatly limited because everything in our experience is new — we are unknown to ourselves and we certainly have little conscious awareness of the world we opened our eyes to. The absence of a conscious definitive reference point for who we are denies us any real understanding of the emotional encounters with our parents. It has already been described how we accept responsibility for the discrepancy between our innate expectation of unconditional love, acceptance and trust and the conditional behaviour of our parents. Accepting responsibility for something we never had any control over represents our first acceptance of guilt. It is insidious in that we are not aware of what we are choosing for, nor do we have any idea what consequences it will have for the rest of our lives.

By accepting the responsibility for the conditions our parents set we become fearful of our own spontaneous impulses and authentic self for fear that expressing them will create a negative response. Should the parent react with a display of annoyance or anxiety, we are likely to accept responsibility believing we are responsible — guilt. We might also begin to believe that we are selfish, uncaring and insensitive if our parents act as if they are victims of their responsibility for us. In these emotional family paradigms, the victim parent expects to be considered before anyone else in the family. His or her vulnerabilities become the controlling emotional benchmark for the behaviour and self-expression of everyone. Their issues form the family paradigm that will control every family member.

For fear of being guilty of causing this parent pain and stress or to become angry and abusive, a child begins to selectively monitor its self-expression and behaviour. This form of guilt will become a permanent feature in its life and act as a severe constraint on way it can be in the world. When an adult, the guilt and the associated fear of causing pain and suffering in others will have the effect of attracting needy vulnerable people because they feel safe with them. If in addition to the guilt, they adopt the victim strategies of their parents they can become just as sensitive and fragile or as aggressive and abusive as their parents were. Just like them they will seek to avoid being held accountable for the negative experiences in life by shifting the responsibility to others or the world. The avoidance of guilt will become their priority in life.

The Inception of False Guilt

Here are some of the most common examples of family paradigms where guilt is the inevitable outcome:

A family where the father is emotionally shut down and will not be held accountable for his actions and behaviours. Feeling unable to express what he feels, he may resort to alcohol or become a workaholic to deal with his emotions and stress. Over time his emotional issues can take him into depression and make himself absent from the family or drink in excess. Amongst his problems is failure and guilt, being a disappointment as a man, his fear of exposing his needs and feelings for fear of appearing weak and powerless which also culminate as his issues with women. Experiencing a deep sense of powerlessness in life — he feels trapped in an emotional existence he believes he cannot change

His partner is insecure but aggressive in her demands and needs and is not afraid to let him know where he falls short of her expectations. His alcoholism and less than appropriate behaviour make him an easy target for her critical judgment and his inability to give a meaningful response increases his sense of powerlessness and thereby his anger. Occasionally, in frustration, he may burst out in aggressive verbal abuse or even physical violence, only to feel the victim and withdraw to the nearest bar.

She feels totally justified in her judgment of him but even though she makes out that he is the problem she does not leave him. In reality her belief in her own powerlessness makes her needy and reliant on his presence in her life. Just like her mother, she fears of facing life independently and therefore cannot exist without the support of a man. The prospect of facing the world on her own terrifies her and this makes her aggressive. She has trust issues with men because her father was an unpredictable and aggressive alcoholic. She does not completely realize that she married a man just like her father because in too many ways she has become the same woman her mother is.

Had you grown up in this family think of what you would be exposed to and how it would have affected you? If you are a girl you would have your mother as the reference point for the development of your femininity. Your exposure to your parents' relationship and how your father relates to you will serve as a template for your future relationships. Their capacity to express love, affection and emotions will come to define how you feel about your self and how you expect others to feel about you. It will determine what your expectation of what a loving relationship should be. None of it provides a great prospect for a happy and emotionally balanced life. There is however much more going on between the girl and her parents.

Though she is just a little girl, she senses that because her father and mother are in continuous conflict, he has issues with women and therefore also with her. She perceives her mother as a victim in the conflict and subconsciously accepts her mother's fears and in securities as her own. Her femininity in respect to men is modelled on that of her mother and this will make a strong contribution to the nature of her relationships with men in the future. At her age it, is unavoidable that her relationship with him will be conditional to his fears, depression or anger. It is also inevitable that she will change her behaviour and self-expression to accommodate her father's issues. By doing so, she unconsciously accepts responsibility —guilt— for his negative behaviour and attitude. This responsibility will become a part of her sense-of-self in respect to all men. In any conflict or confrontation with her father (or men like him), these beliefs will cause her to assume she is the guilty or responsible one and accept a position of powerlessness —just like her mother did.

She will deliberately avoid being open and expressive with her feelings, needs or desires for fear that it will elicit an angry reaction from him or make him reject or abandon her. Just like her mother, her passive-aggressive strategic behaviour is to complain indirectly about all the things she is unhappy with and misses out on but cannot have. She will now and in the future also be the one that will compromise if her father or partner gets aggressive with her. She only feels free and safe to express her discontentment and show her disappointment in him when he feels powerless and inadequate —just like her mother did. Her guilt issues in respect to her father will reappear because she will be attracted and attract men like him. Her mother's belief that she is the innocent victim is likely become hers. She will be convinced that the men she has relationships are the cause for all her issues and unhappiness. It will be unlikely that she will look within herself for the reasons for this and be accountable for them.

Even though the mother behaves like the victim in the relationship, her negative attitude and consistent expressions of dissatisfaction always dominated the family paradigm. Her neediness and discontent received priority in every family situation resulting in her daughter's needs, fear and insecurities being ignored. The mother's neediness for attention and affection and her dependence on men to fulfil these needs make her selfish. This mindset was already present when her daughter was born compounded by her mother's inability to cope with the demands and responsibilities of motherhood. Unable to fulfil her own needs and expectations she feels unable to give her daughter the love and attention she was entitled to experience. She felt under-resourced and powerless to deal with the needs and expectation of her daughter and this amplified her fears and self-doubt. Her daughter, sensing her mother's fears and anxiety, believed that she was the cause and therefore automatically accepted responsibility for her mother's stress. This will stop her from holding her mother accountable for not being there for her emotionally.

The suppression of the authentic, spontaneous and unique self begins very early in a child's life. As does the acceptance of beliefs that she is responsible and guilty for her mother's negative emotions and dissatisfaction. Her unconscious self-suppression will have the effect of intensifying her own unfulfilled need to be loved, to have attention and to get what she wants and she cannot help become needy in her behaviour. She fears asking directly for what she wants for fear of guilt for being a burden and so she resorts to indirect strategies instead. Without realising she emulates much of her mother's behaviour for similar emotional reasons by complaining and nagging. This completes an emotional circle which sets the girl up to repeat her mother's life with a man like her father driven by guilt and never having what she really wants.

A boy would have a similar experience to the girl but would likely model his masculinity on his father. He will be constantly exposed to a dissatisfied insecure mother who is powerless in life and a frustrated angry father who feels he can never be and do enough. His mother is the one who has the most initial influence on him. His is need and dependence for her love and acceptance translates into behaviour that has the intent to keep his mother happy and content. He is likely to become frustrated by the guilt he feels when she displays her discontent and unhappiness because he feels powerless to satisfy her needs. All this sets him up for the same future relationship as his father. Modelling himself on his father's belief that a man has to be responsible for the happiness and satisfaction of women in order to be loved and accepted by them, he will attract and be attracted to needy dissatisfied women. His sense-of-self will define the type of relationships chooses that allow him to play out his guilt issues in relation to women.

If his father is abusive and neglectful he may become defensive of his mother and despise his father's aggression and abuse. This can cause him to suppress the natural masculine assertiveness and sexual expression to avoid appearing as a threat to his mother. Alternatively he may take on his father's beliefs and behaviour and adopt a chauvinist attitude that makes him look down on women. As a result he will blame them for everything that he believes to be wrong in his relationship with them.

Both the girl and boy have learned that the conditions incorporated in guilt are those by which they will be loved, accepted and trusted. Until they accept responsibility for their part in their relationships and deal with that part of their sense-of-self, it is likely to remain that way.

Embarrassment and Shame

We cannot talk about guilt and responsibility without addressing embarrassment and shame even though they are intrinsically connected. We were not born with shame and embarrassment as an intrinsic part of our consciousness. These qualities are acquired from the world we arrive in. When babies we do not care if we are stark naked and urinate in public, if we have food on our faces or demand something in the most inconvenient or inappropriate moment. Shame and embarrassment are learned from others: family or our culture.

We acquire shame and embarrassment by accepting responsibility for the shame our parents (or others) feel. When blamed for causing embarrassment we usually have no idea what we are accused of but never the less feel somehow guilty because we are being told we are the responsible party. The behaviour of our parent and insistent nature of the blame soon makes it clear we must be guilty of something really bad. Initially, we cannot fathom the connection between the embarrassed adult and what it was about us or what we did or did not do that triggered this aggressive reaction towards us. We begin to feel however that we must be responsible because the blame and anger is directed at us. Not conscious of what it is within or about us that causes the negative reaction we can only conclude that **the shame must be caused by who we are**. Once the so called error in our expression or behaviour is pointed out to us, it is made clear why *we* are the cause for their embarrassment. Unable to truly understand the reason, we nevertheless believe and accept that **we <u>are</u> the embarrassment and the shame because of <u>who and what we are</u> <u>when we do or say something we should or should not</u>**. These will over time evolve into a self-beliefs of shame that then form our sense-of-self. We quickly learn to make others responsible for the shame we have accepted from our parents or family the same way it was done to us.

Our physical reaction to shame— blushing — serves to reinforce the sense that we must be guilty even though we do not want to be seen and recognized as the embarrassment. It becomes obvious to a child that it cannot defend its behaviour against the accusations of an adult and therefore has no choice but to accept responsibility. In the future its fear of being responsible for shame will make it behave just like the adult who created the shame in them and blame others for his or her feelings of embarrassment.

Our learned and adopted fears and insecurities will come to the surface in the form of behaviours and feelings but this usually gives little if no indication as to how they are a part of us. Our early upbringing also created the belief that others are responsible for our feelings and causes us to behave as if we are not responsible for what we feel and do. When we try to find the cause for our issues, we can only see that others are the cause for our shame or anger, to feel offended or sad and so on.

The influence shame and embarrassment can have over our state of mind is evident in some cultures where acts of extreme punishment are committed on those that are believed to be responsible for shaming others, the family or community. Murder and disfigurement of women is still a frequent occurrence in certain places in the world with shame and embarrassment as the central motivation.

Accepting the belief that we are responsible for the thought, feelings and emotions of others we also inadvertently accept that others must be guilty of causing the repertoire of emotions we feel which includes shame and embarrassment. Without accepting responsibility for the emotions we manifest, this interpretation for the reasons and causes for what we feel will be perpetuated in the next generation.

Chapter 14

Conditional Relationships

Falling in love is of the most emotionally intense and overwhelming sensations we can have. Our relationships or the potential for one has the capacity to dominate our entire focus and interest in life. In many ways intimate love relationships are central to human existence and paramount to the continuation of our species. We do not exist in isolation of others or the world and generally need partners to have families and friendships in our lives. Experiencing our sense-of-self through the dynamic of our relationships is essential to evolving our consciousness. On an emotional level, relationships serve to create psychological mirrors that allow us to learn about who we are and who we are not.

Relationships between people from casual to friendships and close and intimate are the place where many of critical issues, central to our emotional and sometimes physical survival are played out. If it were as simple as falling in love and living happily ever after we would not have the conflict and unhappiness that lead to separation and divorce. The reality is that being happy and fulfilled in relationships is amazingly difficult for the majority of people. We are convinced by our negative experiences in childhood that in order for a relationship to be successful we either have to compromise our own needs and expectations or make others give up theirs for us. However, neither of these compromises are a solution for the issues that we bring into a relationship. Treating a relationship as if it is a negotiated contract might appear sensible and logical but this will rarely lead to a solution for the dissonance between partners. This almost business-like solution can make a relationship an ongoing negotiation over power, need fulfilment and setting and respecting boundaries of behaviour and so on but is unlikely to be an enduring emotional success.

Many believe that conflict and relationships naturally go together because they have not known it to be different. It is true that being in a relationship almost guarantees that sooner or later differences appear which can become the sites for hostile emotional battles. Most people believe that a successful harmonious relationship is a matter of making the right choice of partner and there are few who would accept that *they* are the real reason why *their* relationships do not work. It must be obvious that each partner contributes to the differences that are being played out with their personal issues.

You will only understand why your relationships evolve in the way they do if you understand who you are as a partner. You can begin by looking at your own behaviour and by becoming aware of your thoughts and feelings when you are in a relationship. If you want to *recognise and accept responsibility for your contribution to the issues in your relationships,* it is essential that you get to know 'who you are' really well.

Attractions and Desires

Our desire to be in an intimate relationship occupies our emotions and focus and well before we get involved. Whenever there is a prospect of meeting a potential partner we tend to become self-conscious of our appearance and how we believe others will see us. Worried that we will not be good enough, we fear being criticised and judged. We commonly measure our self-esteem and our potential for attracting a partner by the confidence we have in our appearance and behaviour.

You are likely to believe that you have nothing to offer to a prospective partner if you can only see yourself in a negative light. Your negative beliefs set the stage for any encounter with your opposite gender because you will expect and anticipate rejection or judgement from the outset. Your conviction that you will never be chosen or wanted because of who you believe yourself to be will control what you will say and how you behave. If this is how it is for you, remember that your critical view of yourself is learned from the way you were treated as a child.

Ironically, we often acquire our negative beliefs from those who have the best intention to teach us right from wrong, good from bad. The problem is that they are teaching us these values without the awareness of their own fears and insecurities. As a result they try and teach us what is right by telling us *what we do wrong and what we should have done instead.* Parents indoctrinate their children into the beliefs, values and standards they learned through their childhood unaware that they are distorted by fear. They remind their offspring through criticism of everything that they supposedly do wrong or failed them. Instead of presenting their children with positive guiding input they create the perception that there is something wrong or bad with them. In spite of the intent to makes us feel confident and loved and present us with a positive self-image they create the direct opposite. Their constant attention on the negatives imprints a child's mind with the *apparent truth of its intrinsic*

shortcomings and failings. These criticisms and judgements become the child's perception of itself — ***the definition of who it is.*** The resulting negative self-beliefs that begin to occupy its sense-of-self become the basis for future intents, emotions and behaviours with inevitable outcomes.

Few parents realize that the way they communicate their expectations of their children can have a negative effect on how they form their sense-of-self. A child may appear to be good and successful because it is meeting the expectations of its parents but often it ***not*** the experience the child has. Our parent's expectations do not necessarily reflect our own passions and desires even if we cannot as yet articulate them. In fact, our zealous need to please our parents will cause us to comply or fit in with what they want us to be or do and cause us never to discover our own. Not having the chance to discover what our potential, talents and abilities, passions and desires are or having them dismissed can be fatal to finding our passion in life. We may please our parents by entering a profession they value but we may thereby also deny ourselves doing what we really want to be. Our natural creative talents and abilities can be lost to ourselves and never find a voice in our lifetime. Living life in fear of the judgments of others can deny us the experience through which we could ***ultimately fulfil our life potential***.

You may well feel that you are the disappointment and a failure to them and yourself should you feel that you do not live up to your parent's standards and expectations. Parents who have specific ideas of what their child should be or do in their life are also likely to dismiss and invalidate anything that does not conform to it. As a result you may miss out on finding out what you are most passionate about and talented in. Even though they are the creators of these expectations, you will be blamed should you fail them. It is also likely that you will naively accept the responsibility for their disappointment by assuming guilt. In fact ***you may accept that you are the disappointment*** as a part of your identity.

A person who has no trust in the value and capacity of their own intelligence will either be passive and lack confidence or try and prove to everyone that he knows and is always right. Unfortunately when they become parents they unwittingly play out these issues out on their own children. They either need to prove to themselves how right and smart they are or cannot instil self-trust and confidence in their offspring because they do not have it in themselves. Not realizing the consequences of their behaviour each actively teaches their children to distrust their own capacities and abilities and to become fearful of being a disappointment and a failure. They either overrule their children's understanding, explanations and choices by constantly correcting them and knowing better or can not giving them confirmation of their intellectual and emotional strengths. They may have the intent to teach them self-confidence but the reality they are undermining the child's trust in its own thinking, judgement, reasoning, perception and ability to draw conclusions, not to mention making decisions and choices. It will feel criticised and judged or unsupported on every level of the expression of its emotional, intellectual and creative mind. Under these psychological pressures a child will potentially grow up convinced that it is emotionally and intellectually inferior. Ether way, it cannot trust its judgement, knowledge and capacity to think and reason and has to rely on strategic behaviour to get through life by avoidance or by proving that the opposite is true.

Expecting that you know, understand and can do something before you have learned or understood it is of course ridiculous but that is often exactly the experience a child has. Parents who by their behaviour need to prove they are right and all knowing frequently unwittingly create this impression with their children. They need to prove that they know and others — even their own children — do not. They do not realize that they are convincing their child through their behaviour that it is dumb, inadequate and hopeless for not knowing something it never had the chance to understand and learn. This places a demand on their child's intellect and competency it can never meet and is guaranteed to fail. Internalising this experience as its sense of self, it faces the future with beliefs that undermine its confidence in its mental capacities as the 'tools' by which to create and manifest success, happiness and abundance. The outcome is not hard to predict because usually the difficulties will already begin when they go to school. For children with these issues, the education systems do not run far behind the all knowing and infallible parent in the way it "punishes" children for not performing to the curriculum's expectations. The question is: Is the system failing the children or are the children failing the system?

Criticism and judgement come in many forms — it can be indirect by continually correcting everything a child chooses or expresses itself and treating it as a disappointment, a failure or a mistake. Alternatively by directly telling it that it is dumb, hopeless, incompetent and so on. The effect on a child will be the similar. In time, the child interprets these destructive exchanges as negative affirmation of who it really is. **Collectively, every demeaning, critical, judgement and correction will form the truth of who and what it believes itself to be.** The outcome will reveal itself in behaviour — either by acting as if they know everything in order to convince others or accepting that they will always be wrong and fail. Either way, both will continue living life in fear of failure.

Developing a Conditional Sense-of-Self

Each child is a unique consciousness and common qualities in their behaviour or physical likeness to one or both parents is not an indication of the true nature of its consciousness. The unique nature of a child demands that it grows and learns at its own pace and in its own way. Unaware of how critical this is to its development they will try and mould its mind to fit their perception of life and the world. They do not realize that the world they see is a product of their own beliefs — negative and positive.

A child's innate drive and desire to spontaneously express its natural authentic self usually puts it in conflict with the values and expectations held by its parents. Their expectations of what their child should be, how it should behave and what it should choose, want and think and so on are a product of what their own parents were expected to be. Parents are likely to respond with judgement and criticism that their child will interpret as rejection. Ultimately, it may feel that it is a failure and a disappointment, unlovable and unacceptable. When a child responds by being disagreeable in its behaviour and attitude the parents do not understand the reasons and automatically blame the child. The issues the parents inherited deprive them from experiencing their child's most spontaneous and powerful state of being. They do not realize that the conditions they bring into the relationship are experienced by their child as a rejection of its authentic nature.

The need to be loved and accepted and the pressure of their innate need for emotional and physical survival forces most children to accept the emotional constraints created by their parent's fears. The fear driven dynamic between parent and child will cause its unique qualities to go unrecognized and dismissed. The impact of not being acceptable will manifest in every aspect of its life.

When a child's attraction and fascination are outside the parents' interest or frame of reference, they are often squashed or just invalidated. Even though a parent may believe that a child's passions and desires are difficult to realize that does not mean this it is unachievable for the child. Unintentionally, the parent's own fears and limitations become the restricted and often-fearful world they create for their children. Their biased perception does not allow them to recognize the potential, talent and ability in their children. It may have an attraction for artistic pursuits and show no interest in physical or material achievements or it may be the other way around. Once the child grows up it will dismiss it own attractions and fascinations because these were made wrong and rejected by the parents. As a result, it cannot find what it wants to do with its life not realizing that it has learned to dismiss what it really wants the most.

A child can be late in finding its passion or fascination and therefore needs time for self-discovery and self-realization. Stimulation, time and space gives it room to let its imagination and fantasy roam freely creating opportunity to discover its own desires, attractions and dreams. A child needs the emotional space to develop its talents and abilities at its own pace and in its own way in order to discover its capacity to creatively deal with life's complexities. Open minded guidance and support are essential to finding its own direction. Exposure to criticism and judgment will only cause it to believe that it is not good enough, a failure and a disappointment. Childhood is a critical stage for our perpetually evolving mind and each aspect of the emotional environment of our family plays a determining role in forming our inner sense of being.

Our parents are victims of their issues just like we are and usually do not realise the impact the emotional expression will have on their children by showing their disappointment and sadness, depression and negativity, worry and stress and so on. Their negative sense-of-self and the emotional state it creates will prevent them being the confident guiding forces their children need them to be.

Expecting to be responsible for a life other than your own can be an issue for a parent particularly when they feel unloved, unacceptable and powerless and their own aspirations have never been fulfilled. How can someone who was never been loved and accepted **unconditionally** and therefore have not learned to love themselves, have the capacity to be unconditional loving and accepting as a parent? The demand to unconditionally respond to needs and expectations of their child can feel like a sacrifice and burden. The innate need of their child to feel and experience unconditional love will be felt as a sacrifice because their own need for love is still to be fulfilled. Their victim state of mind will cause their children to believe that their existence is a burden and their innate needs and expectations are an intrusion on their parent's lives. The only way they can have a relationship with their parents is by suppressing their need for love, acceptance, support, care and protection and so on — they will feel they have no choice. Often this is paired with the child fulfilling the parent's need to be loved by giving love and attention to the parent in order to get validation and acknowledgement.

We need to remind ourselves that we are all born unique and different and that our emotional issues are a legacy from childhood. It is important to first of all accept intellectually that *our issues are not and will never represent who we truly are*. The part of you that feels the negative emotions and experiences negative outcomes is actually more 'the real you' than that part of you that gets lost in these fear-based emotions. By accepting that your issues do not define who you really are, you can at least be sure of **who you are not**.

Blinded by Illusions

Anything you believe or feel about yourself based on fear is actually an illusion and cannot be representative of who you really are.

Once we are adults it may seem that our childhood is in the past but the emotional footprints it has left on our sense-of-self will continue to control our behaviour, choices and perception. It proves that the family legacy of negative beliefs still define who we believe we are and therefore our sense of emotional reality. We need to explore our family history to understand the complex nature of our issues and behaviours in our relationships. Due to the unique nature of each person there are an infinite variety of possible negative family dynamics to which an individual could have been exposed. If, for example, we come from a family that is emotionally turbulent or violent than the evidence of negative influence is obvious and clearly show how our minds were negatively imprinted.

Passive emotionally dysfunctional paradigms played out in families are much harder to recognise because open confrontation and conflict is extremely rare or never occurs. On the surface a family can appear harmonious and peaceful because of the passive and suppressive emotional strategies with which the parents control the emotional space. In this type of family paradigm, the parents unconsciously play out their issues through strategic behaviours and attitude that have their roots in powerlessness and victimhood. They give the impression that they will be negatively affected by the free and spontaneous expression of the behaviour, needs, expectations and emotions of their children. Constantly putting their vulnerabilities on display by acting like victims will cause their children to accept responsibility — guilt — for what their parents fear and do not deal with. The behaviours that come from their fears and insecurities have become the instruments with which they control their emotional environment.

Children can be quick to develop reciprocal behaviour to avoid the guilt that they would feel were they to upset their parents. They learn to fear giving expression to anything that they now believe will cause stress, worry and concern in their parents. Developing independence very early in life is one way they can avoid being a burden to their parents. Compliant and submissive behaviour by the children to avoid being responsible for upsetting the parents creates a façade of peace and harmony. This deceptive picture of the family is not only for outsiders but also for the sake of all family members. Not knowing any different, each family member could well be under the illusion that they are actually part of the perfect family. Reality is, that unconsciously each practices self-suppression to avoid being confronted by their greatest fear — being guilty of upsetting others.

This kind of background makes it more difficult to get a clear understanding from where the emotional harm in your family came from. Parents who feel and believe they are powerless and fear confrontation may unconsciously solicit the protection and support from their children. The guilt this instils in child makes it extremely difficult for them to see their parents objectively when they are adults. The perception that their parents struggled and sacrificed themselves for them makes it hard to accept that their parents are the origin for their own fears and issues in life. This leaves them to have to accept that either they must have been born flawed or that the world responsible for all their ills. Neither of these options will take them to a place were real change and a permanent resolution is possible. Personal change will not be achievable if we allow guilt to stop us from being objective of the relationship dynamic we experienced with our parents.

Depending on the gender of the child, the influence a parent has over a child and its parents can be broken down into specific areas. If a girl, she will instinctively model her sense of femininity on her mother just as a boy will his masculinity on that of his father. Their own definition of the nature of their sexuality will be deeply influenced by interpretation of the same gender parent. A child will either try and reject or embrace the definition of gender represented by the behaviour of its same gender parent. This depends on its own unique nature and how it will serve its emotional survival in respect to its gender. Generally, the kind of intimate relationships it will have as an adult depends on the way the child's opposite gender parent related to the same gender parent and to the child. The strategic and emotional behaviour the parents display to each other and their child will determine the sense-of-self the child will adopt. Constant exposure to the parent's negative behaviour and self-expression between each other and their children enmeshes a child in the parent's gender based fears and insecurities.

The inner-perspective a girl or boy develop because of the relationship dynamic between their mother and father comes to define the sense of their own femininity or masculinity. If these are fear based they will show in every part of life but most intensely in intimate relationship. The expectations and subsequent experiences of intimate relationships are shaped by our subconscious needs, distrusts and powerlessness and so will be our disappointments.

Our lack of awareness of what drives us make it very difficult to recognize that we have issues and how they affect our behaviour, feelings and choices. Initially our feelings often lead us to believe that we have found the perfect partner only to discover later that we cannot live with much of their behaviour, habits or attitude. The inherited issues related to our opposite gender make it difficult to be objective in relationships. We see qualities in our potential partner that are a reflection of our own emotional needs born out of fear-based beliefs. This perception initially creates the illusion that they will fulfil our needs and are a perfect fit for us. In the early stages of the relationship we do not see that we are matching issues rather than just positive qualities. From their perspective the story is exactly the same in that they see their needs fulfilled through us and also do not realize that these are a product of their issues. Sooner or later this will bear out when conflict and discord arises from mutual dissatisfaction and discontent.

When a relationship fails, both parties commonly believe that they have justifiable reasons to blame the other for what went wrong. The accusations can be many and varied but often include accusations of being deceitful at the early part of the relationship. One will blame the other for not being the person they first met or that he or she deliberately misled or manipulated the other. Rarely are the real and fundamental reasons for the breakup — their own fears and insecurities —recognized and addressed.

Misled by Feelings and Attractions

Our consciousness has a simple consistency:
It will only be able to recognize and understand the issues of others once it has realized and transcended its own.

Issues manifested by your negative beliefs alter your perception and feelings by creating false insecurities, needs and expectations. Negative feelings have the capacity to make unfulfilled needs, expectations and insecurities appear genuine and this will cause you to be attracted to someone whose issues seem to be able to satisfy yours. As a counterpart to your issues, their emotional experience of you will in many ways equal your own. For example: Ego driven insecurity is attracted to ego based confidence — ego driven vulnerability is attracted to ego power and strength — a passive insecure victim will attract the ego driven controlling person and of course vice versa. Often it may not be as recognizable and clear as this because other issues can muddy the water but this kind of pattern consistently appears in relationships.

At the beginning of a relationship, both parties tend to get so overwhelmed by their feelings for each other that the real and more fundamental motivations for the attraction are not ever noticed. The love and lust for one another becomes the priority for emotional and physical satisfaction and there is generally no awareness for the deeper reasons for their mutual attraction. They will not see the negative beliefs they have activated in each other and the illusions these have created for each of them. Naturally mutual attraction can consists of many emotional and physical aspects and include love but any of these can be distorted by negative beliefs. Everyone brings their personal issues into a relationship and these will commonly complement those of their partner. This will usually generate the feeling that your needs will be fulfilled by the other. In the bliss of the initial phase of your encounter you will not be aware that you may actually be living an illusion of your own creation. The way your issues interrelate and correspond so perfectly, serves to make the illusion real for you.

Time has the habit of exposing cracks and flaws in relationships and it often does not take long for these to become serious points of conflict that, if unresolved, can break a relationship. For anyone who recognizes the dynamic in play, the outcome is predictable. Often soon after the 'honeymoon period' is over, disappointment, dissatisfaction and criticism are felt or expressed. When the causes are not dealt with, other measures are unlikely to bring lasting resolution. Failing to see that our own issues mirror those of our partner we will fall into blaming and accusing them for what we feel. Unaware of the part we play in the conflict we do not appreciate our responsibility to ourselves first and our partner second and it is probably the same for them. We miss the opportunity to learn and grow from the experience because we are not aware that we are the primary reason for the existence of the conflict. Often, the final journey of a relationship will be in deep contrast to the initial emotional experience you had when you first met.

Relationship issues do not prove that you are the failure but you make it terribly hard for yourself if you do not understand your attraction for a particular type of personality with which you have issues. You cannot change you life experiences if you do not make changes within yourself and that is not possible without being aware of what the issue is.

Relationships are essential to the process of living life not only for procreation but also because they have the capacity to **show us graphically who we believe we are.** Interaction between partners or others cannot only reveal our fear-based illusions but can thereby also provide the opportunity to discover **who we authentically are.** If you keep on choosing the same problematic relationships over and over without questioning your self, you are letting yourself down. Your presence in all of your relationships, points at you as the constant and therefore responsible party. By not accepting that you are the vital contributor to your relationship experiences, you are destined to repeat them. ***The pain you experience*** as a consequence of unsuccessful relationships ***is actually life's prompter for you to look at yourself.***

Remember this is not about what you do or choose but about who you are as the one making these choices and engaging in certain behaviours. Blaming others makes you the victim of the situation without resolution. Blame is your subconscious attempt to avoid responsibility for your choices. Based on what you believe, feel and think, you are the one who decides on the kind of relationship you want to have. You need to understand your inner-processes to see why you make choices that land you in unworkable relationships. You need to have clarity as to why your have the attraction for personalities that lead you into pain and unhappiness in order to know what you need to change within yourself.

Intellect and logic alone cannot undo the reasons for this distorted perception and the illusions it creates. Uncovering the nature of your sense-of-self by releasing your negative beliefs is the only way to raise your clarity of insight and bring you to understand your fears. Changing the core nature of your sense-of-self by releasing your fears will remove distortion from your perception, feelings and behaviour. Without it, manifesting a life that fulfils your potential on a personal level as well as in an intimate relationship will be extremely difficult if not impossible. Emotional issues will always act as a restriction in your life — in relationships and self-fulfilment, and success.

Trapped in Conditional Love

Desire for a potential partner is not simply based on love and physical attraction. Our sense-of-self plays an undeniably part in shaping the nature and context of our desires. Once our self-beliefs are involved so are the fears we harbour about ourselves and others and this will ensure that the object of our desire will be a counterpart to our issues and insecurities. What should be truly alarming about this is that we do this without any aware thought, planning or understanding. Yet, without fail, out of hundreds of potential choices, we will pick the very person who represents a perfect counterpoint to our fears.

It may not occur to you that your potential partner will be going through a similar experience because of their fears and insecurities. The individual issues you both bring into the relationship will also become the reasons for disharmony and conflict. If this astonishes you, then you have not fully realized **the power contained in the intent of your belief systems** and their capacity **to manifest your life experience <u>beyond your conscious intent and will.</u>**

Typically, in a room of full of people, you will be attracted to a particular type of person. You may also have noticed that generally not every one is attracted to the person you are interested in. You may believe that their looks and behaviour are the main attraction for you but it is the emotional energy their presence radiates that will actually win you over. The energetic state of their mind has to complement yours to make your potential partner — in your perception — be the "right" person for you.

For example: *If* you have a need to be the saviour in relationships by engaging in behaviour that makes you appear invulnerable and indispensible. Your strategy is designed to prove your worthiness to be loved and wanted and you will pick partners who have a need to be saved — who are powerless, needy and insecure.

If you are a person who has insecurities and feels in many ways powerless to support your self in life, you will be attracted to someone who appears strong and independent with the capacity to support you without having any expectations of you. Your strategy is to give love and attention in order to be saved and protected. The apparently strong partner has learned to present them selves as strong and invulnerable to their weak and needy parent in order to be loved and accepted by them. Just like you expect them to do this for you.

You could say these two are a perfect match for each other but their union is likely to result in conflict. When the apparent strong partner becomes tired of meeting the endless expectations of their weak and vulnerable mate and withdrawals, their mate will feel abandoned and deserted. The now fearful and disappointed powerless partner will make the other responsible for what they feel. Should the weaker partner change and becomes empowered and confident in themselves and no longer need support and protection, the 'strong partner' on will feel redundant and useless. Each of the two people in this example has an agenda inspired by their issues. Even though each therefore compliments the other, their relationship will still not work in the long term. If they were to look at themselves and each other objectively they would realize that each mirrors the issues of the other. The real difference lies in how each individually deals with it — one by using passive victim behaviour and the other by dominating and controlling.

If, for example, giving and receiving love in your family was conditional then relationships will have become a conditional process for you. Fear and distrust in respect to love and acceptance will become an inevitable part of your life. You will attract and be attracted to partners who through their issues are also conditional in their giving and receiving of love because of the distrust issues that they have. The behaviour in certain types can be obsessive in the way they express love and attention in their effort to convince someone that they are the only person in their life. Relentless communication is used to convince their potential partner that they are the only one for them. Their fear of rejection, abandonment or being alone is extreme. However, because you believe that you are unlovable and unacceptable, you have the need to be convinced before you will believe that someone loves you. Unfortunately it takes an excessive level of persistent attention before you can accept that someone loves you. It is a level of attention that only an obsessive person needy for love and in fear of rejection is able to give you.

Your fear of being hurt by rejection or abandonment will stop you from realizing that your partner is completely enrolled in a relationship strategy — to give love to get love, to give attention in order to get it. By getting you to respond positively to their behaviour they convince you and themselves that they are lovable and being loved by you. This creates the sense that you can trust and believe this love because of his or her persistent attention. Your need to feel loved and wanted and your attraction is usually enough to make you blind to what is really going on. Your desire to be convinced that it is safe to love and commit become the security for your attentive partner. Unfortunately once they have won you over, they can usually not cope with the incessant demands that your need for reassurance places on them. The emotional expectations they have created in you with their exclusive attention for you have become a trap for them. No partner can maintain this level of attention without feeling that his or her own need for love and attention is compromised. At this point they feel it is their turn to receive rather than give 'love'. Their change in behaviour will look to you like a withdrawal of love, affection and attention and this sets your alarm bells ringing. Your fears are well founded because your relationship has now reached a critical juncture. Your fear-based neediness to receive love and acceptance far outweighs your capacity to give these unconditionally.

People who actively and strategically "give love to get love" usually have the need to convince themselves that every member of the opposite gender desires and wants them. Their behaviour with their opposite gender is geared to get the response that will 'prove' this to them. Often, they have lots of 'friends', many of which are potential partners, waiting in the wings. Their deeper insecurities, which are not unlike your own, can also drive them to isolate you from friends and any contact with others, particularly your opposite gender. In order to quiet their fears, they need to own you exclusively and control your life. They will achieve this by being critical of your friends and acquaintances and forcing you to choose them over others. The real problem however, lies with you because without your fears and distrust of love and acceptance, you would have never been attracted to this kind of partner in the first place. You may not have seen it but your need for love and insecurity with the opposite sex have set yourself up for a lot of pain, unhappiness and insecurity.

Once conscious that your issues affect your objectivity it is wise to start exercising greater mindfulness over your choices, behaviours, needs and feelings by closely monitoring these. This would make you more aware of your deeper motivations and potential consequences of your attractions and dislikes. The innate need to love and be loved, including sexual attraction are naturally major influences in any personal relationship. You will only find a dependable level of stability and objectivity in relationships when your relationship with yourself is founded in unconditional love and acceptance. Never forget that the emotional attractions created by the intent of your negative beliefs have the capacity to turn your fears and insecurities into a real relationship experience.

Who is to Blame?

Just imagine that every one of your failed relationships was a crime scene. Would you not be suspicious if the same person turned up each time? ***You are the only one who is consistently present in every one of your relationships*** and that cannot be a coincidence. Who do you think would be the prime suspect in all your failed relationships if you were the common factor? The feelings, attractions and subsequent choices that bring you into relationships are yours and yours alone. You are still responsible for your choices in spite of the fact that you may be unaware of the influences your negative sense-of-self has over them. You can choose not to accept responsibility for your relationship failures but in doing so you decide not to be in control over your life. Only by taking responsibility for what and how you contributed to your relationships choices can you create the opportunity for change and take charge over your emotional life and more. Becoming conscious of yourself by questioning your own attitudes, needs and behaviour can be the beginning of realizing your personal power and embracing your authentic self.

The main reason that loving functional relationships are difficult create is not because of our issues with unconditional love and acceptance, being wanted and trust and so on. Our main handicap comes from our ignorance of knowing who we believe ourselves to be, who we truly are and our unwillingness to take responsibility for this. We cannot avoid realizing what we feel and believe about ourselves in our relationships with others but by accepting responsibility for what we contribute, we would not fall into blame and victimhood. Unfortunately, we tend to throw ourselves into relationships like lemmings running of a cliff, with the kind of desperate commitment that would leave a casual observer breathless. We tend to believe that what we feel about someone represents the truth even if others may not have the same perception.

Our judgment of potential partners is usually hopelessly flawed due to the issues we hold. As a result, no matter what advice we are given, we still follow our feelings of attraction without question because we want to believe what we feel in order to satisfy our fear driven needs. The interesting part of this is that many actually have a sense that something about the object of their passion is not quite what they seem to be. Lack of clarity and the fear that it will interfere with the fulfilment of their desire makes them dismiss these feelings and throw caution in the wind. You may try and convince yourself that you can consciously override or control these negative aspects but you will find that your negative beliefs dominate your emotional life throughout your life.

If you consider that both parties are not only transported into a relationship by their basic attraction for each other but also because of the personal issues that each bring with them, it is no surprise that conflict ensues. Our experience of conflict in a relationship feels therefore very are real and actual. Negative confrontations are a living breathing representation of differences in perception and awareness, needs and expectations when both parties are in a highly emotional state of mind. The intensity with which these differences are often fought over is a consequence of the fear for emotional survival that each party feels. The problems they place at the centre of their conflict are usually the symptoms of an issue rather than the core reasons. Only examination of their own mind set — the emotional issues they brought into the relationship — will reveal the truth of what is really going on between them. Unfortunately, blaming one another will only lead to further separation and less meaningful communication. By making the other responsible for your experience of the conflict you avoid accepting responsibility for your part in it. This is exactly the opposite of what you should be doing

Hold this thought:
At the most fundamental level of our spiritual being we are all one without being one and the same. At this core level of our being all consciousness melts into one unified concept:
One Greater Consciousness that encompasses all uniqueness and power in creation.
This fundamental unity is founded in unconditional love, acceptance and trust. In the absence unconditional love we exist in fear of everything that flows from it.

The Story of "Suspicious Distrust" and "the Convincer"

A woman who has trust issues with men will inevitably be attracted and attract men who are a counter part to this. If she is in fear that men will deceive and disappoint her she will need men who can prove to her that they are dependable, reliable and trustworthy. Her consistent state of suspicion and distrust makes entering relationships extremely difficult and fearful process. She finds it difficult to find men she feels she can trust.

The reasons for her issues will stem from childhood because her mother would have been distrusting of men. Her father may have been a charismatic philanderer or a flirt and a good talker with the need to prove to himself that women desire him. Even though her mother was continuously critical and complained about her father, she never left him. Her mother was far too needy and fearful of being alone to make that choice. Besides, her father would always talk himself back into her mother's life and her mother would always accept the promises he made. She, just like her mother, regarded her father and later men with distrust, something she has never been able to let go off.

A man who has trust issues with women grows up in a similar family. Early in life he will be exposed to his parent's relationship issues and witness some of their conflicts. Through his mother's complaints and discontent they often have early awareness of their father's indiscretions. His mother's consistent expressions of suspicion of his father make him feel judged as a male. This has the potential to make him feel guilty without real cause. His mother's distrust of men also affects the relationship she has with him. She often inquires into his whereabouts and the company he keeps which only reinforces his guilt feelings. Driven by his innate need for his mother's love, he seeks to placate his mother's distrust of him by telling her what he believes she wants hear. He begins to realize that this is the only way he can be free from her oppressive and controlling behaviour. Unconsciously he adopts a style of communication that has the intent to convince her that he would never hurt or disappoint her. This is his way of taking responsibility for his mother's fear and insecurities. His strategic communication style has the intent to prove that he is not like his father or men like him. He wants to convince her that he will protect her by shielding her from anything that could upset or make her insecure.

The beliefs he takes on from his childhood develop into an understanding of how he should relate to women and define what they expect from him. As an adult in relationships, it feels natural to him to be secretive about his life in order to avoid upsetting his partner. He has learned to only give out information that will get him what he wants as long as no-one gets upset with him. This becomes the only way he knows how give love and to be loved.

He bears his mother or women no direct malice, because he perceives them as being the victim of untrustworthy men. The potential of being guilty of this because he is a man stops him giving full expression to his authentic nature and masculinity. His well-meant ways with women will unfortunately always result in them getting hurt and victimized and leaves him feeling misunderstood, unloved and unwanted. On the surface the issues will look like deceit and distrust but the real reasons are the negative beliefs each brought into the relationship. He lives in constant fear of not being able to convince that he will not hurt or deceive them while at the same time living in fear of the responsibility and restrictions that his commitment to a relationship would place on him. She will feel totally justified in her feelings of distrust and therefore believes it is up to him to prove he is different. The only way out is for both to release the fundamental beliefs in relation to their opposite gender in order to see them selves and each other differently.

Women who distrust men are the daughters of the same kind of mothers and fathers that these men once had. Listening to their mother's stream of suspicions and accusations as they were growing up and exposed to their father's often secretive and covert behaviour, girls become convinced that men cannot be trusted or believed. Boys will unconsciously model themselves on their father while the girls model their femininity on their mother. They unknowingly adopt their mothers belief systems about men, relationships and love and incorporate these into their sense-of-self. They see their father and as a consequence all men as deceivers and liars who do not keep their promises and cannot be trusted to be supportive, dependable or faithful. She adopts her mother's strategic behaviour of suspicion and distrust and is inquisitive and controlling in relationships to quiet her fears.

Now, as an adult, she constantly demands that the partner in her life proves his trustworthiness to satisfy her suspicions. However her need to be loved and have a man in her life, just like her mother, defeats her every time. The only relationships she attracts are with men who seem to have the power to make her believe that they are true to their word and would never hurt her but then do the exact opposite. At the onset of the relationship men make her feel that she the centre of their passion and that she is the only one that matters in their life. Greedy for proof that will validate and endorse her need for love and acceptance she is likely to succumb to his promises. She does not realize she is the perfect counterpart for a convincer and that she is in fact attracted to his type of personality because of her neediness as a result of her issues. Living in distrust of the love from men makes her also deeply needy for it.

She is stuck in a vision of the world where men can never be trusted because her experience of relationships has proven this. She does not realize that out of all the men in a room she will be attracted to the one with a charismatic and over-confident articulate manner, while he finds himself unconsciously drawn to her need to be convinced by him. Once they are involved with each other she will not able to resist looking for more security in the relationship. She will start asking questions, which he experiences as being a mirror of his restrictive childhood and this will cause him to become evasive and secretive. His response only serves to bring back old suspicions in her and before she can stop herself she is asking questions that sound to him like an interrogation. What follows should have been predictable for each of them had they understood the emotional baggage they left home with.

In adulthood both the girl and boy suffer the consequences of distrust in love and relationships. We all have the innate desire and need to be in relationships whether they are close and intimate or friendships but when distrust comes into play, issues become unavoidable. A distrusting person feels inherently vulnerable to betrayal and deception, rejection and abandonment and will need proof from their partner that they will be safe from this. It does not occur to them that they are the problem but instead impose their need for proof of trust on others to assure their safety from deceit.

The Story of "Never Enough" and the "Tireless Provider"

Women, who believe they do not have the capacity and intellectual and emotional resources to live without support, fear taking responsibility for their own lives. They feel they are powerless and helpless to support themselves and therefore are convinced they need to depend on a man to survive. Often their sexuality and capacity to attract men become the currency in their relationships and in life in general. The significance of their physical appearance features prominently throughout their lives. They usually grow up in families where the mother has the belief that men are indebted to her and owe her support and care. Convinced of their entitlement to hold men responsible for their needs, emotional and material security, they tend to have an air of discontent and dissatisfaction with virtually everything in their life as if nothing is ever quite good enough for them. The significance of their entitlement is underlined by their criticism of everything and everyone that does not meet their expectations. Designed to give an impression of superiority it is actually their strategy to deal with their fear of being inferior, not being good enough and never getting what they want. They justify that their demands and behaviour to others in order to convince themselves that they are entitled. Their fear of the perceived consequences of being denied can make them go to just about any length to get what they want. She is high maintenance because her fear of existing without material and emotional security rules her emotions, perception and behaviour. She is the one and only priority in her life — everyone else runs a distant second.

Men that are attracted to women with this kind of issue come from families that have mothers with these characteristics. The males in the family learn very early that to be worthy of their mother's love and affection they need to be able to meet her high demands and expectations as providers and carers of women. When they are young they are expected to meet their mother's emotional needs but as they mature into men these become material and financial. In this family dynamic the father and his issues are as great an influence as those of the mother. The father's issues with his self-value in respect to women causes him to be attracted to his partner's pretentious behaviour. She gives him the impression that she is a woman with high expectations and values and a prize for any man she deems good enough. Having her glamour in his life makes him feel special and more significant than other men. Unfortunately, he takes a great deal of pride in his ability to keep on meeting her neediness at great cost to himself. His boasts and need to prove his superiority are not lost on his son who will likely try to prove his worth as a man in exactly the same way.

Their daughter is likely to relate to her femininity according the role her mother plays out for her and to her father. Her father and mother sets the standards and promotes the belief systems that will determine what her future expectations from men and relationships will be. She will be convinced by both her mother that her father and all men like him are responsible saving her from her insecurities by providing for her needs whatever they may be. Her father, true to his role, will in all likelihood believes he has to give his daughter everything she desires so that he can win her heart. If he were not to meet the needs and expectations of women in his life, he fears not being worthy of their love. He has learned to accept that their dissatisfaction, discontent and unhappiness are <u>his</u> fault and so guilt is a strong driving force in his motivation to please. This makes him extremely vulnerable to their criticism and judgement

The behaviour between mother and father is the lesson by which both son and daughter will in time learn to define their respective sexualities. The boy will accept that being responsible for his mother and later women is an indivisible part of his masculinity. The girl will emulate her mother's sense-of-self to become just like her. They both learn that the promise of their strategic behaviours is to be loved and accepted but have no awareness that all the conditions they set for each other distort the sincerity and truth of their relationships. Love for both is conditional and failure to meet the expectations they have of each other will result in the belief that ultimately love will be denied. The potential absence of love and acceptance drives the fear that motivates their behaviour. In adulthood he is unlikely to confront her for her unreasonable demands, needs and behaviour because she will make him feel inadequate as a man for failing her. He will believe that her dissatisfaction and disappointment is always **his** fault. She will not ever be satisfied and content with her life because what she really wants is to experience love, trust and acceptance that is unconditional.

Their needs are interdependent but require individual resolution. Her need to be provided for makes her totally dependent on men and his need to be the provider in order to be deserving of a woman's love makes him dependent on women. These are often a long term relationship dynamic riddled with emotional stress and pain. All family members live in fear or guilt and the only solution they believe they have available in their emotional arsenal is to meet the conditions each sets for the other.

Women and men with these issues have only ever learned to give and receive love conditionally. Neither feels they can exist alone because they are both needy of their emotional counterpart in order to feel they are loved and wanted, significant and special, even if it is conditional.
Even though they use their sexuality to attract men these women are likely to have insecurities with emotional and physical intimacy. Regardless of their issues, these men and women are never long without a relationship. Her fear that she cannot survive without a man results in a desperate need to be in a relationship. Once she has a partner she is in constant fear of being rejected or abandoned. A man can lose meaning and purpose in the latter years of his life if all of his efforts have been used to satisfy the expectations and needs of his

partner while his remain unfulfilled. From the very beginning his passions, desires, talents and abilities were always second to the fear driven needs and expectations of his mother and later to those of his partners.

This kind of relationship lasts as long as he remains the tireless supplier of his partner's needs and expectations and she feels satisfied and secure enough to stay with him. Their relationship is only as strong as his need to create the lifestyle she requires for her ego and her fear of being rejected and having to face life on her own.

Without Feelings Where is Love?

To one degree or another there are many who have an issue with showing their feelings and emotions and dealing with those of others. The causes for this can be cultural and individual at the same time. This fear will create the need to avoid emotional confrontation of all kinds and an attraction to those who are similarly emotionally suppressed. The unconscious intent is to ensure that they will not be confronted by extreme emotions such as anger or sadness and pain.
Each needs the other to be emotionally predictable and stable to avoid feeling overwhelmed by a strong or aggressive emotional reaction of the other. The knowledge that their partner will never emotionally challenge them makes them feel secure in their relationship. However this also means that they cannot make any emotional demands or expectations of one another or hold one another accountable.

They may be attracted to emotionally expressive people but the prospect of living with someone who is frank in their expression is too confronting for them because it demands like response from them. One partner usually appears to be more assertive and confident than the other but this is often only representative of different intensities of the same fears. Neither will openly show what they truly feel and as a result issues, when they arise, are never truly resolved. Avoidance of any negative emotional situation or conflict is their strategy in life, which makes confronting their issues an extreme challenge.

The source for their issues can be traced back to a family upbringing where the expression of emotion — often with the exception of happy feelings — would be frowned upon. Particularly expressing the expectation of love and affection can cause an extreme reaction in this kind of family paradigm. The only emotions that are allowed to have a voice are those that no one will be offended by or confronted. This result is a family environment that totally lacks emotional truth because it leaves only a small range of feelings that can be openly expressed. Children from such families live in doubt whether they are lovable, acceptable or wanted because their parents never directly show love and affection. Without the emotional certainty that physical affection and interest accompanied with loving words would give their children, they are left to question whether they matter at all to their parents.

Unaware of their negative beliefs concerning the expression of feelings and their issues with unconditional love, they assume that they are giving love to their children by physically caring. They may have the intent to love and want, accept and trust unconditionally but their child has no emotional or physical evidence that their parent feels that way about them. Without having the actual experience, it is left in doubt that is lovable and acceptable, wanted and trusted.

The avoidance strategies played by their parents — passively or aggressively — result in different forms of guilt for their children. Their parent's behaviour implies that they cannot cope with the emotional needs and expectations of their own children. In turn, feeling that they are responsible for creating the stress and fear their parent's display and subconsciously, their children suppress their own feelings in order to avoid being responsible. They become convinced that they are and emotional burden and learn to feel guilty for expecting and needing love and affection. They become convinced that they have no choice but to suppress their innate need and entitlement to be loved and accepted and it will be a subconscious condition in every future relationship.

Not knowing any different, children accept the pervading family paradigm as normal. This causes the need to develop a sense-of-self based on fear of the expression of feelings an emotions. Potentially, they will spend the rest their life unconsciously trying to anticipate how others will feel in response to what they want to express for fear that they will upset or offend them and so on. Their choice of what to say or not to say is edited by the fear of upsetting others. They cannot give expression to their spontaneity in their inter-action because of their fear of being guilty of causing emotional upheaval in others and provoke the potential for rejection, criticism or blame. The limit of their self-expression will always depend on their perception and interpretation of the emotional vulnerabilities and potential aggression of others. Rather then just giving expression to how they feel or think, their focus is on the other's fears, needs and insecurities in order to avoid risking guilt, conflict or embarrassment by saying "the wrong thing".

A child that has not experienced physical and emotional demonstrations of love, acceptance and trust becomes an adult who never feels free to express the need to experience this. The question is: If you have **never** been shown that you are worthy and deserving of love and therefore are lovable and that it is safe to give and receive love, how will you conduct yourself in a relationship and what kind of relationship will you choose?

Relationships formed on the basis of suppressed emotions, driven by guilt either become bland or fail. The lack of emotional fulfilment for each partner will make the more aggressive one look for some sort of resolution, which will be unsettling if not confrontational for the other. Whoever takes the aggressive role in this confrontation will be seen to be responsible for the breakup leaving the passive partner as the 'innocent victim'. Resolution for either partner lies in releasing the beliefs of their fear of experiencing, receiving and expressing emotions positive as well as negative. Without the fear of guilt and blame they would show what they truly feel and not feel responsible for the reaction and emotions of others. Assuming there is love between them, their relationship would be very different in the absence of these negative beliefs — fears. Their changed sense-of-self would lead to an alteration in perception, needs and behaviour that would serve to bring them closer to being the spontaneous emotional spirits they were always meant to be.

The fear of unconditional love, acceptance and trust creates an emotional void that unless dealt with, will remain a source for pain throughout ones' life. Our innate expectation to be in harmony with our essence will assure that we will always yearn to fill the emptiness that the absence of unconditional love leaves.

Change without Fear

Even though our families are the source for our sense-of-self, we need to remember that our parents were subjected to the issues their parents inherited from their families. Blaming them for you what are going through will not resolve anything for you. Persisting in holding them responsible will in the long term keep you powerless to make change because you perceive the cause for your problems to be outside of you. It will also leave your family issues unresolved for you. You need to take ownership of your issues by accepting that now, as an adult you are the one holding on to the causes as a part of your sense-of-self. As an adult, you can no longer claim that anyone is doing "it" to you.

By accepting this responsibility you also accept that you are the origin for your problems in life. This choice allows you to regain control over your life and take back your power instead of being disempowered by believing you are the victim of others and negative situations. This change in perception is the most significant you can make because it will transform your perspective of yourself and life, as you know it. By accepting responsibility for your issues, you are ready to objectively explore your past, your emotional family history in respect to yourself.

Becoming aware of your behavioural patterns that are responsible for conflict, unhappiness and discontent and so on, is the first step in understanding yourself and others. The knowledge you acquire can bring you to realize why you feel the way you do in those situations. Everything you learn and see will be a piece of the puzzle that will ultimately lead to discovering the negative belief systems that are at the source. In the knowledge that fear distorts your sense-of-self, becoming self-aware and how you relate to others and the world will allow you to see yourself in a different light.

In the past, forcing yourself to behave differently may have got you positive results. Not only is this kind of solution difficult to maintain but it also does not address the core reasons for your issues. Over time it is unavoidable that your fear-based beliefs will manifest. ***Real transformation comes by changing who you are*** and not just by a change in behaviour. ***Releasing false beliefs rooted in fear will transform who believe your self to be*** and as such ***change the doer/ thinker and*** this will ***automatically change the doing/ thought***. Changing our inner-identity will also change whom you are attracted to and who is attracted to you.

By changing who you are, you will create a new relationship with your self and this changes the dynamic of your relationship with others. Accepting responsibility for your negative contributions to a relationship is an important part of this for you. It is the same for your partner. Remember that your current partner is your choice and a result of your attractions, needs and expectations, none of which you can hold her or him accountable for. If they turned out to be unlike who you thought they were, you have no choice but to take responsibility for your own distorted perception that caused you to be attracted to them in the first place. If you can recognize how this distorted perception in regard to intimate relationships became a part of you, it will show you how you deceived yourself. Your negative or positive belief systems hold the key to the nature of your attractions, expectations and desires in relationships. These are 'the programs' that shape your perception of the person you are attracted to and will ultimately choose to be with. Your negative belief systems have the affect of blinding you to their issues because they complement yours so perfectly. Actually they are a part of the attraction between you. No matter what nature your negative beliefs are you will find or bring out complimentary issues in your partner, as they will in you. Although it may initially be hard to accept, no one but you is responsible for the experience you have of your relationships.

If you are in the middle of a relationship break up, you may find it difficult to accept this point of view, particularly when both parties are emotionally affected. Each has their own emotional response to a breakup but whether passive or aggressive, whether in guilt or blame —both are likely to believe that the other is responsible. Do not believe for a moment that anyone can escape the negative outcome — you will not be able to and neither will they. Whatever pain, anger or resentment you may feel, they are a direct result of your own emotional processes even though the situation with your partner may have triggered them. If you feel vindictive because you believe they have done this to you, you are showing yourself up to be the victim in the relationship with the belief that you are not responsible for any of the issues you shared. This prevents you from holding yourself accountable and accepting responsibility for choosing this relationship in the first place. If you do not do anything to change your self, you are likely to repeat your relationship story with similar personality types again and again until you realise that *you are the one who must change.*

Resolving conflict within a framework of self-responsibility requires complete emotional frankness by each party. Instead of confronting issues when they reach a crisis they need to be addressed in the moment, as they become apparent. By communicating your personal experience of the situation without blame, you can stop disagreements from growing out of control. Try and explain the motivations, feelings and intent for your behaviour, actions or choices and let your partner do the same. Your focus needs to be on understanding your part in it as well as your partner's experience of the situation and their mindset. Speaking with emotional clarity and honesty is more likely to create positive results than blame, avoidance, accusations. Telling your partner what you think they want to hear to avoid conflict will only postpone the situation to the next time.

Not withstanding that this can be very difficult to do, with practice and patience you will find that it will reveal answers that have the capacity to bring you much closer to your partner. You must remember that you cannot take this approach independently of your partner and that they need to be prepared to address relationship issues with a similar frame of mind. Speaking openly and truthful from the heart will get you positive results. Sometimes the outcome may not be what you would expect it to be but remember that you can only flourish as a spirit in a relationship that is based on truth and honesty.

You may not always totally understand the basis for all of the feelings, thoughts and behaviours that represent your part of the issue but by giving expression to what you *do* know and understand you create steps towards resolution and growth. It all comes down to being self-responsible in life

Emotional "Genetics"

It is obvious from our examples that that it appears to be unavoidable that we pass on our beliefs to the next generation. The emotional imprint we receive in childhood becomes the template for how and why we live our lives and create relationships. If do not release our fear based beliefs before we have children, we pass on the emotional patterns inherited from our parents to them. Unaware of the true nature of our being and in the absence of any understanding of the process by which we manifest our life experiences there is no other outcome possible. The conscious and subconscious belief systems of the parents become theirs and in the absence of real change, they are doomed to repeat this process when they become parents. Only you can disrupt this generational repetition by changing who you are and seeking to live life as your authentic self in the absence of fear.

The expression of negative patterns of beliefs can often be recognised through the type of behaviour that is displayed. Behaviour can also strategically disguise the real fears and insecurities someone has but on the surface can appear very functional. For example, very confident and absolute behaviour can hide the fear of being wrong and not knowing. This behaviour seeks to convince others of the opposite and is generally successful with those who are passive and also not too sure of them selves. The problem with negative beliefs and their supporting behaviours is that if they are not transcended, they will persist for generations.

In that respect your emotional family tree is in many ways much more interesting than your genetic one. Consider that who you generally attract as a partner and the person who is attracted to you is an emotional reflection of your parent's individual fears and issues. If you were to trace the emotional issues of each family member and the partners they marry you will realize that your emotional family tree will show this. If you also combine this result with that of the emotional 'genetic' tree of these partners, you would discover many common qualities that prove that these attractions are almost inevitable. Once you recognize the patterns of attraction and the cause for conflict it may give the impression that you have little or no control over your life. It may seem that it is your destiny to perpetuate these emotional patterns but this is not true. Only by remaining ignorant of the truth and the fear of facing yourself will make it inevitably that you repeat your family's negative emotional heritage.

Separation from our authentic self appears to be a gradual process where each subsequent generation finds itself at a greater distance from their inner truth and spiritual reality. Our individual misconceptions and illusions instilled through fear also have deep ramifications for the society we ultimately create with them. Sharing our illusionary fears with others gives them justification and makes them acceptable and potentially these distortions become "new truths" by which a society then makes its rules, lives and survives. This does not necessarily happen in a lifetime but it is an ongoing process that can be measured in many generations, over many hundreds of years.

Empowered Being

Changing the world starts with each individual taking responsibility for their life without exception. There are no shortcuts or simple solutions that magically make issues and the feelings that go with them disappear. Reclaiming your power as a creative and manifesting consciousness is essential to fulfilling the potential of your unique authentic being.

When you are lost in your issues, positive results are hard to create because you are fighting your own negative beliefs that oppose your efforts to fulfil your potential. Although for you this conflict may appear to be with others or the world in which you want to achieve your aspirations, in reality you are in conflict with yourself. Your own negative self-beliefs are the actual barriers to your achievement or success.

We generally believe that only our conscious thoughts and choices create our reality experiences but nothing could be further from the truth.
We incessantly manifest our life through the intent of the beliefs we hold — consciously and subconsciously, negative or positive.
Whenever our fears are activated they will by their very nature seek to dominate our mind.
Realise that whenever issues just seem to appear in your life that you must be manifesting experiences from your fears in the most effortless of ways.

You will manifest positive life experiences by living life in the absence of a fearful sense-of-self, supported by beliefs that are in harmony with your essence with the same effortlessness you did your issues and problems.

The process is easier than you might think because it all depends on who and what you believe yourself to be, in respect to yourself and in relation to the world. Looking for your life solutions beyond the obvious will take you to the source of your limitations and releasing these will create the space for your authentic and unique self to be present. Each change will contribute to the positive basis by which you manifest your life.

We are generally unaware that ***who we believe we are***, operates on individual and collective levels. The power the intent of our sense-of-self has over us as individuals also influences our society and the world as a shared consciousness. The negative or positive emotional consequences of expressing our sense-of-self are present within us and visible all around us. Prisons, armies, poverty and starvation, unequally distributed wealth, discrimination of all kinds, drug taking and all forms of abuse are ***manifestations of human consciousness living in illusion controlled by fear.***

Chapter 15

The Quest for Happiness

The quest for personal happiness is at the top of the list for most people. At first glance this appears to be logical because who, after all, would not want to be happy? Happiness usually appears only for short periods in our life and it is rare to meet someone who is truly in a constant state of happiness or bliss. So why is happiness so important to us and should we not ask why and what is behind this quest that most seem to think is the nirvana of life?

Before we can go any further consider what the nature of true happiness is so that we can become a reference point in understanding our relationship with it. The dictionary defines **happiness** (as in "emotional state") *n.*: state of well-being characterized by emotions ranging from contentment to intense joy.

A more spiritual description of happiness might be as follows:

True happiness is felt
- *by living life in a state of unconditional love, acceptance and trust with the freedom to express the power and potential of your authentic self unconditionally*
- *by living life true to the essence of your spirit in the absence of fear.*

Anything less, becomes happiness that is conditional to the absence of all manner of fear. Our innate desire to find happiness is intertwined with our innate drive to exist in harmony with the essence of our spirit. Achieving this harmonious state connects us with the true source for happiness and joy. Our feelings can be extremely deceptive making it possible to have emotional experiences that parade as happiness and joy but are actually poor facsimiles. Without knowing what true happiness and joy feels like we lack the meaningful reference point we need to recognize it.

Our unique nature makes the general idea of happiness differ from one person to another. While one feels happy watching the sun go down, another feels it by seeing their favourite sports team win. One will find contentment and happiness helping others, while another will only be satisfied when they have what they always wanted.

You may be happy not to be fired from your job or not getting killed in an accident. A lottery win may keep you smiling for a long time because of the way it changes your life. At long last finding a partner to share your life with may well keep you happy for a while. Finding your way out of a critical predicament will probably do the same thing. Going on vacation after a year of slogging it out in your job may be your version of happiness while others are convinced that getting blind drunk or high on drugs is the way to feel 'happy'.

Obviously there is any number of examples for what happiness is, which only illustrates that our idea of happiness on the surface appears very individual and contextual. Chasing this kind of happiness is very different from the happiness experienced by being in harmony with the essence of our spirit. We generally do not want to face the fact that much of our idea of happiness depends on the issues we have. The security of food and shelter can be a source of happiness for the homeless and displaced, just as power is to the powerless. In the awareness that we create our own life experiences, it follows that **our concept of happiness** often **depends on escaping what we fear**.

Whenever pain or fear has been replaced by a positive outcome we are likely to feel happy about the absence of the negative. ***This kind of happiness is a product of the absence of fear, loss, guilt, powerlessness, anxiety, worry, pain and so on is a result of escaping from what we fear.***
On the physical level this can be job security over unemployment, having a holiday and freedom over constantly having to work and bear responsibility or just having a secure income over having to survive from day to day and so forth.

On an emotional level it can be having power and control instead of being powerless, having choice in life over having to do as you are told or being loved over being rejected and so on.
Each time you achieve the positive over the negative you are likely to feel happy but it is unlikely to be a lasting state. The reasons why you manifest negative experiences in your life in the first place are still a part of you. It may appear that your positive emotions — feeling happy — is an indication that you have dealt with your issue but that is part of the illusion. The emotion you experience is produced by external circumstances and not a result of innerchange. Without releasing the reason for the negative, this will not be an enduring.

Using strategic behaviours to achieve happiness is fraught with pitfalls. Its success depends on accommodating, controlling or having influence over those around you and this may not work. The fear of being rejected, disappointed, unwanted, and denied and so on drive your strategies and this ensures that your happiness will always sit on the edge of failure. Feeling happy will be totally dependent on your capacity to maintain control and influence over the way other react and respond to you. You dependence on their positive response in order for you to be happy makes it highly probable that sooner or later this will fail. The intent created by fear will always win out and as a result happiness will be denied. If strategic behaviour is your only means to get what you want than your only option is to repeat the exercise all over again always in hope that this time you will succeed. The problem is that in your perception, the fundamental source for your happiness lies outside of you and you are therefore dependent on how others respond. The reality is that strategies can never give you control over your happiness; that is just your illusion.

If for example you believe you are unattractive, undesirable and not good enough, you will probably think that no one would want to be with you. Assume for a moment that you discover a behavioural strategy with which you can appear confident to the opposite sex and get them to like you. The successful implementation of your strategy will make you feel happy because you believe that you have made someone want you. However, you are now worried that they will lose interest in you if they find out who you really are because you still have the belief that you are not good enough. Even though your behaviour is not sincere, you have no choice but to continue with your strategies in fear that if you do not you will be rejected. You may be happy each time your strategy works but your fear of being found out to be the inferior person you believe yourself to be will always be lurking in the background of your mind. This kind of happiness could be called strategic because it depends on conscious behaviour to manifest.

We confuse relief or escape from loss or disaster or anything we fear or cannot cope with as happiness because it makes us feel relieved that we are not subject to the consequences we fear. Not being the victim of a negative experience or event cannot be truly described as real happiness, even though elevated feelings of relief from suspense and fear of disaster are obviously welcomed and embraced. We need to be able to recognize and make a distinction between these feelings to avoid misinterpretation between what is a temporary relief from fear and true happiness.

Happiness Without Fear

Language may actually contribute to the problem when we try to put our feelings into words. In many cultures the vocabulary used to express feelings of love, joy and happiness are limited when we think of all the different shades these feelings can have. In English the words 'happiness' and "love' are readily used in any number of the circumstances.

Happiness as a result of experiencing love by giving or receiving it, can become complicated when we try to distinguish the love for a friend to that for with the love for our self, our partner or our children. Accepting that we do know within ourselves what the differences are because we feel them, communicating this to others is usually not so clear-cut. Often, the finer layers of what we feel get lost in translation because we cannot find words to express these nuances in our feeling of love and therefore happiness.

True happiness comes from being in harmony with our spirit through being at oneness with the unconditional love, acceptance and trust with All That Is and oneself.

This concept of happiness refers to the core foundation of this feeling in our being and is new emotional territory for most people.
How would we experience the world if our state of mind were harmonious within and without?
What would it be like to live life without fear, powerlessness and distrust and accept accountability for everything we create in our life?
How would we express our sense of being — emotionally, physically and intellectually — if we were openly truthful, spontaneous and free, suspending all judgment and criticism of our selves and others?
How would we experience and conduct our intimate and other relationships in the absence of fear and guilt?
What would be the nature and quality of our parenting in the absence of our own fears and insecurities?
How would we raise our children and what would be the focus in their education if evolving their consciousness were a priority?
What would be the nature of our health care if we understood the connection between spirit, mind and body and our energetic being?
From what kind of vision would we create a world society if we had a mind that is emotionally self-responsible and feels connected to everything?
With what economic and law structures would we govern and support each other's existence?
What kind of world would our eyes see if they were uncorrupted by fear?

Finding Happiness Within

You might say that happiness and joy come in different layers of which the internal harmony between mind and spirit forms the core. Once we achieve a level of inner harmony that is more dominant than our fears, our experience of pleasure and happiness will be greatly enhanced. The resilience created by our harmonious inner-core will diminish the depressing impact that our remaining fears can have on our perception thoughts and emotions.

Fulfilling the potential of our authentic self by living life unconditionally — in freedom and absence of fear — is central to finding true and consistent happiness and joy. This kind of happiness comes from the achievements that support the growth of our mind and spirit. They do not depend on the recognition or adulation from others or having to prove ones superiority over others. Instead, inner-change expands our consciousness and leads to greater fulfilment of our spiritual potential.

The only triumphs in life that truly matter to human consciousness are those we achieve within: Through fulfilling our potential by releasing our fears and giving unconditional expression to our inner- resources in order to manifest our lives in full awareness of our responsibility as the creator of our own reality.

All creative acts of manifestation begin and end with our selves. An imaginative thought, supported by beliefs and their intent, actioned with the will to make it real through the application of the mind and all its faculties, is an act of creative manifestation. All creative acts and the results they achieve are both a learning experience and a mirror for who you are. Your responses and reactions to any outcome are a reflection of the nature of your belief systems — your sense-of-self — and the level of inner-harmony you have at this point in time. The balance between fear-based beliefs and harmonious beliefs ultimately is the determining factor for the presence or lack of happiness in your life. When the balance leans towards harmony with our essence, everything in life is sweeter.

Happiness by Avoiding Suffering

Your life happiness should not depend on relationships, material security or need-fulfilment because it is not a product of escaping or avoiding your fears. Sharing oneself and contributing to others in the process of self-fulfilment and learning from their unique perspectives is a substantial part of discovering inner-happiness. Once we live our lives from this inner-context, our happiness cannot fade or disappear in the face of negative external circumstances. Instead, we would manifest a world, which nature and experience would correspond to the new intent of the harmonious belief systems within our sense-of-self.

We need to stop blaming personal unhappiness on others or circumstances in our life and begin to question the nature of our own mind to understand why we create the events that cause us to feel that way. Were we to take this approach we would give ourselves a chance to go to the root of our unhappiness issues. For instance, once we feel "unhappy" with our job, we will find a million things wrong with our work environment and the people we share it with. Holding our work place responsible for our dissatisfaction gives our discontent a target and justification and allows us to convince ourselves that *we are not the problem — work is.* There may be many reasons why work can be an unhappy experience but your choices have put you where you are right now. The question you should ask your self is why you made those choices in the first place because the answers would show that you are the cause. Unresolved, they will re-appear in other places in different ways until you deal with the reasons for them within you.

Every choice you make in life whether for work or relationships is a product of your mindset coloured by the beliefs you hold — positive or negative. Your choices in life will always place you in environments where your issues will manifest. Your understanding of negative encounters also represents opportunities to overcome the fear based belief systems that underpin these experiences.
Remember that your experience of life is a product of the innate and incessant creative intent of the belief systems that make up your sense-of-self.

The truth you hold on to may be that your parents invalidated your interests, passions ands desires. This convinced you that what you were attracted to and excited about is worthless and insignificant. Rejecting your passions because your parents did, you may have chosen a career that pleases your parents. In your mind, meeting their expectations has become a condition for their acceptance of you.

Fear of confrontation, being held accountable or fear of failure may represent another reason why you do not like your work environment. Your fears may cause you to perceive others in your workplace as aggressive and critical, demanding and judgmental of you. The issues you have are all within you so you do not have to look very far for the culprit who created your problems.

The question is: Do you have the courage to face yourself without fear or judgment and accept the reality of your beliefs in order to transcend them?

Happiness and Relationships

Those who depend on relationships to find their life happiness are likely to be disappointed. Relying on another for the fulfilment of your emotional needs, dreams and expectations are bound to fail. This kind of happiness is usually the product of a heart that does not love and accept itself and seeks to feel love and acceptance through being loved by another. This version of love is always dependent on what someone else is prepared to give and makes us feel powerless, emotionally needy and vulnerable. The expectation that another should complete what is missing in oneself is learned through the example our parents set for us in their relationship with each other and how they related to us individually. Your experience of their expression and understanding of love becomes your definition of what love is. You will seek recreate the same conditional love, acceptance and trust you were exposed to by your parents by choosing a partner who will fulfil this subconscious requirement in you. The person you choose will naturally have complementary issues to your own and which will be a facsimile of those of your parents. The process that is life will ensure that you will replicate the conditions you have learned to believe exist for love in a relationship in order to transcend them.

Happiness that comes as a result of one person compensating for the fears and insecurities of another will usually be short lived. Someone who feels weak and insecure will be attracted to someone who appears to be strong and in control as a resolution for their fears. Their chosen partner will be someone who has learned to be loved and accepted by strategically presenting themselves as strong, capable and dependable. In reality it is their way of dealing with their fear of being unlovable and unacceptable and this totally complements the fears of the weak partner. Unfortunately the idea that one can compensate for the other's fear and insecurities is an illusion and therefore an unrealistic expectation for both. In time, usually the more aggressive or assertive partner will give up because they feel there is no end to the dissatisfaction for which the other holds them responsible. Eventually discontent will lead to conflict, as each is likely to blame the other for what they feel is missing. Happiness will have left the relationship a long time before that.

Consistent happiness in relationships can best be achieved if both parties in principle accept responsibility for their emotional experiences in the relationship even if how and why is not clear to them. Should there be conflict than each will take responsibility for their own feelings and look at them selves for the reasons for their part in it. Open and truthful communication over the emotional matters that are at the core of their individual issues will allow them to support each other in finding resolution within themselves. By helping each other through fears and insecurities they will develop a deeper understanding of one another and make their relationship more intimate rather than less.

Working towards our own happiness and the happiness we share with others is an inner-process that asks us to investigate all and any reasons for the fear based conditions we place on love, acceptance and trust in ourselves and others. Our fears create critical emotional limits and processes representative of our fear-based beliefs. These will always lead to unhappiness and discontent. With closer observation we will invariably find that our conditional self-beliefs mimic the conditions that our parents acted out between them and with us. Letting go of these negative beliefs will alter our thoughts, perception and change our feelings, behaviour and choices because we — our inner identity — will have changed.

The moment we open our eyes to this new world, we embark on the journey of finding happiness within, through existing in greater harmony with our spiritual essence. Every time we release a negative belief, we allow more of the essence of our spirit to come to the surface and reveal new aspects of our authentic self. Each progressive change brings us closer to our spiritual being and allows it to find greater expression for our amazing potential. Every time we release an issue in its fundamental form we are in greater harmony with our essence and this is what will create a new level of true and consistent happiness within all of us.

Chapter 16

Power Without Fear

These are some of the dictionary explanations for the meaning of power:

Power is the capacity or ability to direct or influence the behaviour of others or the course of events.
Power is a measurement of an entity's ability to control its environment, including the behavior of other entities. The term authority is often used for power perceived as legitimate by the social structure. Power can be seen as evil or unjust, but the exercise of power is accepted as endemic to humans as social beings.
The use of **power** need not involve coercion (force or the threat of force). At one extreme, it more closely resembles what everyday English-speakers call "influence", although some authors make a distinction between power and influence – the means by which power is used

The problem is that none of these explanations of power take into account that no matter what kind of power and in what situation it is wielded, the effect it has on others and the environment depends entirely on the inner nature of the persons controlling it or are being controlled. Issues, fears and insecurities will always distort the values and standards, integrity and principles for those who pursue power for its own sake.

When we say power corrupts *it is not that power as such is actually responsible for corrupting a person. The issues — fears — within the individual who acquires power will cause them to misuse and abuse it.*

Someone with fears and a distorted sense-of-self will be seduced into using and abusing the power at their disposal because it becomes a resource to satisfy or overcome their personal issues. They will always find justification for their actions and choices that are consistent with their mindset, often in total disregard of the consequences this has for others and the environment.

It is not surprising that power and control have become important values in today's society where it seems nothing can be attained or achieved without involving these two elements into the equation. The words power and control are used in many a slogan promising change. Their acquisition promises to give you the capacity to get all the things you want, wish for and desire. The power to have what you want in life and the capacity to "Control Your Destiny" through personal power is a seductive idea. Most of us assume that if we have control over every tiny aspect of what we and others do and think, their behaviour and choices, we will also be in control of the outcome. We are convinced that it is the only way to be sure to have what we want when we want it. The truth is that we can develop or inherit strategies that work and achieve positive outcomes but generally and over time they will fail us in one form or another. The strategic approach to life tends to ignore the greatest influence of all — YOU as the instigator. What your life will be and how you will experience it will ultimately be determined by ***who you believe yourself to be.***

What you do and ***how*** you do it may initially bring you a level of success but your negative beliefs — fears — and the intent they hold cannot be denied expression. The process of living manifests the nature of who you are as an emotional and physical life experience through your choices.

The thought that we can acquire anything by knowing strategic "how to do behaviours" appeals to those who believe in magical solutions to overcome their fears and insecurities. They are always looking for that one concept, strategy or idea that will take away their fears and let them get anything they want. For those reasons alone being in control and having power is a very desirable notion.

Should the acquisition of power and control be the main goal in life, you might be wise to look really closely at your reasons and motivations. From your perspective it may seem normal to strive for this but potentially there are negative reasons for this desire. Without knowing the true nature of your sense-of-self you will not recognize the negative consequences your quest may have for yourself and others.

Before we go any further consider these statements:

One only needs power and control in life
if one is in fear of being powerless and without control.

Only those in fear of powerlessness and without control
have the need for power, control and the domination over others
in order to feel empowered and in control.

The general notion of personal power is the ability to get whatever you want, when and how you want it, regardless of external influences or the effect this may have on others or the environment. It is generally accepted that should external influences prevent you from achieving your goals, you need to become more strategic and tactical, more aggressive and assertive in the application of your power. This paradigm disregards the nature of human consciousness and the consequences this approach can have on others and the world.

Extreme versions of this such as the use of violence, threat, torture and fear as weapons to control individuals or a population are seen by most to be unacceptable. Our judgment changes, when we are made to believe that these same methods are used for the greater good — our welfare and protection The same fears and insecurities that had us reject this kind of violence now causes us to sanction and justify them. They form the perception that we are no longer isolated and therefore safe from this kind of threat and generate the fear that we could be the victims. By playing on our pre-existing fears and insecurities and sense of victimhood, the emotional state of a population can be manipulated to manufacture consent. By convincing a fearful population that certain actions and choices are absolute necessity for their security and safety and by creating alternatives that are made to be obviously shocking and unacceptable, approval can be extracted. Believing it to be in defence of our own survival and security, we are usually prepared to accept inhumane and cruel methods even if it means that we thereby corrupt our personal and innate values and standards, integrity and principles. Unfortunately, the idea that 'the end justifies the means' and "we have to sacrifice for the greater good" is still very much alive and used extensively and inappropriately when individuals and institutions seek power and control.

Naturally we are entitled to defend ourselves if our life is under threat but what if the perceived threat is a product of deception reinforced by our own illusionary fears and insecurities. In many cases these illusions are product of generations of fear-based misconceived beliefs. Is violence or aggressive control still justified if the reasons for our fears have no foundation in truth or the real reasons have long dissolved in history? These are questions that need to be answered by both sides of any potential conflict if there is to be a basis for enduring peaceful resolutions.

The Beginning of Powerlessness

How and why do we come to feel powerless when at birth we generally seem to be without fears and insecurities?
How does our sense of powerlessness become a part of us and why does it have such influence and control?

Even though we are helpless to survive independently at birth we do not feel controlled by fear or powerlessness. A baby shows no concern that it has no "power and control" over its survival in the new world it has entered even though it will call out if in discomfort, not fed or kept clean. By all account, it is clear that there is an inborn trust and expectation that it will be loved, taken care off and protected. This inner confidence has to be innate as it appears in all babies without exception. Its' expectation to be unconditionally supported — loved and wanted, accepted and trusted — by the environment in which it arrives is unequivocal. This sense of trust originates from its unconditional spiritual nature that also forms a strong part of the bond it feels with its mother. This sense of its own being becomes the only reference point by which to form its inner identity — its sense-of-self.

A child is driven by the innate intent to develop and evolve its physical and emotional independence not only as part of a physical survival strategy but primarily to acquire the capacity to fulfil the multi-facetted potential of its creative consciousness. The process of living becomes its journey of self-discovery, self-expression and an opportunity to evolve every element of its unique and authentic self. In just about every instance a child will begin this process with trust and in the absence of fear. Fear and powerlessness become only a part of its mind when the conditions set by the parent and its own expectations are in consistent conflict. Sensing that its authentic and unique self is not able to meet the conditions set by the parents makes it feel powerless and separated from unconditional love. Once powerlessness gets a hold, the fear of failing to meet the conditions becomes its faithful companion and will dominate its development throughout its life.

The first and probably most difficult part of a child's life-journey is transcending the emotional environment of its family. The ground-rules for emotional expression and interaction are already determined by the parent's insecurities and limitations. Any fears or issues they inherited from their families will become a prominent part of the emotional paradigm characterising the relationships between all family members. Every negative belief a child takes on as its personal truth instils either a direct sense of powerlessness or represents a version of powerlessness.

The real reason that you feel overwhelmed by a verbally aggressive person or by being rejected by your lover, feel demeaned by someone's comment or ignored when wanting attention is your own sense of powerlessness. Our individual relationship with personal power or powerlessness will determine how we experience either. Although it may not be not obvious but using dominating behaviour — passively or aggressively — to be in control over others is just as dysfunctional as being powerless to be in control of your life

The child's trust in unconditional love, acceptance and trust is severely compromised by the parent's unconscious rejection of its innate authentic self. Failure to meet these expectations creates inner-conflict and because it is powerless to be unconditionally accepted as its authentic self. Each time it cannot meet the conditions set by the parents its sense of powerlessness deepens.

The incessant pressure to conform causes it to be convinced that giving in to the parent's conditions is the only way it will be loved and accepted. Unconsciously it is taught to give away its power— initially to its parents and later to others. Gradually, it learns to depend on outside approval and endorsement in order to be accepted and acceptable. Every new dependency on others creates more needs in a child and causes it to experience powerlessness in different ways. In maturity, this will prevent it from living life to its full emotional and physical potential. Personal powerlessness goes hand in hand with not being in control of your life. Nearly all of our fear-based issues contain this emotionally disabling element. Rejection and abandonment makes us feel powerless to be loved and wanted. Being judged and criticised makes us feel powerless to be good enough to be acceptable and so on. Our response is to become strategically passive-powerless or aggressive-powerless

Living in Powerlessness

Your fears are proportional to your sense of powerlessness and vulnerability in relation to a perceived threat. Once you are convinced that your strength and resources lack capacity to survive or cope with what you think is an overwhelming emotional or physical confrontation you will experience fear. It has less to do with the size of the threat than it has with your perception of your own power and capacity. Fear will dominate your mind if the threat or confrontation appears to be larger or stronger than you believe you are. In the case of a physical threat this can be totally justified but even under these circumstances our self-perception plays a major role in respect to how we will respond to it. The evaluation needs to be very different when confronted with strictly emotional fears because these are illusionary. The perceived consequences and their effect on us have no basis in reality. Our experience of rejection or blame, shame or criticism and so on will not cause us to suffer real injuries or terminate our existence.

Living in the belief that you cannot survive, confront or overcome a range of emotional issues will make you generally fearful of living life. The consequence of issues such as rejection and abandonment, anger and aggression, making 'wrong' decisions and choices, initiating new ideas and potential failure, expressing your feelings and speaking your truth and so on will not kill you even though it may feel that you cannot live with the outcome.

Your desire to avoid any of these negative outcomes and your inability to do so consistently successfully makes you feel fearful and powerless. Your process of living your life will be tainted by the fear of negative consequences in all of decisions and choices. Issues of this kind are more common in people than one would think. Fear of living life can spiral into an ever-greater vortex of avoidance or/ and dependence on strategic behaviours and the support of others. It can feel emotionally as well as physically debilitating. The influence and power of fear can become so great that once the self is overwhelmed it can cause an emotional shutdown that begins to affect the function of the body. This can be felt as deep fatigue and issues in the digestive system when there is a strong need to avoid negative emotional confrontation. What is essentially an emotional fear has now found physical expression in the body.

People with these issues unconsciously choose to become very strategic in how they live and conduct relationships. Their constant fear that their behaviour, actions and choices will elicit negative responses from others results in suppression of their spontaneity and emotional truth. They are actually trying to control the emotional process in every encounter in order to avoid conflict and guilt. They usually present themselves as ultra caring and considerate of others, which hide the stress and anxiety they live with. The people they often attract have the fear that they will not being able to do what they want or be who they want to be. They are aggressive-powerless and often use aggressively demanding and controlling strategic behaviours. They unconsciously are attracted to the company of those who will not refuse them or hold them accountable — passive-powerless individuals.

Being in fear of life is often paraded as personal choices that are an expression of very unique likes and dislikes or behaviours that is forced on them by others or circumstances. Power over their emotional life is given to others and the world around them. They commonly hold others responsible for the negative circumstances or experiences in their life and thus make themselves to be the victims. They make themselves powerless to address their issues. As long as they believe themselves to be victims they will not hold themselves responsible. Each time we avoid taking responsibility for our issues, the process of living life has the inevitable characteristic of presenting every one of us progressively with ever bigger and more intense experiences of our fears.

Powerlessness plays a role in every fear we hold. Together with related negative emotions, it drives us into developing strategic behaviours as a counter-measure to our fears. If we are passive by nature and feel powerless to be loved and accepted by our parent, we will try and avoid rejection by whatever means at our disposal. We may use avoidance strategies to never display behaviour that might trigger a negative response. Or we may choose to engage in submissive and accommodating behaviours — pleasing — to gain approval. If our fear is intense enough, we can be driven to use aggressive, controlling and confronting behaviours. Our aggressive strategies are intended to challenge those we believe do not love and accept us in order. **We try and elicit a response that will prove to us as well as to them that they do not care.** All these strategies have a use-by date and will sooner or later fail.

In the course of all this our parents unwittingly keep proving to us with their fear-driven behaviours that our spontaneous authentic self is not lovable and acceptable in one form or another. This will generate the feeling that we can never be who we are supposed to be for them to gain their love and acceptance. In a deeper sense, **we can literally not be other than who we were authentically born to be.**

However, when parents feel that who we authentically and spontaneously are is in contradiction with their expectations of us they seek to change us to suit their sense-of-self. The expression of our authentic and unique self raises all manner of issues in them. They therefore demand we change to accommodate their fears. Our ultimate compliance with their expectations of who and what we should be convinces us to dismiss our authentic nature and suppress our spontaneous self. Instead we are coerced by their fears and our own need for their support and approval into accepting self-beliefs that do not represent our authentic nature. Even if we behave according to their expectations there is no guarantee that the approval and acceptance we seek will be permanent or given at all. Hence we are always in fear of losing love and acceptance and experience rejection.

In reality, all we want is to fulfil our innate expectation to be unconditionally loved, accepted, trusted and wanted. The only way to arrive at that state of being is to release beliefs that convince us that we are not lovable and acceptable and do not qualify to receive it.

Living life subject to fears that create feelings of total powerlessness and helplessness makes for a terrifying existence. It is easy to refer to extreme cases and forget that there are many who live every day subject to constant fears. Passive powerless people are mostly subjugated by their fears and generally use avoidance strategies to survive. They are also most likely to become the target for aggressive powerless people who deal with their fears by being controlling, intimidating and dominant over their passive counterparts.

Aggressive powerless personalities may overcome their fear with self-assured behaviour, sometimes underpinned by a level of intimidation are often placed in positions of power and control. Their family background often promotes the value of competitive behaviour to prove who is best and their dialogue is designed to prove they know and are right. This will give those similarly minded trust and confidence in them. Powerless passive people however are attracted to this kind of person because they have no self-confidence and determination. Lacking trust in their own power and abilities they will choose *to be led rather* than take *responsibility for their life* — decisions and choices. This will make each needy and dependent on the other.

From Powerlessness to Anger to Violence

Anger is an emotion we are all too familiar with because at one time or another we have all been at the receiving end of it or felt and expressed it. Every time we find ourselves in a state of emotional powerlessness, there is the potential that we will respond with anger and aggression or with avoidance and repression.

Anger, aggression and powerlessness are intrinsically connected emotions that are part of everyone's minds. Some will not ever dare to give expression to their anger because they have learned to believe it to be wrong and unacceptable. They fear it will cause love and acceptance to be withdrawn and therefore strategically suppress it. All emotions require expression but none more so than aggression and anger emotions. Suppressing anger can over time result in unpredictable and extreme aggressive outburst of aggression over something that does not appear to warrant this behaviour. Consistently internalized negative emotions such as powerlessness will ultimately demand and find expression. If not emotionally it may find expression in your body and manifest as physical health issues.

Your family is the source for any beliefs that convince you that you are powerless and have no control over your life. There are generally two ways that a sense of powerlessness can be instilled and both can be present at the same time in a family dynamic. Being exposed to either aggressive, intimidating, dominant behaviour or to passive powerless victim behaviour will create a sense of powerlessness in a child.

Physical and emotional intimidation and aggression will obviously overpower a child's capacity to respond to protect itself. Repeated exposure can therefore cause it feel completely overwhelmed and powerless. To survive the onslaught it may use passive avoidance or become aggressive to protect itself. Neither of these behaviours will save it from the emotional damage that has been done to its sense-of-self.

Parents who are in fear of taking emotional and material responsibility usually perceive themselves to be the victim of the demands and needs of their partner and children. Their strategic behaviour can either be aggressive-defensive (blame) or passive-defensive (guilt) or adopt total avoidance as a strategy in order to prevent confrontation with their fears. Regardless of the behaviour employed they are always the victim and those that depend on them the aggressors. This will cause their children to withhold and suppress innate and normal expectations for fear of being responsible for the parent's anxiety and stress and risking emotional abandonment. They assume that if the parent gets resentful when they express their needs and wants that they must be guilty and emotionally responsible. In truth a child can never be responsible for the parent's feelings because they have no control over the pre-existing fears held by their parent. Unfortunately the parent's fears become the child's sense of guilt for wanting and needing support, care and protection. As an adult, this guilt manifests as a lack of entitlement paraded as independence and self-sufficiency.

More then often it is the male in the family who is the aggressive figure and the female partner is the passive on but it can just as easily be the other way around. Generally, women tend to be emotionally dominant and controlling but not physically threatening. They control emotionally by a display of vulnerability, anxiety and stress whilst aggressively complaining about their dissatisfaction and disappointment in their partner or their lot in life — by being the victim and powerless. This kind of parent sees themselves as a victim of their children's needs and expectations and that their discontent is caused by their own offspring.

In this context, a parent can use aggressive and dominant behaviour to avoid perceived blame and accountability, often acting as if they are beyond reproach to hide their own feelings of powerlessness and inadequacy. Trying to prove that they are all knowing and never wrong, they expect to be listened to and obeyed. To cope with the emotional pressure created by the fears they live with they may use ways to avoid what they feel by finding relief in other ways. For example consuming alcohol in excess or just being absent from the family. When held accountable for their behaviour, it is not uncommon that they default to anger and aggression or behave the victim. Either response is caused by their belief that they are powerless helpless victims of the demands and expectations of others, circumstances and the world.

The unfortunate reality is that children exposed to this kind emotional paradigm have a strong potential to become just like the parents that raised them. Children exposed to fear-motivated behaviours develop the need to be constantly aware and alert in order to be prepared for the unpredictable aggressive or powerless responses of their parent. Avoiding being the target of aggression becomes and essential part of its behavioural strategies in relationships for them. A child will adopt strategies to avoid being held responsible and accountable for the negative feelings and behaviour of its parent. Often it will adopt similar strategic behaviours to those role-played by the parent. It learns to believe that aggression or avoidance is an effective defensive mechanism against being blamed and accused or feeling guilty and to blame. Unconsciously it becomes just like the parent.

The assumption that parents naturally want the responsibility for the family they create ignores many of the reasons why people are attracted to form intimate relationships in the first place. As has been already pointed out, an individual's issues play as much if not more a decisive role in the attractions individuals have for each other. These fears and insecurities make themselves most apparent in intimate relationships and when families are created because love, acceptance and trust are the currency between all parties. The interdependence this creates makes a strong demand on each individual's capacity to love, accept, trust, support, care and protect and so on, unconditionally. If not an issue as yet between partners, usually their children will challenge everything that is conditional in each parent with the expression of their needs and expectations. This emotional environment brings their fear-based beliefs in the parent's sense-of-self to the surface as behavioural strategies begin to fail.

In the reality of life aggressive-powerless victims are subconsciously attracted to those with a passive-powerless sense-of-self and vice versa. Ironically, they complement each other perfectly because the root for their issues is powerlessness and so one is an emotional mirror of the other.

Control Without Power

By now you may be confused about how anyone can have any power and control over their life. It is important to know how to make the distinction between the power within and power outside yourself. If you ***have to*** exercise power and control by using strategic behaviour over others or the world so that you can get what you want or to feel safe and secure, it is likely you are responding to the fear of being powerless or being without control. ***Your behaviour driven by your feelings are a manifestation of your fear of being*** *powerless to get what you want and being without control.* Whatever the circumstances responsible for activating these issues may be, *your need for strategic behaviour proves that you are definitely not self-empowered*. That is not to say you cannot be pro-active in your behaviour and choices but it does means that your inner-motivations and intent come from the fear of being powerless. If this fear is at the core of your behaviour, any resultant experience of power and control is in reality an illusion. It will depend on the environment in which you can strategically play out your fears.

Dominant Control

Rather than contain and suppress your need for recognition and feeling special, you may adopt controlling and dominating strategies to proof to others that you are significant, special and entitled in order to be accepted by them. Your strategies would create constant stress for fear that your strategic behaviour might not succeed and you will be judged to be worthless and insignificant. This behaviour is a product of the same fears that make others passively compromise themselves — become pleasers — to gain significance and be valued. The differences in behaviour are a display of passive and aggressive attempts to resolve very similar negative belief systems.

By understanding the relationship between behaviour and the negative state that underpins it, we can identify specific emotional characteristics about ourselves and others. Powerlessness underpins both passive powerless and aggressive controlling behaviour. The attraction that aggressive powerless individuals have for passive powerless personalities reflects a dynamic, which fulfils both their emotional needs. One uses strategic behaviour to have power and control and the other surrenders and gives their power and control away. Each finding reality in the expression of the fear-based beliefs they individually hold.

Passive powerless people tend to use pleasing and putting others before themselves as their strategy to fulfil their need to avoid confrontation with rejection and judgment. They will attract aggressive-powerless individuals who find their sense of power by engaging those who are passive pleasers. Both were powerless to be unconditionally loved and accepted by their parents and as adults by others. Both ultimately compromise their authentic self and finish up living life subject to the emotional whims of those they are attracted to.

True Personal Power and Control

The simple truth is that the human mind can be convinced to accept to believe almost anything. Our minds have enormous flexibility and capacity for change. ***This inbuilt mental versatility also means that we are equipped to change who we have been convinced to believe we are.*** We are naturally capable of changing the nature of our sense-of-self and recover our unique authentic origin. ***Our negative beliefs are founded in fear therefore illusions and not real.***

Whether we know it or not, but we constantly and incessantly create our own sense of reality. The intent held in the beliefs that form your sense-of-self controls the unique focus of your mind, which then determines how you express and perceive your world. The intents in your beliefs are the directors of your mind and as a consequence your life energy.

You as the originator of your intent — positive or negative — are actually in control of your life experiences through the beliefs that form your sense-of-self. You, as the keeper of your own beliefs are the one who has the power to be in control of your existence.

You have not realized that you are already controlling your life even though you may not feel it because you are convinced that others and the world are responsible for what you experience. Accepting ownership of your negative beliefs and responsibility for the outcomes they create is your first step towards taking control. You can begin to be real and truthful with yourself by letting go of the emotional and behavioural strategist you have become in order to deal with a multitude of issues that limit your life. It will create the freedom to take stock of your fears, insecurities and negative or self-destructive behaviours. This can lead you to understand the beliefs that are at their core. Each step constitutes a move to take charge of the nature of your own being and the acquisition of the real personal power you are innately endowed with.

Once you have taken ownership of your sense of self you need to decide which beliefs you are prepared to accept as your truth and which are based on fear and are therefore negative and illusionary. By doing so you are not just taking control over your belief systems but you are automatically taking control over the negative intent that originates from them. Releasing these beliefs will then alter the intent of your sense-of-self and the kind of life you will manifest and experience as a result. You are also opening way for your unique authentic self to resurface and become the dominant voice in your self-expression.

Your sense-of-self contains both negative and positive beliefs, the balance and intensity of which is different for everyone. Letting go of disharmonious or negative beliefs gradually moves the overall balance of your intent towards the positive and harmonious, creating a happier more positive life experience. Each change contributes to a greater sense of wellbeing and a reduction in negative feelings and emotions and therefore negative feelings and stress. Depending on the issue you are dealing with and the system of negative beliefs you release, you will see an improvement in a specific area or there will be a general improvement in your state of mind. The influences these changes have over your life will astonish you as will the way others will change their perception of you. You will come to realize that the potential of your consciousness is only limited by the restrictions placed on it by your own fears.

True personal power lies at the heart of your sense-of-self. As your sense-of-self reaches greater harmony with the essence of your spirit, you will become aware of your confidence in every aspect of your being and self-expression. The power to create the life you want lies within you and you do not need to have power over others or anything else in this world to attain it.

The personal power to create and manifest your life potential through the nature of your authentic self lies in accepting the unconditional nature of your spiritual essence — unconditional love, acceptance and trust.

UNCONDITIONAL LOVE and ACCEPTANCE are the only true source of power for any human consciousness.

Each person has the innate power and entitlement to live life as their unique and authentic self.

We are born with the innate capacity and resources to fulfil our unique potential without restricting, diminishing or controlling the lives of others.

Our existence is intended to be harmonious and cooperative with that of others and complement and support the evolution of each consciousness.

Collective Powerlessness

The nature of the world we live in today is almost exactly the opposite to the world of our ideals: Controlled by fears rooted in powerlessness, people living their lives in absence of emotional responsibility, with a lack of self-awareness and understanding of the process of life. Nearly all are constantly engaged in strategic behaviours in every aspect of their life and therefore are never present as the person they were really meant to be. In some respects they may as well be walking in their sleep. Humanity as a whole, lives in a state of fear that has become so much a part of the fabric of life we consider it to be normal.

Although the reasons for our fears appear to be in the world, they are actually within us. What we experience in the world is only a mirror for the many layers of fears we individually and collectively hold within our sense-of-self and act out in the world.

The Story of Fear

Fear's powerful intent to get you to respond to its message is extremely persuasive because it seeks to trigger your fear for emotional survival and than take control of what you will manifest in your life.

Fear is like a sly friend who tells you that he will protect you from danger, which in reality does not even exist because it is an illusion. By convincing you that your emotional or sometimes physical survival is at stake, it capitalises on your emotional vulnerability and insecurity. *Fear* deceives you into believing that your feelings of anxiety, worry and insecurity are real in order to create the emotional pressure you will ultimately give into. By surrendering your power to your seemingly protective friend, he now owns and controls you and whether you like it or not *you will be doing 'fears' bidding*.
It will promise you that if you totally rely and depend on your strategic behaviours — aggressive or passive — you will avoid any of your *fears* becoming true.
Fear has made the illusions it has created in your sense-of-self seem like reality. Fooled by your emotions and feelings, you cannot help but dance to its tune.

If you want to take control over your life you need to conquer your fears by realising that they are illusions and then take the steps necessary to release the beliefs they control.

Some notes about power, control and powerlessness to think about:

*Aggressive-Powerless people will only feel powerful
by being in control of those who are Passive-Powerless.*

*Passive-Powerless people are always in constant need to feel safe and seek
to be protected by those who appear to be strong and in control
— Aggressive-Powerless individuals*

True Personal Power can only exist in the absence of fear.

*True Personal Power is NOT a product of control
over those who are weak and fearful.*

*True Personal Power comes from being in harmony with your spirit and
has no need for control over others or the world.*

*True Personal Power does not fear losing 'power or control' because it
resides within.*

True Personal Power naturally serves to <u>empower</u> others.

Chapter 17

Transcending Fear

Experiencing emotional pain and suffering, fears and unhappiness are such a common aspect of life that we do not really question how we get to have those feelings. How we deal with negative events depends mostly on how our parents coped with their issues in life. Their emotional reaction to life and the behaviours they engaged in, become self-defining for us, their children. This is not to suggest that dealing with life is a skill or a trick that you just need to learn however for many it appears to be exactly that way. A lack of confidence in the capacity, power and integrity of our sense-of-self plays a major part in how we will deal with life. To understand this, we need to remind ourselves that we are the creators of our life experiences and every event we are a part of reflects aspects of our sense-of-self.

Commonly, our first reaction to emotional pain or sadness is to try and avoid, suppress or dismiss it. This becomes more difficult when our negative feelings threaten to overwhelm us. Once we are caught up in negative emotions, our thoughts, behaviour and perception will be affected. They can feel emotionally so encompassing that they will totally control how we will act and respond.

Activities that we normally engage in for pleasure can become a means to escape from what we perceive as a threat to our wellbeing. We are usually so convinced that our negative feelings are the issue that we do not realise we are only dealing with the symptoms and not the cause of the issue. By not confronting the origin, the kind of experience you are trying to avoid will repeat itself. This is the nature of manifesting your own reality. If you have a strategy to deal with your issues, you will have to keep on using it in order to escape the consequences, in the hope it will not fail you.

Common avoidance behaviours are transference of responsibility and disassociation, emotional and physical withdrawal. Often together with partying or relationships, sex or sport, 'medicating' your self by drinking alcohol or taking drugs. Whether you will choose avoidance over confrontation depends on the nature and intensity of your powerlessness. Your sense of powerlessness relates directly to the belief systems of your sense-of-self — powerless to be lovable and loved, acceptable and accepted and so on. Any or all of these will make you vulnerable to: rejection, low self esteem, stress, pessimism, aggression, abuse, sadness and so on. Once you have chosen for avoidance, you will use whatever works to try not to feel the negative emotions that come from your fears.

It is quite common to be resistant to therapy for emotional issues even though there is deep suffering. The fear of admitting and accepting that we have a problem is often felt as proof of inferiority and inadequacy compared to others. We try and convince our selves and others that ***we know what we need to do*** to overcome our issues. Frequently, we only consider asking for help when everything we have done has failed and arrive at a point of complete powerlessness. Even then we can be extremely reluctant to accept support. We can be even more resistant to the idea that we are responsible for creating our negative experiences. Yet, it is the only perspective that makes a real solution possible.

When you cannot see that you are the originator of your emotional issues, you are likely to look for the cause outside of your self just like your parents would have. If your parents suppressed their feelings you avoidance behaviour is likely to be the same. You may suppress or deny your negative feelings to avoid dealing with who or what you believe to be the source. In the course of your life this behaviour may become intolerably painful.

Pretending that what you feel is not an issue or does not matter is an invalidation of your true sense of being. You convince yourself that you negative feelings do not effect you because you have learned it is unacceptable or even aggressive should you show what you really feel. By doing this you close the door on your senses and innate awareness of what is a disharmonious emotional state in you. Your denial also diminishes the value and relationship with your own emotional being. You may not realize that there is only one door through which your feelings flow and that closing it will cause you dismiss or diminish positive as well as negative emotions. Denial proves that you have become fearful and distrusting of your emotional nature — positive or negative. Unfortunately, once in denial you are not likely to question your own state of mind and try and uncover the reasons for your behaviour.

Victimised by Beliefs

The greatest source for pain and suffering are the fear of rejection and abandonment, guilt and shame because they will control the dynamic of all of your relationships. If the behaviour or dialogue by your partner, friends or even strangers is construed to be criticism or judgement, rejection or abandonment, it will immediately trigger related negative belief systems in you. The same goes for guilt and shame; each is an extremely powerful and influential emotional force that can drive human behaviour to extreme levels. Your interpretation of their behaviour or words confirms for you that the beliefs of being unwanted, unlovable and unacceptable in its various forms are about to become reality. You response can be one of high anxiety or even panic but also anger, aggression or sadness. Once these intense feelings overwhelm your senses, you will either be prepared to meet almost any condition at any cost or feel the need to aggressively confront or blame others to protect yourself from your fears.

We are not aware that because we exist, we are by definition lovable, acceptable and wanted in the core of our being. We would not be in existence if we were unlovable, unwanted and unacceptable.
Every spirit consciousness comes into existence through an act of creative manifestation, founded in unconditional love and acceptance, belonging and trust. This act is the source of our being and represents the innate natural state of our consciousness from which we cannot be separated.
They are innate psychological reference points that are truthful and consistent and provide us with inner guidance.
The origin and very nature of our consciousness makes us a creation and a creator, a manifestation and endowed with the capacity to manifest.

The fact that we exist is in itself proof that we belong and therefore matter. Any notion that contradicts this is just a belief and does not represent spiritual reality. As part of our capacity to create and manifest our reality we can use our will as a force to drive our intents in order to fulfil our potential. The essence of our spirit contains the capacity to accept or change our intent by changing what we choose to believe. *If* any of what **we accept** is a result of **conditional love, acceptance or trust as our truth, we will create and manifest from** a state of **fear**. It would prove that the fears of our parents have become our fears and thereby their illusions have become ours

All objectivity is lost when negative feelings dominate and your capacity to be rational in respect to your issues becomes questionable. Even if you have an understanding that your parents did not want or love you, you will not necessarily realize that just because ***they did not want you, it does not mean that your life or existence is unwanted.*** Your parents are but two individuals in a world of billions and they are the only ones that you had this experience with. By accepting your parent's treatment of you as your truth, you are allowing it define your identity. You assume that you must not be lovable, acceptable or wanted by anyone else either.

Logically this does not make any sense at all but our almost childlike emotional mind makes its own rules. It does mean however that ***your parents' capacity to love and accept***, support and be involved with you unconditionally ***was limited by their fears and insecurities.*** Now, as an adult, the problem is yours to deal with because the distortions lived out by your parents have become self-defining beliefs held by you and no one else. At this time, you are just as lost in fear-based illusions as your parents were at the time and maybe still are. Only an open-minded examination of your emotional origins will lead to a greater understanding of the reasons for your fears and recognize the beliefs that have held you in their painful grip for too long.

The Origins for Negative Events

For many it is hard to accept that external forces are not the cause for the negative events and encounters they experience. Once perception, feelings and behaviour are distorted by negative belief systems, it is difficult to recognize what is true and what is not. The energy you give out depends on the state of your sense-of-self and this will determine who and what you will attract to become involved with. You will bring people and events in your life that will be complicit in making your fear-based issues a reality. In this sense nothing that happens in your life is an accident; the people you attract also play out their issue driven sense-of-self in concert with you. Everyone's self expression carries the intent shaped by their sense-of-self. Our mind's intent will manifest regardless whether it is driven by negative or positive belief systems, there is no escape from that.

Since the origin for our fear and suffering or anger and resentment are an intrinsic part of our sense-of-self, no one but us can take responsibility for the beliefs we hold. While this may sound harsh it makes it obvious that the quality, nature and intensity of our pain in life are generated by each and every one of us. Once we accept this we will also see that negative events and others cannot be blamed for what we feel. As much as ***unconditional love and inner-harmony*** are the basis for happiness and joy, ***conditional love and acceptance*** create the fear that drives disharmony and inner-conflict, which is the source for pain and suffering. Our sense-of-self holds the key to our negative or positive life experiences. Our perception that that others and the world are the cause rather than we, is a handicap to personal change and a distortion of reality.

Probably one of the wisest statements ever made is:
Do not to try and change those things that you cannot change (i.e. others and the world) but change that which you can (i.e. yourself).
This very much applies here. Realize that you cannot change your partner, your mother and father or anyone else in the world. Spending all your effort and energy trying to change others does not change you or your life experiences. Regardless of what strategies you apply — passive or aggressive control, manipulation or any other kind of influence — you will remain as you are. Even any strategy is to some extend successful; it will be just in that moment and for that situation. You will have to spend your life repeating your effort over and over under constant pressure of the fear of failing.

The only have real power and control you can have is over your self. As the creator of your life through your sense-of-self you also have the capacity to change yourself by releasing the negative beliefs systems that are a part of it. Reality is that you can be the one who is in control over your pain and suffering by letting go of your illusions and by accepting the true nature of who you are.

In Life and Death

The loss of a loved one is a major emotional event and feelings of abandonment and grief are a natural emotional response. How we experience and process such an event in the long term is not totally dependent on our emotional connection with the individual. Here too, our belief systems play a major role in how we will go through times of loss and how we will continue to live our life in their absence.

Your personal beliefs about the nature consciousness and life also define your perception of death. If you hold the belief that life is essentially physical and consciousness depends on the existence of your body than death is a step into non-existence. Losing someone when you hold this as your truth makes their departure extremely painful because they went from being into nothingness. The impact created by the effort, involvements and confrontations of a lifetime will come to a permanent conclusion. When there has been pain and suffering throughout someone's life it often appears that they died without ever experiencing any benefit, pleasure or happiness.

The belief that you will also eventually leave this existence and go from being someone into nothingness, will not only determine the perception of your own eminent demise but will also influence the way you will live your life. This kind of belief system creates the perception that life beyond procreation of the species has limited purpose and value. How and why we exist become meaningless questions that complicate a life that is lived essentially without a sense of higher purpose and meaning. This state of mind denies itself a future beyond the term its physical existence. What you believe to be true for yourself you will hold to be the same for others and this will add to the sadness and pain felt at a time of great loss.

The concept of spirit, mind and body sees the process of death as an inevitable part of its eternal journey. Without spirit neither mind nor body would exist because it is core essence of our conscious being. The mind is the vibration of our awareness of self and knowing of our state of being. The body is a vehicle for our spirit and mind in material reality and is essentially a creation of consciousness itself. The body is intimately connected to spirit and mind through metaphorical patterns that relate energetically to our mind directly. As a consequence anything that happens in the mind will also finds expression in the body and all of its workings. As our bodies come to the end of physical functionality, death creates the transition essential for the spiritual expansion of our consciousness and evolvement beyond physical reality.

The origin of our consciousness or spirit is a source for endless religious, philosophical and scientific debate. Since each demands its' own particular proof, you need to look within yourself to access your inner knowing for what is true for you. Being totally objective in your judgment is extremely difficult considering the concepts and beliefs of your culture, inherited religious beliefs and society you grow up with. By allowing your intuition and inner senses to lead you to your truth you will find your own understanding.

Once you recognize that our spirit and mind are intimately related to our bodies, it is easier to accept that our spirit continues to exist after death. Surrendering our body by releasing spirit and mind from their material bondage recognizes the continuation of our spirit. Acceptance of this transition from the physical to other states of being can alter our perception of death as an end of existence and change how we see the departure of a loved one. Death is as much part of the ongoing journey of their spirit as it will be of ours. Every life lived is a learning-experience to expand the infinite nature of our consciousness. Although most of us have been culturally taught that death is a bad and negative event, the transition into our next state of being should be a celebration of the life lived by the person on their journey to greater being.

Emotional Suffering

When tragedies occur in our lives there are no glib solutions to deal with the emotional pain and suffering we feel as a consequence. We often hope that the passage of time will create emotional distance between the event and us but many constantly relive their pain to one degree or another. To avoid the pain, some will change their lives through making new determinations to deal with their loss. Emotional support of others is desirable but usually over time this will fade as friends return to their own lives. Ultimately we are left to face our tragedies alone because we are the only ones that can do this for ourselves. Even though certain strategies will be effective to allow us continue our lives with some normality, these do not necessarily deal with the reasons why the pain may have taken on such an enduring form.

There will always be emotional pain when we are separated from those we love by death or even severe illness. The fact that we each can have a different experience of the same event shows that it is not as simple as that. Our personal issues related to rejection, and abandonment, powerlessness and being unwanted for example, play an undeniable role in the way we will experience trauma and the stress of loss. Someone who believes they are unlovable, unwanted and unacceptable and then loses their partner is very differently affected than someone who does not have these issues. Their dependence on their partner to be loved and accepted makes them extremely needy and fearful of abandonment and therefore extremely vulnerable to loss. Their emotional security and identity is dependent on what they received from their partner whom they relied for the fulfilment of their emotional needs. Their absence can plunge them into an abyss of fear, loneliness and unhappiness. Their own fears and insecurities serve to intensify the experience of their loss and this will exacerbate and prolong their sadness and suffering.

An event such as this can take them back to re-experience the childhood fears, which were compensated for by their partner. If they were to deal with their fears it would off course not change that they have lost someone dear to them. Inner change will however alter their self-perspective and therefore how they will feel about their loss and potentially can make it bearable. Life and death are intrinsically connected and natural elements of the existence of everything including us. Everything changes and transforms and this is a natural aspect of consciousness. As such as much as we want to experience life we must accept death as the natural course taken by all consciousness in their journey of existence.

Someone with a harmonious sense-of-self will deal with emotional trauma very differently than someone who is needy, dependent powerless and so on. The beliefs they hold in relation to themselves, life, death and dying are from a point of self-power and eternal existence. This awareness helps them to accept the journey of a departed and still continue the meaningful path of their own life. Whether one chooses to have a new relationship or a different direction in life or not, becomes a matter of choice and should not be a product of fear. Life does not have to become an ongoing journey of loneliness, misery and pain.

Someone who goes into depression or becomes suicidal after a big financial loss already has their sense-of-self-worth and identity rolled up in material wealth prior to the event. Someone who cannot cope with the breakup of a relationship and does not look at the negative contribution they made to this outcome. If you attract events or people in your life that cause you pain or anger, powerlessness or guilt, you need to accept that you must be implicated because you are the constant factor in it. There are an endless number of examples of these. Your understanding of these will allow you to clearly define the difference between the authentic pain of loss and trauma and that part that is created by your own pre-existing emotional issues.

While it may be difficult to examine yourself when you are in this state of mind the reasons for doing so are extremely relevant and legitimate if one is to find inner peace. As odd as that may sound, those who cannot cope with traumatic emotional events very likely already have pre-existing belief systems responsible for intensifying their experience. Dealing with unresolved emotional issues related to loss or trauma can make an amazing difference to your perception and feelings in respect to the event. You do not need to worry that your personal changes will make you an uncaring or insensitive individual. Your grief will still be sincere but releasing the cause for these issues will exclude that part of your emotions that were really about you and not about the one you lost.

CHAPTER 18

Fantasy and Imagination

So far our focus has only been on belief systems being the source for the creation and manifestation of our experience of reality. They are the decisive and determining elements in the process of manifesting life but there is much more to the innate capacities of our consciousness to make this possible. Faculties that that are inherent in consciousness give us the power to manifest our lives in accordance with the beliefs, which make up our sense-of-self.

We have an incessant drive to create and manifest our thoughts, fantasy and imagination. The desire of consciousness to learn and know, understand and experiment is never ending. All of this feeds the all-encompassing force within all consciousness to expand the nature and capacity of its own being in order to evolve. Consciousness always seeks to become more than what it is. The direction it chooses to achieve this is determined by its perception of reality created by its sense-of-self. Negative experiences versus positive will notify the mind that it is **manifesting life from fear** (conditional love and acceptance) **rather than unconditional love.**

Being conscious that the essence of your spiritual being is present in all of your beliefs and feelings, behaviour and self-expression is the only way to be aware that you are manifesting a harmonious existence.

Anything invented, built and achieved by man started out as an idea, inspiration or fantasy or imagination. Anything that is physically created or a tangible idea or concept begins as an energetic construct of the mind initiated by our imagination. Application of our intellect and judgment, choices and actions, talents and abilities, competencies and skills and commitment can bring, what was an inspired idea into physical reality. Whether it is the pyramids or a box of matches, a mathematical equation or a painting they all start within our mind as a creative concept or inspiration.

Our imagination and fantasies are essential elements of your life tools which when driven by our innate desire to learn and manifest, can result in amazing outcomes. They are the source of new ideas and concepts that can transcend current perception. Without them we would not have had the advances in every area of our existence that are now a normal part of life. They give us the means to tap into realms of creative contemplation that transcend the limits of convention and accepted logic. They allow us to bend laws and rules of reality established by conventional knowledge and logic and go beyond norms that act as limitations and restrictions in the physical or emotional world. They serve to challenge our perception in order to transcend accepted convention. These innate faculties are extremely precious aspects of human consciousness and they serve us in our quest to grow and expand the nature of our being.

Each of us has the capacity for fantasy and imagination, which is particularly obvious in young children, who's minds flow easily and freely between reality and fantasy. When fantasies and imaginings are encouraged, children learn to use them as a place of experimentation and to test their veracity of their imagination against the physical world. You might be surprised to learn that children are innately aware of the differences between their imaginings and reality without feeling that they have to dismiss them as invalid concoctions of their minds. Each has value in its own context and they are — from a creative perspective — intimately connected to one another. Because of this, dismissing one or the other could be damaging to their minds. Invalidation of their fantasies and imagination diminishes trust in the nature of their own consciousness and separates them from the gifts they are endowed with. This can severely restrict a child's future capacity in becoming confident creators of their own life. Fantasies and imagination are a resource that allows consciousness to find a creative outlet for the fulfilment of its potential beyond accepted norms.

The nature of your sense-of-self plays a major role in the expression of your fantasies and imagination. Your trust or distrust in these innate capacities will affect any creative ventures your mind considers to undertake. Your relationship with your creative impulses and desires, talents and abilities can be a resource for the achievements of your aspirations. Your rejection or distrust in your creative imagination can act as a limitation on your creative self-expression.

Suppressing Your Creative Self

It is easier to be in suppression of the natural creative capacities than what you might think. When we first display and express our creative imagination in play, story telling and games they are often not accepted by our parents. Their dismissal, criticism or comments can make us feel wrong about the voice we give to our spontaneous imaginations. We learn to reject and suppress our creative imagination from our parents because it is likely they had the same experience in their childhood.

People who feel powerless in life often have the expectation that their offspring see the harsh reality that they believe exists. They see a world in which there is no place for fanciful imaginations and fantasies. For many, the general view of life is that it is difficult, a struggle and full of hardship. They do not realize that they use their creative imagination in concert with their negative beliefs to paint a gloomy negative picture of reality.

If you grew up with parents whose issues and therefore fears consistently created negative life experiences you will assume that this is how life is. Their belief that life is a struggle will become your expectation in life. Growing up in a family with negative and pessimistic beliefs, you may use your fantasy and imagination to escape from the terrible world you come to believe exists. On the other hand you might reject your fantasies because you have been convinced that they are unrealistic. Locked into the negative perception inherited from your family, you believe the experience your family presents you with as reality. You would not have known that your parents are the creators of their life experiences and yours and consequently cannot imagine that it could be different. By negating your own imagination you inadvertently invalidate that of others if for no other reason than to be right. Even though may not actively discourage your children in their fantasy play, your pessimistic behaviour and attitude would transfer the pain you feel in living 'a life of struggle' to them. Others may judge you for being cynical and pessimistic but in your own perception you believe yourself to be a 'realist'.

Pessimism, negativity and the anticipation of disaster — generally all fears tend to undermine our faith in the whole creative process that is life. Imagination and fantasy project negative potentials if driven by fear. Highly creative personalities i.e. artists of all kinds, who have fears and issues tend to express their creativity with a pessimistic slant that encompasses their pain and suffering. It kind of romantic to think that their pain is the source for their art but more than often they only feel comfortable or safe to express what they feel by using the voice of their artistic abilities. Their art becomes the language by which they communicate their pain or anger or any other emotion. Deeply affected by emotional issues, they show their true feelings through their artistry. In this respect art also can be a therapeutic bridge to find free emotional expression for those who have difficulty giving a voice to their feelings. Art can be optimistic, revealing and inspiring and this also shows the nature of the artist

Escape from Reality

Consciousness is amazingly clever when it seeks to survive in the face of perceived limitations, restrictions and in the absence of love and acceptance. It will use any tool at its disposal to ensure its emotional security and the most powerful of these is strategic behaviour. The nature of our negative beliefs and the manner in which they are acquired steer us to strategic behaviours. They become the means by which to retain our relationships with our parents. They delude us into believing that meeting their conditions is the way we will be loved and accepted. Once adopted, become our means to overcome our fears in life.

Our fantasies, dreams and imagination can become a strategic tool to escape fears and insecurities, disappointment and restrictions, instead of being the source for creating life. The children in families in which negative, pessimistic and restrictive ideas and beliefs are promoted through passive or aggressive behaviour are pushed to find ways to survive emotionally. Each child will be limited and controlled by the parent's emotional issues without realizing that they cannot be responsible for their parent's negative emotions and feelings.

Under emotional suppression and in fear some children may look for escape by withdrawing into fantasy and imagination. It can seem the only place where can be totally free to be who it wishes to be by creating an imagined existence without restrictions. In your fantasies you are the creator of your imagined reality and in control and safe. Often such children come to believe as adults that their imaginations can never become reality and this can stop them from taking steps to deal with their fears. Another child with the same powerlessness to be accepted, may rebel with anger and aggression and fight for its right to express its true self.

Our mode of escape can take many forms from sport, books or computer games and so on. Escape from suppression can easily alienate us from socializing with others and become alone and lonely. By reacting aggressively to being suppressed we find ourselves in constant conflict and that too does not bring us happiness and peace. Without realizing we will come to accept our patterns of behaviour as normal, as if part of our personality. This can lead us to becoming the same as our parents and potentially repeat the cycle of their behaviour.

Lost in Fantasy

The disparity between real life and your imaginary life can be so wide that you may believe that you can only ever have the life you want in your fantasies and imagination. Remember that we create our own reality no matter what. ***Believing you can never have what you want in reality creates the intent that you never will.*** In your fantasies you may have amazing love relationships, enjoy immense success and live in great abundance even if you hold beliefs that you are not lovable and acceptable, not entitled and unattractive, not good enough and dumb.

Once you are convinced that ***you can only have what you want in your fantasies, dreams and imagination and not in reality*** you have set the stage for how you will manifest your future.

The consequence of this kind of belief system is not easily seen but can have an extremely limiting effect on someone's potential. The context and intensity of this issue varies enormously from person to person. Those with this issue are usually not aware that they themselves are the cause for many of their frustrations in life. Without imagination and fantasy at the disposal of their creativity, life cannot turn out to be anything else but a disappointment. Convinced in their expectation that their wishes and desires, hopes and dreams will never be fulfilled, how can they project an optimistic future?

Everything we manifest in life and in the world starts as a creative projection manifested by our imagination before it ultimately becomes reality. By accepting our negative beliefs as truths we stop our imagination from ever being realized by us. Without making an effort to understand why this is our experience of reality, it is likely that our life will be disappointment.

Potentially, people with this mindset have the tendency to make their fantasies disproportionally ambitious. As a result their expectations become so incredibly outlandish that they cannot possibly be realized. Imaginings of romantic relationships with incredibly wealthy and successful handsome men or beautiful women, becoming famous or successful may sound like obvious fantasies but are more common than you might think. In their real life they are not actively involved in anything that could lead them to make their fantasy a reality. Putting their ambitions far beyond the reach of their own capacity to deliver gives them justification why their dreams have not become reality. Consequently the outcome they experience will be will be a faithful reflection of the negative beliefs they hold and confirm that they cannot have what they want in reality.

Even though we are actually free to believe, think and behave the way we want, the emotional forces under which we were raised define how we will be in the world. Every quality of our consciousness plays a role in the manifestation of who we are in life. Our fantasy, imagination and dreams play a significant role in our creative capacity to project our future existence and collectively a future world. We can restore the innate human capacity for fantasy and imagination by releasing of these emotional restrictions than we will be able to turn our dreams into reality. There are no limits to the capacity of your consciousness other than the fears you hold in your sense-of-self.

Considering our perception of our limitations is determined by who we believe we are it not surprising that we easily dismiss the proposition that *we should naturally be experts in the process of manifesting our own reality*. Our perceived limitations make it seem impossible to have control over our life but this is entirely achievable. *The capacity to be the conscious creator of our own reality is innate in every one of us.* There is no doubt however that in order to be an 'expert' creator, you need to become the 'master of your own consciousness'. For this you need to first of all develop a clear and intimate understanding of the fears held by your own consciousness. *A master would engage in the process of creating life in the absence of fear with complete trust in the purity and power of his or her intent.*

This is why strategic behaviours as a solution have only temporary value and should be treated as such. In the process of becoming the master creator of your own reality you have to deal with your fears. Every release will bring you closer to that goal. Fantasies and imagination are essential tools for a master creator in the process of inventing and initiating new life challenges so that his or her consciousness can evolve. Through manifesting intent, they allow you to project a potential for a different life into the future. By forming a clearly defined idea or intent for the future and engaging in activities in the present designed to make it reality, you are creating your dreams and aspirations.

Chapter 19

Living Your Unconditional Potential

Who you believe yourself to be and the feelings this creates in you will determine the choices that lead you to experience your unique life journey. When we encounter emotionally challenging issues and our existing strategies fail, we usually try to find new strategic behaviours to replace them with the intent for a better outcome. We should always see this behaviour as a temporary stopgap solution. These new strategies do not deal with the fundamental cause of why we are confronted by issues in the first place.

If you want to address your issues at their core, you have no choice but to explore the nature of your own mind. You have to stop being preoccupied with changing **what you do** and begin to focus on changing **who you are**. Real personal change requires the release of negative beliefs that cause you to manifest your fears and insecurities as a life experience. What you do may appear to be the cause but your behaviour is a learned response and an attempt to avoid your fears.

Defined by Fear

While it may be difficult to become absolutely unconditional in every aspect of your being, you can be sure that every time you release a fear-based belief you are bringing yourself closer to that goal. Before that can do that you will need to examine everything about yourself — your behaviour, your feelings and choices and responses to others and what you create in your life with them.

You may find for example that many of the things you want from life or from others are aspects that you believe to be absent within you.
- If you have **the need** to be accepted by others, it is because you do not accept yourself.
- If you **have to prove** that you are special and significant to others it is because you believe you do not matter to yourself.

- If you **need others to prove to you** that you are lovable and acceptable, it is because you believe that you are not lovable and acceptable and do not love and accept your self.
- If you **expect to be forgotten and ignored**, it is because you believe your presence and your existence is insignificant and does not matter to anyone. You may believe that you are not wanted.
- If you **anticipate being blamed and accused**, it is because you are convinced that whenever someone is upset or things go wrong, you must be guilty or implicated.

Your negative sense-of-yourself acts as a motivation that leads you into getting *proof from others that you are NOT what and who you believe yourself to be*. Your subconscious strategy is to make others believe that you are lovable and acceptable, significant or special and so on through your behaviour. The truth is that you are trying to convince others in order to provide proof for yourself that you are not who you fear yourself to be. You have think that if others believe you are special that this proves that you must be special and so on. You can apply this to being lovable, acceptable, being innocent and so on. The obvious problem is that you will always be dependent on the response of others as so to convince yourself that you are not who or what you believe you are. You do not realize that *your behaviour gives others power over your sense of being*. Any success your behaviour achieves will only be momentary and in respect to those involved. Next time, driven by the same fears, you will have to play out your strategies all over again.

This approach to your issues can be either aggressive or passive and for some both (but not simultaneously). Through behaviour and dialogue you can try and convince others that you are significant, special or important and so on, to avoid that they see who you believe you really are. Alternatively you may identify so completely with your negative beliefs that you feel you are a victim of them. You will become who you are according to your beliefs and live your life as if they are the truth about you.

- *If your issues cause you to fear being unhappy and sad*, you will focus your efforts on those things and situations that you believe will **make** you happy and avoid those that you believe will not. Your mother or father (or both) would have been modelled these issues through their behaviour and attitude. Their pursuit of happiness will be marked by constant dissatisfaction and disappointment with each other or their life experiences. Their negative beliefs causes them to give excessive importance and focus to everything that disappoints them or makes them unhappy and sad. This only serves to emphasise their despondency to their children who begin to accept this as being true about themselves and life. They expect others and the world to bring them happiness, not realizing that *happiness can only be created by them and can only come from within*. Their perception however is coloured by their constant pessimism and sense of powerlessness to find happiness and contentment. Exposure to your parent's constant state of disappointment and criticism sets you up to believe that this is how life is and what to expect. You will either accept it as a truth or do anything possible to avoid it. Should you accept that your expectations will never be met you will believe your life will be filled with disappointments. This may cause you sidestep anything in your life that has the potential to make you unhappy, sad depressed or disappointed. Alternatively you may obsessively engage in activities chosen to make you feel good and distance you from your fear based negative of feeling. Instead of directing your focus within to discover the causes for what you feel and experience, you have made yourself dependent on others and the world to feel good about your self (just like your parents have always done).

- *If are a victim of aggression or the manipulative control* of your parents, it is likely you will have been made to believe you are powerless. Your powerlessness is probably a result of having an aggressive or dominating parent who may have openly or indirectly blamed you and held you responsible for their discontent, frustration or anger. On the other hand your parent may have acted as a passive-powerless victim transferring the responsibility for their feelings of pain and suffering to you. In both scenarios you become the guilty party for which you can adopt either passive or aggressive behavioural strategies in order to survive. You may form the belief that the only way to avoid being a victim is to behave in the same way as the person who intimidated or dominated you. On the other hand, you may have accepted the belief that you are powerless. This belief can cause you to wait for approval and be given permission to do or have what you want. If you believe you are powerless you may be attracted to becoming the follower of someone who you believe is powerful and significant. Their display of power and control will give you a sense of power by association.

- *If you feel that you do not matter and are insignificant together with the belief that you are not entitled*, will cause you adopt aggressive or passive strategies. Aggressive by ensuring that you will always be the centre of attention *or* passive by making yourself 'invisible' to avoid being noticed. Secondary behavioural strategies in response to this kind of belief system are; extreme independence, not being able to ask for support, help or for what you want. Besides having a childhood history of feeling ignored, forgotten and blamed you may also feel that you are a burden to your parents and later others. Their lack of interest and involvement with you convinced you that you are uninteresting and insignificant. Their dismissal of what was special to you have made you feel that your interests and your excitement over them did not matter and therefore you believe you do not matter. This took away your desire to challenge yourself in order to achieve. You may even fall into depression because of the constant cycle of negative thoughts your sense of insignificance and powerlessness bring up in you.

The reasons for these family paradigms are many. Parents who feel the pain of being denied love, attention and acknowledgement in their childhood will be so needy for what they never had that they cannot give this to their own children. We would like to think that our parents are perfect people but the reality is that they have fears and insecurities that become most evident in relationships and parenthood. Unfortunately, their issues become ours because their incapacity to love and accept us unconditionally results in making us just as needy as they are. Consequently we are likely to repeat their pattern of behaviour.

The way out of these consecutive patterns of generational negative belief systems is clear. Your first response to any negative emotional experience should be to look at your self to discover your part in their manifestation in your life. Arriving at an objective understanding of the nature of your own belief systems can only come from a mind that does not judge, blame and criticise but is open and unconditional. Recognition of illusions and distortions in your sense-of-self enables you to see the form in which you hold you negative self-beliefs. It will lead you to understand the fears and conditions that you subconsciously place on living life, on your relationships and self-expression. You will become aware that **you** are and can only be the one responsible for your issues and **you** and no one else holds on to them. As a consequence ***you are also the only one that can change yourself*** by releasing them.
The truth is that:
Our negative beliefs do not attach themselves to us; our childhood fear of rejection and abandonment causes us to hold on to them.

The Lies Fear Creates

Fear promises that **if** we respond to the conditions it wants us to believe are true and real, we will receive love, acceptance and trust. Fear never reveals what the real consequences will be if you accept its truth. It convinces you that as long as you respond to its call, you will be safe from abandonment and rejection, criticism and judgement, shame and unhappiness, loneliness and exclusion and so on. As children we feel we cannot do anything other than accept the conditional form love and acceptance we are presented with. If we do not there will be no one to support our existence —at the time we think that we have no choice.

Using fear-based strategic behaviours to create love and acceptance in our lives gives others the power and control to determine the conditions under which we will feel and experience love acceptance and trust. Due to way our psychology has evolved the nature of our beliefs over the ages, our personal and collective awareness and perception have become severely restricted. The aim of true personal transformation is to reclaim your authentic self and personal power to reconnect our inner-self and thereby expand our awareness and become conscious of who you truly are. The results of releasing negative beliefs are literally life changing and permanent in how they change the way you are in life. The absence of fear alters you sense of who you are and therefore how you believe others will perceive you not to mention your behaviours, feelings and perception. Everyone has to content with their own fears but without real change, our functionality in the world will depend on the ongoing effectiveness of our strategic behaviours.

The Battle for Control over Your Mind

Fear is constantly in contest with unconditional love for control over your emotional mind. If the absence of unconditional love is our deepest fear, **why do we not just give into love, acceptance and trust unconditionally** and thereby resolve all of our issues? It is obvious that we have extreme difficulty doing exactly that from the way we live life. There are a number of emotionally compelling reasons to explain why we do not only have major issues with confronting, recognising and accepting our issues but also why we do not release them easily.

The reasons for these are explained here in the approximate order in which these emotional barriers become a part of us.

Distrust of our authentic self is a major obstacle when we want to change. Our identification with our fear-based sense-of-self and our dependence on it for our emotional survival, convinces us that if we should release our fears we will be left without a sense of who we are. We learn to distrust our authentic self and its unique and different qualities because they did not fit the expectations, norms and values of our parents. Their fears and insecurities of anything that different from what they hold to be true and right caused them to make your spontaneous unique and authentic self wrong and unacceptable. This leaves you no choice but to accept the values and standards shaped by their fears as your 'truths'. The acceptance of their negative mindset will contradict the innate nature of your authentic self but your need to emotionally survive gives you no choice but to accept the conditional love and acceptance offered by your parents. Unconsciously, your choices have brought you into a state of mind that makes you fearful of being your authentic self and expressing your authentic nature. You are now convinced that if you do, you will attract or provoke conflict or aggression, criticism or judgement anger or resentment, powerlessness or guilt and so on. You will unconsciously suppress and reject who you authentically are to protect yourself from the consequences your fears present you with.

Emotional neediness and the feelings our fears create are compelling forces that will cause us to reach out to our strategic behaviours, as the only emotional tools we believe will get us emotional fulfilment. The fear of having to live without what we believe we need to feel loved, safe and special provides the impulse to search for ways to fulfil our needs. Under constant pressure from the fear of not having what we believe we cannot exist without, we live life at in a constant level of anxiety. The fear of missing out or being neglected, being unnoticed or never having what you want, feeling worthless and so on are all different forms of neediness with fear at their centre. Each will create different levels of stress that cause us to resort to strategies.

We become so conditioned to believe that love, acceptance and trust are conditional that we usually will not even recognize or accept unconditional love. Strange as it may seem but it is usually so foreign to us that should it cross our path, we tend to treat it with suspicion. In the belief that love is conditional, the absence of these conditions makes unconditional love strange and in some ways even perilous. Being unconditional in love and acceptance appears terrifying because it would seem to make you vulnerable to the pain of abandonment and rejection. Surrendering the conditions you believe are real is like giving up the protection from pain and suffering experienced in childhood.

So instead of choosing for unconditional love we are subconsciously drawn to people who carry the complementary part of our issues or are a direct mirror for them. The fear of living in the absence of love and fear of loneliness intensifies the neediness for a partner and closes our eyes to the emotional causes for what we feel. Your neediness will control your behaviour and responses such as pleasing and attention seeking for example but can also trigger controlling and dominating behaviour.

The fundamental problem with neediness is that it always represents an expectation from others. By being needy you transfer the responsibility for what is missing for you within yourself to others or a partner. Your counterpart will likely be someone has learned in childhood that they will only be loved and accepted if they take responsibility for the needs of others or their potential partner. They will prove to you that you are lovable and acceptable by putting you before themselves and giving your needs and expectation priority over their own. Eventually this will create resentment in them because it will feel to them that their needs are never taken care off. At the same time your own constant neediness make you dissatisfied and disappointed thereby making your partner feel that they can never please you. The cracks that appear in your relationship can only be healed if both parties individually release the core reasons for the issues displayed through their behaviours.

Fear of being powerless in the world can be so intense that just the experience of living life can feel like an overwhelming confrontation. When controlled by these feelings, you are likely to try and avoid engaging in anything that will be perceived as a potential challenge, risk or threat. The belief in your own weaknesses and vulnerabilities creates a world in which you are the potential victim of threats and aggression. Living becomes a constant battle for emotional and sometimes physical survival. Your strategies can be passive or aggressive — either focussed on the avoidance of anything that creates stress or fear in you or you feel driven to resort to aggressive or manipulative behaviour to gain power and control. Either way, your fearful, negative or pessimistic outlook on life is a reflection of your fundamental fears. Trying to avoid being seen to be weak and powerless ensures your dependence on your strategic behaviours to maintain the outward illusion that you are in control. Unfortunately this will also cause you to avoid facing your emotional issues and dealing with the core reasons for your fears. Any failure to maintain emotional control over your life will likely to be blamed on others or circumstances and a justification to be more aggressive, cautious or mistrusting. You do not realize that by not accepting responsibility for your beliefs, you actually justify maintaining your sense of powerlessness. ***Your fears will always try and sabotage your attempts to find their origin.*** In an effort to protect yourself from what you feel afraid off, you turn your attention to everything and everyone that could be a threat. Your belief that the reasons for your fears are external will keep your focus on your environment, which ensures that you will not look within for the reasons for your state of mind.

Your dependence and trust in your strategic behaviours as the only means, by which you can have power to make the choices to get what you want keep you in a state powerlessness. The conditional relationship with your parents will have taught you that if you get it wrong, you will be blamed and suffer the consequences. At the same time the conditions they set also educate you how you can meet them in order to be eligible for love, acceptance and so on. If you fail to meet the conditions by not being who they want and expect you to be, you will feel powerless to have control over your relationship with them. As a child it will feel as if you have to choose between being yourself and suffer rejection or being what they want you to be and being acceptable. You will most likely choose the latter in order to have some form of love and acceptance. But, not every child will conform to accept behaviours that do not represent who it feels it is. They can become the children that we perceive as difficult and contrary because they refuse to submit to the parent's ideas, values and standards which can potentially come from fear.

No matter whether you took on passive or aggressive strategies, should they fail, it is likely that you will try and find a new and better strategy to regain control over your life situation. You do this automatically because it is what you have learned to do and alternatives are invisible to you. You do not see that the emotional circumstances you are in are a reflection of who you believe you are because you can only think in terms of doing. As a result, the prospect of letting go of these instruments of power and control over your emotional security — your strategic behaviours — feel like an unacceptable proposition. In your understanding of how life works you would feel powerless without them. Often, you will only consider the potential that you may be implicated in your life issues after suffering emotional pain and stress because of consistent failure of your strategies.

The fear of being seen to be wrong or imperfect, a failure or inadequate, responsible or guilty and so on by others can make acknowledgement and owning your issues feel like an admittance of guilt, inferiority or not being good enough if not ashamed. Accepting that you have fears, issues, insecurities or shortcomings and so on contradicts what you are trying to prove to others through your behaviours. You want to appear strong, powerful and in control, as someone who has total self-confidence and trust. Failing this, you will again feel like the child who was insecure and self-doubting because of constant criticism and judgement. You probably adopted the same strategies your parents used on you — by making others wrong and yourself right in order to give yourself an air of superiority and thereby hide your insecurities. Potentially you are your own worst critic and beat yourself up for not being whom and what you believe you should be. Your desire to be perfect in the eyes of others can be so intense that admitting your flaws becomes virtually impossible. Instead, you completely rely on your strategic behaviour to create the image of yourself you want the world to see.

In your job, you may work yourself into ground to make sure you do not fail the expectations of others because that would mean that they would be aware of your weaknesses and insecurities. Your excessive commitment might make you the performance star in the workplace even though it is at great emotional cost to yourself. This same approach will fail dismally in relationships where your desire to be seen as perfect creates expectations that are difficult if not impossible for a partner to live with.

The prospect of being totally unconditional in love and acceptance poses huge emotional challenges for us because it ***demands that we live life in the absence of fear.*** Unfortunately, our issues no matter how small or large, are all a product of fears caused initially by our separation from unconditional love, acceptance and trust. You become attached to the identity your negative beliefs create even though they confine and restrict your life through the conditions you believe have to be met. When fear, distrust and suspicion and the strategies they cause you to adopt have been lifelong companions that kept you safe, the prospect of letting go of them can make you feel extremely vulnerable. Letting go of fear can feel like becoming powerless in life

Unconditional love in the form of unconditional acceptance and trust are so terrifying because we unconsciously place so many conditions on our emotional life. What we really want is a guarantee that the outcome will be according to our expectations ***before*** we become unconditional but that in itself is a condition. No one can say that it is easy and that is why we should not expect that becoming unconditional is the same as flipping a switch. It is a process where your levels of being unconditional become greater as you release more fear-based beliefs.

The fear of the consequences of being spontaneous makes us contrived in our behaviour and responses. One of the major benefits of releasing your fears is the return of spontaneity lost in childhood. Fear will always make us question our initial impulse to be spontaneous resulting in strategic behaviour. It can also make us doubt our instinctive and intuitive actions, creativity and inspirations and can cause us dismiss them. Fear will cause us to become calculated and contrived in our self-expression by making us question our perception, interpretations, judgment and choices. Soon our lack of self-trust and self-belief will give fear the power to make our choices for us and take control over our life. Fear separates us from being and existing within our own power and makes us hide our spontaneous and unique authentic self. Ultimately fear will stop us from being at one with unconditional love and being connected to Everything That Is.

You can see that potentially, there are quite a few bridges to cross on your journey to real change but if you really look at each of these obstacles you will realise they are all part of the illusion you have been living in all along. You will find that are all interconnected and overcoming one, supports transcendence of the others. ***Reality is that there is nothing more motivating than fear, pain, stress and suffering to create the emotional necessity for personal change.*** It is also true that setting out on this journey before your life hits a crisis point can save you from a lot of anguish.

Dependence on Strategies

Emotional strategies have a role in life because they give us results in the short term but their success always depends on how others respond to them. Regardless of the outcome you achieve with your strategies your relationship with yourself and that with others will remain conditional and rooted in fear. As long as we stay strategic we will always find reasons to justify our behaviours.

Over time, life will present us with progressively more intensely confronting events and situations until eventually our strategies will let us down. At the time we may think that we have failed but we are actually experiencing the fear-based version of ourselves we have been avoiding by being strategic in our lives. Each negative event is in fact a reflection of our emotional issues — our negative sense-of-self. If we do not suffer an obvious emotional effect from these self-created negative experiences, they may eventually show as issues with our physical health or in both. In life, there is no escaping the outcome of the consequences of the process by which we manifest our reality. This is as true in the negative sense as it is in the positive when coming from a state of inner-harmony.

We are often not prepared to explore the nature of our minds for fear of what we will discover. However if we choose not to confront our issues before we reach these physical or emotional extremes the negative consequences will be inevitable over time. Without accepting that we are the instigators and creators of our own life experiences, it is doubtful that we can achieve permanent change in our sense-of-self.

Strategic Relationships

Usually, those who are looking for the perfect partner do not realize what they are asking for. Unaware of their issues they do not appreciate that their idea of perfection actually incorporates their fears and insecurities. Someone who feels powerless and vulnerable will automatically look for someone to protect and look after them. If you are in fear of being trapped in responsibilities you will look for someone who is over-responsible and has no expectations of you. If you are aggressively controlling in your life you will want a partner who is passive compliant and will not challenge you.

We unconsciously seek out and attract partners who compensate for our insecurities and are willing to take this responsibility. Of course they also have to be good looking, financially well off, have a sense of humour, be intelligent, socially engaging, trustworthy and so on. Generally those who depend on their relationships to make them happy, safe and fulfilled also believe that their appearance is their most important asset to get what they want. Usually in denial of their emotional issues and vulnerabilities they depend on how others see them to attract who they believe to be the right partner. How others may judge their appearance becomes the focus of obsessive attention because it is the only part of them they feel to have any direct control over.

Once you are convinced that others cause your issues, it is an easy stretch to accept that only the perfect partner will make us happy. Reality paints a very different picture. Instead of attracting a partner who will save us from our fears, we will attract someone who will bring complementary issues into the relationship. Expecting that our partner will not only make us feel lovable, acceptable and wanted, we also demand that they protect us from our fears and insecurities. The consideration that our partner may have needs, expectations and issues of their own does not figure in their idea of the perfect relationship. In the belief that our partner's only desire and focus in life should be on us, this romantic idea of a relationship is unlikely to be sustainable. Your own issues will guarantee that our partner's issues will surface an in the course of time, which will mark the beginning of discontent.

It is quite common for both partners have the same underlying issues but play these out using contrasting strategies. One will use passive strategic behaviours while the other is strategically more pro-active or confronting by comparison. In relative terms, this makes one appear strong and the other vulnerable or weak, which is also the perception they have of each other. Unconsciously, each depends on the other to compensate for their issues. This exchange of apparent power and the dependence each has, can function reasonably well for a period of time. Sooner or later however one or the other will begin to feel that the power and support is not genuine and begin to question the nature of the relationship.

Couples who are both very fearful of confronting and living life are a good example of this. By sharing their fear of confrontation and guilt and conflict, judgment, powerlessness and rejection and so on they share a similar perception of the world. As a result their issues and fears and the avoidance strategies they employ to deal with them as likely to complement one another. Everything to do with living life generates fear in them including openly expressing ideas, beliefs and emotions. Even though they are both passive, one may take a more dominant role by, for example, using logical reasoning to justify why certain avoidance strategies are perfectly sensible to be safe from the world. By knowing what to do and how to do it to avoid confrontation, the more aggressive partner makes the other feel safe. Their fears place severe restrictions on the expression of their feelings and emotions, choices and decisions and makes. Their inter-dependence also causes them to be in fear of losing each other. This makes them cautious in the way they relate to each other for fear of upsetting one other and rejection or abandonment. Their fears have turned their 'perfect' relationship both into a safe-haven and an emotional jail. In this environment, their sense of self will not evolve to its potential and they are unlikely to ever come near knowing what it would be like to exist in the freedom of their authentic self. This is not the kind of relationship any of us should aspire to.

False Needs and Expectations

It is not simple to create the life you want if your issues control you. Realize first of all that *you are always— consciously or unconsciously — manifesting your life experiences*. We generally think that the only time we actively do something with a specific intent is when we put strategic plans in place for a project or to achieve certain goals. This is a total misconception. The intents attached to the beliefs that form your sense-of-self are active every moment of your existence. Your subconscious intent seeks to find fulfilment with much greater vigour in every moment and aspect of life than you are aware of. *The fear-based intents propagated by your negative beliefs can and will override your consciously planned and created intents immediately or over time.* Positive or negative, your intents will attract, create and manifest life experiences that fit their nature.

Going after what you feel you want and need may seem very natural until you question your motives. Without being conscious why your needs and motivation are so significant to you, your pursuit may be destructive or irrational. The needs and feelings that make then so prominent for you might have their origin in the fear of missing out or being denied, being insignificant and worthless and so on. Even though these fear-based beliefs are nothing but illusions, their emotional influence will control how and where you will spend your energy and effort in life.

Knowing full well that all of us have emotional fears of some description it is sensible to question yourself in respect to your needs, expectations and desires. Your aspirations could be a product of your fears and then the way you go about realizing them can have undesirable consequences for yourself and others. It is therefore important that you **make yourself aware of — why you want what you want/ why you need what you need/ why you do what you do** and so on, to ensure that it is not a product of your negative beliefs. Justifying your desires, needs and aspirations because others act like you is highly misleading because you do not know what belief systems drive them.

If you are powerless, you will believe you need to have power, if you are poor you will aspire to be wealthy, if you are a failure you want success or have someone successful in your life, if you are lonely, you have to have a partner, if you feel vulnerable you want to be strong or be protected and so on. By not questioning the motivation for what you want, you risk that your aspiration or desire you are actually are distortions based on illusions created by fear. Trying to create the opposite of these negative beliefs is your habitual way to avoid what you fear. Actually, your choice of solution does not change anything because you remain the same. Even though you may have manifested wealth and established a position of power in your life, you have to depend on the success of your strategies in respect to others and the world to hold on to them. Despite giving the appearance that you have transcended the issues of your past *you have only changed what is outside of you but not who you are— your sense-of-self.* The same applies to those whose avoidance strategies have kept them from confrontation and conflict. Whether you like it or not in spite of your perceived success of your strategies, your negative beliefs still control your emotional state of mind. The consequences of your fears are likely to reveal themselves in other areas of life (or in your body) of which you may as yet not be aware.

We commonly want those things we were denied in childhood. We want to do the things we were not allowed to do and give a voice to that part of us that was suppressed, criticised and judged or made out to be a disappointment. The problem lies in how we go about reclaiming our freedom, our power and ultimately our authentic self. **We live in a world that has convinced us that all we need to do is opposite to what we fear in order to change our life experience and get what we want.** It appears that regardless of how we interpret our life issues, just about everyone follows similar patterns of response, which is to discover new strategies to overcome negative outcomes.

Your sense-of-self would have developed very differently had your childhood been experienced in an unconditional family environment. As a result you would not have acquired fear based belief systems and feel confident and empowered. Free to follow your inspirations, talents and abilities without concern for failure you have the opportunity to fulfil your every aspect of your potential. You may discover that you have more than one passion in your life and many talents and abilities to give expression to. One thing is certain that if you choose out of neediness you are not in control and your fears are doing the choosing for you.

How to Be Authentic

The journey to find yourself assumes that you have lost who you are and therefore you must find who and what you truly are to be able to change and evolve. The good news is that your authentic self cannot be and was never actually lost. On the other hand to expect your real self will reveal itself like a Jack-out-of-a-box is unrealistic and unlikely to happen. Add to this that you have learned to suppress and hide most of what represents the authentic self it becomes difficult to establish who that is. Without the aid of emotional reference points it is difficult if not impossible recognize what part of you represents your authentic self and what is not.

The end result is that we unconsciously disassociate ourselves from who we truly are. With the passage of time, our authentic self will already be buried by fear driven beliefs, needs and strategies before we had the chance to realize its true nature, capacity and power. Now, we no longer trust our authentic self to bring us the unconditional love, emotional security or self-fulfilment it initially promised. Instead we put our faith in our fears and we expect that they keep us safe. There is no greater illusion than to believe that fear will save you from creating a negative reality.

Describing the actual qualities that would make your authentic-self recognizable for you is not possible other than to confirm that it is in harmony with your spiritual essence. The authentic self is not so much a fixed state of being than it is a representation of a collection of qualities that are unique to you. Everything that makes up your authentic self exists in a state of greater potential and has the capacity to evolve into something more than what it is. It is not predestined to become anything specific although it may have certain leanings and biases in the direction it may develop under your auspices. The potential intrinsic in our authentic self, together with our innate drive for creativity and capacity to formulate intent makes it the most potent aspect of our psyche. There is also no limit on how or how far it can evolve because that depends on us. "FEAR" as a concept and emotional state of mind is the critical limiting factor in your discovery and development of your authentic self

Your fear-based beliefs have buried your authentic self and overlaid it with behaviours that have the intent to make you loved and accepted to others even though it is all conditional. This ensures that your true self is seen to be unacceptable by you and never given a voice. Even though your authentic self reflects your authentic spiritual identity, your negative beliefs, feelings and strategies are now your resource for survival in the world they caused you to perceive. Nevertheless, even though denied presence and self-expression your authentic self is still the essential nature of your consciousness. The consequences that are implied by your fears are the reason you do not allow yourself to be authentically yourself. Your negative beliefs and behaviours are like are like a fortress that keeps your safe from the consequences of your fears but simultaneously keeps you its prisoner. Your fear driven convictions portray themselves as saviours while in reality they contain and control your self-expression.

Transcending Your Illusionary Self

Becoming your authentic self without dealing with the fears that caused you to distrust and suppress it in the first place will probably be unsuccessful. Your conscious desire to be your authentic self is contradicted by the intent of your negative beliefs. Your fear-based intent will warn you that accepting your authentic self will recreate the fears of your childhood all over again. Guess which of these will win out? Since you have learned to mistrust much of what is your authentic self, you need a different approach to bring it back as your conscious being.
Your dependence on your fears and their strategies to survive in your life make it highly unlikely that you can instantly switch from your fears to being your authentic self. Overcoming emotional fears in this way is extremely difficult to achieve, particularly if you cannot identify with your authentic self. The only thing you can be sure off is that your authentic self does not come from fear.

The secret to becoming your authentic self is simple:
Release all fear and your authentic self will automatically begin to reveal itself.

Once you start this process your authentic self will reveal it self layer by layer, through the way you feel, choose and in what will manifest in your life.

After you let go of certain fears, the next step is to accept and trust what any newly discovered quality or aspect of your self. However you need to be mindful at all times that your new discovered aspects are not newly discovered fears.

You may not always immediately recognize those beliefs that truly represent your essence. If fear is a dimension of a newly discovered aspect of your self you can be sure you that it is not your authentic self. However you need to trust these emerging new and unknown aspects once you know they are not based on negative beliefs. In time you will go through this process without feeling uncertainty because your growing awareness of what is fear based and what is not.

Most people believe that their authentic self has to be the opposite of their issues. Feeling powerless and helpless in life will make you believe that your authentic self will be powerful, dominant and in control. Feeling insignificant will cause you to believe that your authentic self has to be very special and unique in the eyes of others. The point is that you think that once become your authentic self your life will be total opposite to your current experience of your self. It is true that once you release your fears, the related issues will dissolve but it does not mean that this will manifest the extreme opposite experience of reality. In other words you will not automatically rise to become a recognized dominant figure from being a passive compliant victim. To believe that once your fear of commitment, intimacy and giving and receiving love you will immediately fall in the most amazing and perfect relationship is unrealistic. This is not to say that you do not have the potential and that there is not the possibility for this to be manifested by you.

Understand that the changes you have made are within you. Transforming your sense-of-self has changed the potential of what you will choose to manifest in your life. A big part of changing your sense-of-self is the absence of neediness of all kind and how this alters your idea of what you want out of life and relationships. The other major change comes from realizing that you have choices you could not even imagine you could have or make because your fears used to decide for you.

You will only feel and experience giving and receiving unconditional love, acceptance and trust in the absence of your negative beliefs. There appears to be no shortcut to this because for as long as fear dominates the mind, it will always prioritize your fears for the sake emotional survival.

Chapter 20

Our Conditional Mind

Undoing the negative impact of your childhood will take you through all manner of mental and emotional stages. Even though we try and avoid negative and painful emotions, our feelings are essential to our understanding of who and what we are in our life. Our emotional experience of life is essential to our emotional growth and survival. We would not be aware that something is very wrong within us until we experience intense and enduring negative emotions. Without feeling the many different forms of pain or happiness and joy, we have no way of knowing whether we are manifesting from our essence or from our fears. In the absence of negative feelings there would also be no motivation to try and resolve the inner conflict that creates them. We would not care about the consequences our fears manifest for us and others. Negative feelings are an indicator that our experience is a result of actions and choices, which are in disharmony with our essence.

Commonly our immediate response to negative feelings is to find the source for what we feel outside of us rather than within. It usually does not occur to us that *who* we believe we are is the problem and therefore a key to a solution. This limits how we deal with emotional issues. .

By working on the symptoms of an issue instead of ourselves, we remain deluded that we are actually resolving our life problems. It is exactly in this way that our parents tried to change us to deal with their fears and insecurities. We, just like them, believe that we can solve our issues by changing others and the world. By transforming your sense-of-self, you will ensure that your issues will not be passed on to future generations — your children.

Our emotional survival mechanism is triggered by the fear of being separated from unconditional love by raising the acuteness of our awareness so that we pay greater attention to any emotionally threatening encounter. It is an innate defence and survival strategy for our consciousness (and on a physical level for the body) that generally serves us well. The trouble starts when we lose the capacity to differentiate between a real threat and one that we create in our mind in response to a fear-based belief accepted in childhood.

Once we cannot differentiate a real threat from a self-created illusion we have lost the connection with what is real and what is not. In that case, fear will dominate our perception, behaviour and emotions, our view of reality and what we experience. We will be controlled by illusion not reality and live with the negative consequences it manifests.

Our distorted perception makes our fears feel real and this will usually override any sensible reasoning or responses. If we were to asses our feelings before acting we might finish up with a more objective and responsible perspective and respond differently. Giving into your feelings without any consideration to anything other than what you feel will ensure that you stay in old patterns and learn very little. It is important to acknowledge and analyse your feelings and try and recognize the part you have played in making a negative event come about.

Obviously if you start out with the belief that you could not possibly be implicated, it is unlikely that you will accept responsibility for what you create in your life. It makes more sense to assume that you must be in some way responsible rather than to than thinking that you are totally innocent. Painting yourself the victim of others or circumstances will do nothing to advance your personal growth. Blaming others makes you the victim and therefore causes you to take a position of powerless. This will not address your issues and you are likely to perpetuate them in the future.

You must not be judgmental or critical of your self or others on your journey of self-discovery. There is nothing to gain from self-blame, guilt or blaming others because none of these are a true representation of being self-responsible. Indulging in this will only distort your perception even further and make it harder to understand what it takes to change your life.

When seeking to determine the nature of your negative beliefs you may wonder how you can be sure that the conclusions you come to are as unbiased and objective as possible. The notion that one can be truly objective when making personal judgments is misleading. Even if you are without fear, your perception will always be effected by the unique nature of your mind. Resolution for your issues does not in fact rely on your capacity to be objective as much as it does on your acceptance that *your present understanding of causes for your issues has been learned in childhood.*

The reality is that your issues are a product of a fear based sense-of-self and therefore illusionary because this contradict the unconditional nature of your spirit. The fear context of these beliefs excludes it from being representative of who you really are — your authentic self. Your childhood interpretation of the negative emotional events created by the dynamic between you and your mother and father have formed these beliefs but that does not mean they are real. However by matching childhood relationships and experiences with your current issues, the negative beliefs the origin for your issues will become obvious.

The standards and values you can apply to test whether your findings represent positive or negative belief systems are as follows:

- *Any behaviour, response, action, choice or feeling motivated by FEAR is a product of negative belief systems that form your sense-of-self.*

As soon as you recognize that *fear is involved* in your feelings and behaviour you have an indication that you are dealing with a negative belief that you believe to be real but is not. Fear is always a negative influence no matter what justification or reason might be given to the contrary.

- *Any behaviour or response, action or choice or feeling motivated by GUILT or SELF-BLAME is a product of negative beliefs — Fear.*

Unless you are guilty of knowingly and with premeditation of causing pain and suffering, your guilt feelings have no real basis in reality. Guilt feelings and self-blame are products of feeling over-responsible for the issues, pain and suffering of others. You are most likely to experience guilt in relation to people who perceive themselves to be victims and powerless. Their behaviour can be aggressive in their blame of others to shift the responsibility for their issues to prove they are the victims. Or, they can also present as passive powerless victims of life. The core for these issues will be in your childhood with a similarly affected parent.

- *The only truth that counts in your search for emotional truth is your personal perception and experience of an event or relationships.* In searching for the truth in your childhood, your version of what is true in your past is the product of your translation of events and represents the emotional experiences that shaped your sense-of-self. Your conclusions need to explain the nature and reasons for your behaviour and feelings, choices and perception. The negative beliefs that make up your sense of self will always hold the key to the reasons for your behaviour and feelings. Asking others for their perspective in relation to your upbringing can provide you with helpful points of view but they do not necessarily have to correspond with your own experience and understanding. Sometimes it can verify what you already believe to be true and at other times someone else's opinions will be at odds with your own. Ultimately you can only accept information you believe to be true and corresponds with your own perception at that time. ***Even if it were distorted and not true to fact, it is still your version of the truth*** and therefore has formed the basis for the negative beliefs you took on board. If you come to the right conclusions they should reveal the beliefs you hold that drive your feelings, actions and behaviours.

- ***Parents who consciously express the intent to be loving and accepting*** for fear of being the parent to their children the way their parents were with them do not realize they are sending contradictory messages.

They will have inherited the issue that stops them from being emotionally expressive of love and acceptance and probably other feelings therefore find it hard to show love and affection to their own children. Their fears of displaying emotions and feelings of love contradicts their conscious effort to connect emotionally to their children. Their sincere intent to give love is hampered by their fears. They can be very caring and supportive on a physical level and even verbalise that they love you while their actual behaviour around the expression of emotions and feelings contradicts this. When this is the case and you will be left with a lot of confusion in terms of expressing love, affection, closeness and intimacy. The reality is that when it comes to love, ***it is difficult to give to others what you have never received unconditionally***.

Most parents will say that they accept and love you unconditionally because that is their intent. You need to accept that if they set conditions due to their fears and insecurities, you would have experienced their love as conditional. The end result is that a child will believe that it is unlovable and unacceptable until these conditions are met regardless of what the conscious intent of the parent might have been. Fear of revealing feelings and emotions to others denies a child the actual physical and emotional sensation of being loved, feeling special and wanted. This emotional void this creates demands to be fulfilled. The consequence will be that once the child becomes an adult, it is likely behave in the same manner and experience the same emotional difficulties as its parents did. The absence of having the experience of being loved generally results in an inability to love one self and to act with unconditional love towards others. Instead it creates an empty well that yearns to be filled by the love from others, which causes selfishness and neediness. The intent to love and accept does not replace the actual act of being unconditionally loved and accepted. The same can apply to any emotional state that children require confirmation for such as: being supported, being praised, being trusted and being able to trust, expressing truth, being listened to and so on.

- ***You must be truthful with yourself about your issues.*** By being in denial about your contribution to the negative events in your life, you deny yourself the opportunity to change your life and your future. Even if your part in it is not totally clear to you, you need to approach your issue with the understanding that you must be involved. Only than will you begin to look in places that will show you why that is so
- ***Do not put any conditions or limits on your search for inner-truth or the process of your change.*** Limiting ideas will ultimately become restrictions that will hold you back from finding your truth and being who you were always meant to be. Bite the bullet if you have to face issues that you will find extremely confrontational and follow through — in the final analysis your issues and beliefs are nothing but illusions and so you actually have nothing to fear. ***Know this: The intensity of your desire to avoid your issues is usually proportional to the fear of the negative consequences you believe they have the capacity to create.*** Push yourself past your fears and the outcome will be more than you can imagine.
- ***Do not set expectations or standards and conditions as to how the outcome of change should appear in your life or in the experience of your self.*** Pre-conceived ideas of what your changes should look like or how they should appear in your life may cause you to miss what the real results are and you will not appreciate the value of what you have achieved. The truth is that you do not really know who you are without your issues and you are discovering a part of yourself that has been foreign to you since childhood. Allow yourself to be amazed by discovering your 'new' self.

Deciphering Your Illusions

The level of control that negative beliefs have over you depends on your fear of the consequences should you be unable to meet their conditions. Feelings, perceptions and behaviours that come out of fear are your guide to the source that created them. On face value it always seems that the person or situation you are afraid of is also the cause for your fear but that is not true. Even this aspect of your perception is a product of beliefs. By blaming something or someone you may think that you have found the reason for your issue when you are actually experiencing an illusion of your own creation.

Fears of all kinds are driven by a variety of negative beliefs in unique contexts and with different consequences. The first step in your search for your emotional truth is to take a deep look at the reasons for your emotions and behaviour. The nature of an event and the emotions of those who are involved are essential pieces of information that can lead you to understand the nature of the beliefs that brought the situation into being. Connecting current events and outcomes with historical ones in childhood can help you to recognize the original experiences responsible for your negative beliefs you still hold.

If, for example, you have a strong reaction to criticism than you can expect to find the answer in your earliest experience of this with one or both parents. If rejection and abandonment are your issue than you can expect that there were strong conditions in your relationship with your mother and/ or father. The relationship between them also deserves investigation because also exposes you to their issues and insecurities. You will find that differences in your own perception and that of others make reality and the truth not always as clear cut as you probably would like it to be. Just work with what you found and begin to trust your intuition.

The belief that an emotional issue has to be the result of a traumatic or critical event in childhood or later in life is erroneous and misleading. You start manifesting your life experiences from a very young age— 10-12 years, and this becomes more conclusive as we enter teenage— 12-21 years, and then adulthood. It follows that because our foundational belief systems are acquired from 0 to 8-10 years old and we therefore gradually incorporate them in our sense-of-self. They will reveal themselves through our choices and decisions, actions and reactions and so on. Our beliefs lead us to attract and be attracted to certain personalities and situations throughout our life and these encounters create our negative or positive life experiences. These outcomes are manifested by the intent held by our beliefs but a negative experience later in life will generally not be the origin for our emotional issues. If you have been exposed to violence and abuse in childhood you are likely to suffer from being powerless or the fear of being powerless. This can make you a passive anxious compliant or aggressive angry controlling individual. Your beliefs and their complimentary feelings and behaviour will control the way you will manifest your life.

Your search for answers lies in discovering a truth that can in many ways only be unique to you. Your personal truth distinguishes itself from that of others in that it is totally based on your perception and experience at the time. The true nature of the personality of the person involved being a family member or sibling is not the point for your search for the reasons for your issues. It is also not a search for the truth of the experience of an event in your family if such a truth even exists. Each family member may see the emotional aspects of a situation or event in a different way but the effect on you will be the only thing that matters. If, for example, your parents favoured you brother or sister over you, their experience of your mother or father or both would be a very different from yours. Feeling ignored and forgotten will cause you to believe that you are unlovable, unwanted and do not matter while they may think they were special. Even if later in life, your parents assure you that they love you, your belief that you are not lovable will still create your reality right now. This means that the original reasons for your beliefs are still valid and active within you regardless of time.

Your original perception as a child remains the foundation of the belief systems that now make up your sense-of-self. Once you can accept that your own conclusions are accurate to the best of your knowledge, you are ready to put it into a form that is representative of a self-belief. In the final analysis your conclusions are not open to judgment by others. They may have the perception, for example, that your parent is good and kind because they did so much for every person in their circle of friends and acquaintances. You however may have experienced them as being selfish and uninterested because in being involved with others, they ignored and neglected you. To you, the only version that is of value in your process of change is the one you perceived as a child. There are a host of reasons why each sibling in a family is likely to remember their relationship with their parents very differently. The original nature of your unique being and order of birth, gender and favouritism are strong influences on your being. Add to this the individual emotional issues your mother and father brought into their relationship and the family unit and you can see how each contributes to make childhood different for each sibling. The perception of outsiders to a family only reflects what is true for them but you cannot allow that to invalidate your own interpretation and understanding of your childhood.

Owning Your Fears

Taking ownership of your issues can be challenging even if you have the intent to be serious about change. Not many of us would jump at the concept that they are the origin of all of their life issues but refusing to accept this will be a barrier to self-change. Accept responsibility for your issues after spending most of your life blaming others and the world for your ills is a big turnaround in perspective. This is particularly confronting if your strategy is predominantly based on dominating and controlling behaviour. You are likely to fear that you will become powerless and defenceless without your aggressive approach. In addition, being in a dominant and controlling position can create the assumption that you are superior to others which than makes it also difficult to admit and accept that you have flaws.

Passive strategic individuals have a different problem with taking responsibility for their issues. They are commonly deeply affected by guilt and therefore accept responsibility and blame for the negative emotions in others even though in actuality they cannot be held accountable for their creation. Their sense of over-responsibility causes them to try to avoid situations and people where guilt may become an issue. Exactly the opposite becomes the reality of their life. Their apparent willingness to take on responsibility causes them to attract and be attracted to individuals who resent or avoid taking any responsibility for the issues and dramas they create in their life. Their strategy is to blame all their fear, anxiety and stress on others. This kind of person intuitively senses that their newly found friend will never confront them and hold them accountable for the negative experiences they have manifested in their life. Again, each is just an emotional mirror for the other in respect to their guilt issues.

On the positive side the assumption of guilt by an over-responsible person makes it easier for them to seek help because of their fear of being the cause for pain and suffering in others. Understanding their inner processes and the beliefs that underlie them is a major step towards emotional resolution. Letting go of their negative beliefs liberates them from their burden of guilt and allows them live life without being controlled by the fear-based emotions of others.

Understanding Life's Purpose

If you cannot see how you are involved, it is hard to accept is that you are the creator of every life experience. The causative triggers for any event in your life are very individual and commonly not easily fathomable by others. If you cannot recognize that you are central to all of your life experiences and others cannot confirm it than what is true? It is therefore just as difficult to accept that we do not live in an accidental universe. If you cannot even relate to the nature of your own being — your sense-of-self — how can you feel connected to the consciousness of others and the reality you in which you exist? Your awareness of your inner being is also the pathway to deeper connections with the nature of all consciousness that forms reality. When you begin to realize that all consciousness is interconnected and relates to one another it is also easy to accept that reality and the events we experience cannot happen by chance. The manifestation of our life experiences is both individual and collective act and is the result of the interconnectivity of consciousness. No consciousness acts in isolation of all others and the intent expressed by one individual has an impact on all others. Our general lack of awareness at this time makes this difficult to appreciate.

We are not aware how our perception has been altered because we are unconsciously indoctrinated into believing that emotional experiences are most commonly a product of outside forces. The truth is that the incessant process of creation is an indivisible part of all consciousness. The potential to be in or out of harmony with itself — the positive or negative nature of consciousness — is an interactive influence within the overall state of universal consciousness.

The intent within human consciousness will attract and be attracted to others whose consciousness resonates with it regardless whether it is harmonious or disharmonious in nature. Their interaction will bring about events, which will reveal the true nature of their intents — positive or negative, unconditional love or fear.

The deep personal nature of any creative act makes it difficult for an outsider to fathom the intents and motivations for the manifestation of a particular event because the behaviour that supports it can either be sincere or strategic. It is then difficult to see what the true and what is not and what the real issues are if they are acted out. Their behaviours act as a disguise if fear is the motivating force behind their intent. In addition, an observer is likely to have issues of their own of which they are unaware and these will act as filters and distort their perception of the person and the event. All these elements make it difficult if not impossible for many to understand the deeper motivations and intent for someone's behaviour and the life situations they create.

Without any real insight into the fundamental emotional forces at play, we often try to explain the negative outcomes experienced by others by looking for guilty parties associated with such events. We may label the events as accidents and misfortunes or create aggressors and victims. If this is your approach to negative events in your life and that of others, it is predictable that your first impulse will be to reject the concept that you are the creator of your own life and therefore responsible.

The most common approach used to try and prove that we are not creators of our own reality is to list various disasters in which many suffered or lives lost their lives. The deeper reasons for involvement in a disaster or horrific event are often completely incomprehensible to an observer. From their perspective pain, suffering and death occur indiscriminately and without apparent reason and purpose. The victims of a disaster can of any age or gender, from babies to the old and infirm. At another level of consciousness, those who are involved in it however, may well understand and be aware the reasons for their participation in the event. Excluded from knowing the deeper nature of the mind and consciousness of those involved, it is difficult for observers and survivors to comprehend the reasons for this. Much involves our understanding and belief in the nature of death and life and our own responsibility for the expression of our consciousness. The actual reasons for being a victim of a disastrous event are difficult to argue because the chairs of those who could provide the relevant information are empty. It helps to deal with life and death if we can accept that all consciousness is connected and transcends physical life. If we begin to recognize that everything that is in existence, is a product of intent and that we are participating creators of this intent, we may realize that every experience is of our own individual and collective making.

Remind yourself, that your existence goes beyond the life span of your body and your spirit is on an infinite path of evolution.

From Issues to Negative Beliefs

We need to delve a bit deeper into our own state of mind and family dynamics to understand why our negative beliefs take a particular form and how we can become clear about their nature and intent within us. ***The clues to our negative belief systems are within us, as feelings, perceptions and behaviours and outside of us as events and experiences mirrored by the people and situations we are attracted to and attract.*** Negative experiences are the most obvious place to begin because they are direct evidence that we are manifesting from a place of fear.

The personality and behaviour of your friends are also a good indicator of your own state of mind because like attracts like in the negative sense as well as in a positive way. Your friends do not only reflect your interests but they will also compliment your issues, fears and insecurities. Throughout this material there have been examples how certain negative traits will attract others who match those traits and the friends you make are not an exception to this. Objectively appraising your friendships can be useful in discovering more about the nature of who you are. This may be new for you but it is part of your learning process.

You cannot fail because every new understanding and realization is a triumph for your consciousness and the essence of your true self. You will find that your path of self-realization becomes easier as your clarity and insight progressively grows, taking you to a new level of self-awareness. Once you understand the nature of the different elements that make up your negative beliefs, you will also appreciate why they are such a powerful psychological force in your mind.

The Elements of Negative Beliefs

The structure of a ***negative belief system*** is complex because it ***contains intent, cause, context and consequence***. Each element of a belief plays a decisive role in the hold it has over us, how, where and with whom the belief will become activated and the consequences this has for us. Some of the previous examples show what to look for when exploring your psychological family history. Going beyond the obvious is essential if you are to discover the causes and in what context and consequence our fear-based beliefs operate so you can understand the basis for their potency.

Appreciating the contribution that each element makes to the structure of your negative belief systems is important when you want to understand your beliefs in order to release them. You cannot let go of a negative belief you neither own nor understand and appreciate in detail. Trying to release belief systems by using their most contracted and basic form — I do not love myself / I am unacceptable / I do not matter / I have no value — simply does not work. While the general intent of a belief is sometimes easy to recognize, it is not specific or detailed enough to address the unique reasons why it has such a hold over your emotions and behaviour. In other words it is too general in concept to have any real meaning for you in order to release it.

Our minds are already extremely sophisticated in our earliest state of consciousness and register an immeasurable amount of detail in abstract form. These emotional and physical impressions form an integral part of the future function of our minds. From the vey beginning our perception, responses and reactions are influenced by how we experience them emotionally. Our yet unevolved mind is a receptacle for every bit of emotional and physical information it is exposed to but lacks many of the specific reference points necessary to make sense out of them. ***A child's only frame of reference is its innate expectation to be unconditionally loved and wanted, accepted, be trusted and be able to trust.***

Even though this sense is vital to the child in order evolve the capacity of its spirit and mind it does not provide it with an immediate understanding of the nature reality in which it just became conscious. Nor does it give a child the tools to deal with the life experiences it will be exposed to. In a deeper sense this innate reference point serves a much greater and higher purpose in its consciousness. Regardless of how the child will turn out in life and no matter to what level it consciousness has evolved, this reference point will remain central to the nature of its sense of being

Unconditional love and acceptance, trust and being trusted, wanted and belonging and so on will always be the reference point for your understanding of which beliefs are positive and which have their intent and foundation in fear.

Cause, Context and Consequence in Negative Belief Systems

Emotional issues are a product of beliefs held as a sense of your self that contain conditions founded in fear. These beliefs hold the threat that if you do not meet these conditions there will be severe consequences which you than seek to avoid. Appreciating the value of intent, cause, context, and consequence in belief systems is extremely important for your understanding of your sense-of-self.

Take for example that you hold the belief that you are unacceptable.
THE PRIMARY INTENT *within the belief that you are unacceptable is to convince you u that you are not only unacceptable to yourself but that you are also not acceptable to others*

THE CONSEQUENCE *is that your belief causes you to be in fear of rejection and abandonment and the expectation that you will be alone and lonely.*

Understanding **the cause** is extremely significant because it can lead you to understand how negative beliefs became a part of your sense-of-self. Your insight into causes will also reveal **why** you create certain negative outcomes or events. All causes responsible for establishing negative beliefs share similar emotional elements. Every event or encounter responsible for the formation of negative beliefs will contain any of the following derivatives of fear: exclusion, abandonment or rejection, criticism or judgment, embarrassment or shame, blame or guilt, powerlessness or vulnerability. There are others but these represent the most common emotional elements of fear based causes.

The behaviour and attitude of your parent's in response to your presence and natural expression of who you are and your innate needs and expectations is the origin for your the experience of these negative emotions. Their reaction could be in response to your appearance, gender or being present or just by being different from what your parents expected you to be. Even though it is their issues that make them respond in this way you will feel responsible. Once you accept the experience of their behaviour as your responsibility you will unconsciously internalize it as a conditional belief as a part of your sense-of-self. It will automatically become ***the cause*** for developing strategic behaviour that seeks to meet these conditions and determine your attitude towards yourself and others. You may justify your negative state of mind by becoming a judge and critic of yourself, turning negative behaviour into a virtue or taking the role of the justified aggressor or the vulnerable victim: none of this will represent who you truly are and meant to be.

THE CAUSE *is a product of a specific set of emotional circumstances* in which an issue was initially experienced, realised and accepted. This is brought about by being treated or dealt with in a way which contradicts unconditional love, acceptance and being wanted and trusted in childhood. Some examples of this are judgment, rejection, treated as if you are a burden, being ignored, being invalidated and blamed, criticism and judgement, having your needs and expectations dismissed and so on, the list is close to endless. Fundamentally, it comes down to not being unconditionally loved, accepted and trusted and celebrated for who you truly are — your authentic self.

THE CONTEXT is a product of the unique circumstances and personality types involved in the emotional events that were experienced at the inception and formation of your negative belief systems. Even though our consciousness defines and records these elements, it is handicapped by the lack of a clear frame of reference (other than unconditional love) in order to have a clear realization of who is responsible for what. The ability of a child's naive mind to make value judgments is constrained by its unevolved awareness and lack of external reference points when trying to make sense out of its emotional experiences. What it will ultimately accept as real and true is largely determined by its innate need for the survival of its emotional being and physical self.

THE CONTEXT *within a negative belief* represents the kind of situation and the type of personalities and their emotional intent and expression involved at the inception creating your negative beliefs. These elements will still be active later in life and manifest the same issues. They are the circumstances and conditions unique to you connected to negative belief systems that when activated will define your particular perception, feeling and behaviour within a framework of fear.

For example: If you were raised by a controlling and domineering father or mother, involvement with people with similar emotional characteristics will trigger the same emotional response you had in adulthood. Men that grew up with a needy, dependent and insecure mothers and have learned to be protective and responsible for her fears and expectations will attract women with similar issues and exhibiting similar behaviours.

Should both your parents come from a family background that denied them and made to feel guilty for expressing their needs and expectations, they are likely to be selfish and self-centred or behave as if they have no needs and expectations. Both the selfish and the parent who cannot express their needs will make you feel guilty for having needs and expectations. Their needy selfish or guilt driven behaviour will create guilt in their children or make them aggressively needy for fear of being denied. As a consequence a child may feel compelled to deny its needs and expectations and instead put others before itself as a way to avoid guilt feelings. This upbringing can cause you to believe that others are more entitled than you. Without realizing you may either strategically put yourself always first in order not to miss out or put yourself last because of lack of entitlement and guilt. In the end you could turn out to be just as needy and selfish or disentitled as your parents.

The Ultimate Intent of Your Beliefs

Together, these different elements that make up a belief system have the capacity to turn it into an extremely powerful psychological instrument for the expression of our consciousness. The axe our minds wield in its process of creating its own reality is both conscious and subconscious. Although the focus has been on negative beliefs to show you how you they influence and control your life, the power and influence of beliefs operates in the positive and negative sense.

The same power and influence that gives a negative belief the capacity to create a negative event is also present in positive beliefs to manifest positive events and relationships.

Cause, context and consequence are elements that contribute to the specific nature of the intent of any belief system and the environment in which it will be activated. Jointly, they define what will activate a belief and what it will create if the implied conditions of the belief are or are not met. Without the inner reference point of unconditional love, you might well be totally indifferent to what a belief system creates for you in life. Fear or love, anger and resentment and so on would cease to be different and discernable emotions. Potentially, you would not be able to tell what their nature is because you will not be able to differentiate a negative emotion for a positive one nor would it matter to you. An event no matter what the impact or outcome would be just that: an experience without emotional context. Only threats to your physical survival would elicit a response from you.

Your spiritual foundation rests on unconditional love, acceptance and trust and this provides the context in which fear and powerlessness, distrust and unacceptance acquire meaning and make an impact on our lives. On deeper levels of your consciousness you are always in the awareness of this and the intent this holds creates the emotional bias that allows you to recognize and experience unconditional love and fear.

Whenever you find yourself back in the emotional context of an issue, you revert back to the child you were at the time when these events first occurred. Your naïve acceptance of the truth of what you learned to believe ensures that you will go back to the same childlike behaviour that is now framed in adult justifications. Once our childhood fears take centre stage, our intellectual, logical adult reasoning and perspectives go largely missing.

In actuality our belief systems are interchangeable and can be released if negative and fear-based or evolve if positive and harmonious. Our individual and collective reality will change dramatically once we transcend first our negative childhood beliefs and than our limiting social and other structured belief systems. To that aim we need to focus our efforts first on dealing with our personal fears so that we can release them at their origin. Not doing this can result in creating an existence that translates into a life of unhappiness and disappointment and we will pass these same negative beliefs on to our children.

Once you have incorporated negative beliefs as a part of your sense-of-self, we will without exception manifest WHO WE BELIEVE WE ARE — our sense of self.

Consequences in belief systems articulate the basis for your fears. They represent the outcomes we fear should our behaviour fail to meet the conditions we are convinced exist in order to be loved and accepted. The fear of being judged, criticised or punished for being a failure, inadequate and unacceptable because you do not meet expectations. Being made to feel guilty and responsible for upsetting others because you are blamed for being insensitive, uncaring and aggressive. Being told that you are unwanted and unlovable because you are a nuisance and a burden to your parents and therefore you now live in fear of being rejected and being alone — and so on.

Once you recognize the particular consequence you fear will become reality you can begin to trace how it became a part of you. Try and remember in what emotional environment and circumstance this became a fear in you. You may have the fear of being alone and being without your friends without realizing that it proves that you have abandonment and rejection issues. You may avoid confrontations with others and tell yourself that this is a good thing while in reality you are terrified of having to deal with aggression, disagreement and conflict. You were not born with these fears and so you need to question the dynamic of the relationship with your mother and father in childhood in order to find out the cause for your fears. Uncovering the issues your parents had at the time by Discussing the emotional experiences your parents had with their parents can reveal many of the reasons why they behaved the way they did with you. It may show how they acquired the fears and insecurities they played out as your parent. This could be good for them as well as for you.

Consequences go hand in hand with the conditions contained in negative belief systems and all of our fears are generated by the expectation that the consequences we believe exist will become reality.

Here are a few condensed examples that show how children can respond to the consequences implied by the conditions set by their parents' fearful sense-of-selves:

A mother who is afraid of failing, making mistakes and getting things wrong will also fear being unable to meet expectations. She is likely indecisive and not deal well with the pressure of responsibility for raising a child. She will have little or no idea how to respond to situations and problems created by her newborn because for her every choice feels critical and essential and therefore creates and emotional crisis. Confused and overwhelmed by the possibilities of every decision, she is unable to set priorities, instead she physically withdraws and emotionally disconnects in an effort to hide from her potential to fail her child and attract criticism and judgment. Often, she will try and get advice from others in order to make some sense out of her indecisiveness but then is still ensure of what to do.

The emotional scenario that she lives by is a product of her negative belief systems and is only true in her perception. Her lack of self-trust and belief and conviction in her own vulnerabilities and powerlessness gives her a victim mentality. She needs to release the negative beliefs responsible for her victim mentality and lack of self-confidence in order to have a different experience of herself and life. In the absence of her fears she will find her innate power and confidence.

If you come from this family environment then the following may apply to you:

The causes for your issues were manifested in through the fears your parent inherited from their parents. Once your mother was convinced and accepted that she was weak, powerless and vulnerable because of the fears with which her parents raised her, your childhood experience was predetermined. As a consequence of her fears, she felt that she could not cope with the responsibilities of motherhood and life. She could only give love and acceptance and trust to the point where they did not challenge her fears and insecurities and that made the love she could give you conditional. As a result you came to believe and accept that your authentic self and innate needs were a burden and imposition on her because you thought they were the cause for her stress and anxiety. You concluded from her behaviour, stress and anxiety, pain and unhappiness that you must be unwanted and unlovable, insignificant and do not matter.

The strategic behaviour you adopt to compensate generally falls into two types: You may believe that you are a victim of the needs, expectations and feelings of your mother and others and adopt behaviours that will pacify and please. On the other hand your fear of being guilty will make you take on aggressive behaviour that ensures that you are not going to accountable or responsible for anything that others feel, need or experience. You will be more likely to blame and accuse others than accept responsibility. Regardless whether a child's behaviour falls in the first or the second category, later in life the negative beliefs that support these behaviours will become ***the cause*** for its life issues.

The context of your belief are the people, women or men, with who their particular issues mimic the childhood experience in which your issue was created. You could say that they are using the same dysfunctional script your parents used when they parented you. In this particular context they are indecisive, emotionally disconnected, are fearful, anxious and insecure, have issues with emotional expression and feel powerless, act as victims of life and the world, worry and cannot cope. ***The consequences of the belief*** in this case are: The fear of being guilty for causing pain and suffering and insecurities in others — Suppression of your authentic self or the imposition your needs and expectation on others — Attracting anger and resentment from others if needs and expectations are expressed — The fear of being blamed and accused. Side effects of this type of behaviour are the inability to refuse and simply say no, fear of confrontation and speaking your truth, general fear of being spontaneously authentic with others and an incessant fear of upsetting or offending others.

Understand that you have been convinced that you are the guilty one by a parent or parents who believe they are the victims of you. They have issues that convince them that they are powerless and vulnerable in life and cannot cope with responsibility, the expectations of others or emotional confrontation. Instead of taking responsibility for their issues they have made you directly or by inference responsible for their fears and insecurities because they are felt in response to you.

As a consequence, if you are a girl you may become just like your mother or try and be the opposite. Should you be a boy then you will either become attracted to women who are needy and insecure and try and save them from their plight or instead be in complete avoidance of all intimate relationships for fear of having to be responsible for the needs and insecurities of others.

The intent and cause, context and consequence are core elements of every belief and of particular significance in respect o negative beliefs because of how they control our lives.

A primary version of this belief system looks something like this:
Because my mother is always upset worried, stressed and unhappy, upset and fearful, powerless and helpless, cannot cope
- I have to live in fear, be worried and concerned —
- that if I express my presence, my needs, expectations and wishes and desires, fears and insecurities —
- my mother will get upset, worried, stressed, unhappy, stressed and anxious (and so on). —
- and — it will be my fault, I will be to blame, I will be the guilty one —
- and so because of that — I have to suppress and hide, never show and reveal —
- my innate need to be unconditionally loved, wanted and accepted, trusted and supported, cared for and protected, my authentic self and my personal power etc.—
- to avoid being guilty, responsible and to blame for my mother's pain, worry concern stress, unhappiness (and so on) —
- because it is always my fault — I am always to blame — I am always the guilty one.

There are many variations possible but the core elements always remain the same.

A father who will not tolerate being contradicted or have his ideas and values challenged may use aggression to be in control. He cements his need for intellectual and emotional superiority by being critical and dissatisfied with everyone around him. At the same time, he never takes responsibility for anything he creates through his actions, behaviour and choices. He believes he is justified and that others and the world are responsible for his reactions and responses and blames them when the outcome is not to his liking. He becomes indignant and responds with anger and aggression when held accountable to create the impression that he is perfect and never wrong. Often he will see himself as sacrificing his life, freedom and opportunities by being the provider, partner and father.

When in a negative state of mind, he is easily provoked by anything his child does with anger and critical blame. His child comes to live in fear of finding itself at the brunt of his father's anger and abuse. In order to cope with its fathers often unpredictable behaviour, it unconsciously develops and acute awareness of its fathers habits and behaviour, physical cues and moods as an emotional survival strategy. The moment its father is in its vicinity, its senses are heightened by its fear to increase its awareness of how the father might behave or react. Commonly a child will suppress its own presence to avoid attracting the attention of the father. Obviously, the child cannot feel loved, wanted and accepted by its father and will not trust him. It lives in constant fear of the consequences should it fail to meet its father's unpredictable expectations.

The father's issues are generally: fear of being powerless, inferior, failing and being wrong. He has to prove he is more intelligent and knows more than others because he feels inferior and inadequate. He fears the responsibility for the expectations of his family because his inability to meet them would expose him to be the inadequate failure he fears he is. Potentially these expectations would also challenge his unfulfilled needs and expectations and loss of freedom.

For the child, being yelled at and accused by an aggressive grown up and not knowing why it is the target serves to make it feel truly powerless, helpless and ultimately guilty and responsible. The consequences are manyfold: fear of physical and emotional violence and abuse, fear of being demeaned, criticised and put down. Everything in the attitude and expression of the father and tells it that it is not only to blame but also that it is a burden, stupid and inadequate. It is possible to recognize the father's negative beliefs in the issues he creates in his child.

The internalisation of responsibility and guilt for its father's emotional abuse results in the acquisition of a guilty and demeaning sense-of-self by the child — it is my fault my father cannot love and accept me, is angry and critical of me and so on. By now it will be convinced that it is not good enough and a failure, a disappointment and an unwanted responsibility, unwelcome and so on.

It has the choice of one of two strategies to overcome its fear of the consequences of not being what it should be for its father. It can take on the behaviour of its father and potentially become a bully like him in order to prove to everyone that it is better, is more significant and is stronger than anyone else. Alternatively it can become passive and adopt avoidance strategies, which are likely to be very much like those adopted by its mother. Adopting passive avoidance strategies with the overall belief that it is a powerless victim in life can in fact cause it to become the target for bullying.

The cause is the oppressive experience of the aggressive anger and abusive behaviour by your father that caused you to accept a system of beliefs that convinced you that you are powerless and unwanted, unlovable and unacceptable, a failure and a disappointment etc. These beliefs will than define your sense-of-self and become *the cause* for your issues in your adult life.

The context is the people and in particular men, who are forcefully aggressive, dominating and controlling in getting what they want in the way they want it. They are the type that are never wrong or never fails nor can be held accountable because they are always justified in their behaviour. In their world everyone else has issues with exception of them. If confronted and held accountable they commonly revert to the base negative beliefs they hold, which are the source for their aggressive strategic behaviour — they will then act as if they are the victims of every one else
People with these beliefs and aggressive behaviour are attracted to those with the same issues who display passive powerless behaviour. This allows them to play out their fears through dominating and aggressive behaviour and convince themselves that they are right and others are wrong. Vice versa those who are passive powerless subconsciously choose environments in which they will be exposed to these aggressive personalities

The consequences are that we live our lives in fear of aggression and abuse, blame and guilt, fear of failure and being a disappointment and ultimately rejection and exclusion, the withdrawal of love and acceptance. We will try and avoid all this by suppressing our needs and expectations, wishes and desires, by hiding our feelings, fears and insecurities, power and spontaneity — by not being our authentic self.

A primary version of this belief system looks something like this:
Because my father is always aggressive and angry, abusive and upset, can never be pleased, and is always unhappy and disappointed, critical and judgemental etc.

- I have to live in fear and I be worried and concerned that if I express my spontaneous authentic self, my power, my truth, my needs and expectations, what I really want and feel etc.,
- my father (and others) will be angry and resentful, aggressive and upset, abusive and critical of me, violent and judgmental, offended and disappointed in me,
- and so because of that — I have to suppress and hide, never show and reveal my personal power and authentic self, the capacity of my intellect and potential, my emotional truth and expectations, my feelings and needs etc.,
- because it is the only way I can avoid being the victim, the cause and the reason for my father's aggressive anger, resentment and abuse,
- because it is always my fault — I am always to blame — I am always the guilty one.

You are getting ready to let go of your conditional beliefs, once you can clearly see the cause and intent, context and consequence within the beliefs you hold.

Something to be aware of: Our attachment to our individual fears contributes to the collective of fear and distrust that humanity lives with every moment of every day of which the consequences are evident all around us. If we were only prepared to recognize them for what they really are we might initiate an effort to deal with fear on a large scale and eliminate much of humanities self-created suffering. Taking individual responsibility for your issues by addressing your fears makes a significant contribution to changing the collective. You are the place where all change in the world has to start and this makes taking responsibility for what you manifest in your life an act of much greater importance than it may seem. As long as the emotion we call fear is in control of how we manifest our lives individually we will not change the outcome to which our collective fears are taking us. The absence of unconditional love and acceptance, rejection and exclusion, abandonment and guilt, powerlessness and the absence of control are such influential negative forces in our emotional lives that they control our human destiny.

Chapter 21

Uncovering Self-Deception

To uncover the negative aspects at the centre of your sense-of-self, you need to become a 'forensic' investigator of your childhood and present life.

Our behaviour proves that we are generally convinced that our feelings tell us the truth of what we experience. We do not realize how they can mislead us and cause us to misinterpret the nature of our experiences. Feelings can cause us to believe that something is true while it is actually an illusion which than allows us to justify our perception and behaviour. To break this habit of blindly responding to our emotions, we need to first of all question our feelings because they act as the primary reason for our responses and reactions.

It can seem as if our feelings and behaviour conspire against us to keep us in a state of powerlessness and fear but that not true. It is actually relatively simple to recognize erroneous feelings by realizing how they affect you and others.

If what you feel is in anyway negative — anxiety or stress, powerlessness or feeling insecure, pessimistic or anticipating disaster or others in the same vein — you are influenced by beliefs driven by a version of fear.

If your interactions with others or situations make you feel angry and aggressive, judgmental and critical, blame and accuse others and so on, you are also responding to fear.

If your behaviour in response to your feelings benefits you but disadvantages others it is highly likely that it comes from fear.

Feelings that are a product of fears will always result in disharmony within your self and with others. Once you see yourself capitalizing on the weaknesses and insecurities of others, as the only way to feel powerful or safe, superior or in control you can be sure that your fears are dominating your mind. It shows that the emotions that initiated your strategic behaviour had to come from fear because of the intent displayed in your behaviour. Your need to be in control or dominant, avoid responsibility or confrontation and so on is proof that negative beliefs based dominate your expression in life.

In the act of playing out your issues to others and in the world you will probably not realize that your behaviour is all about you and no one else. Fear makes you selfish and self-centred regardless whether your strategic behaviours are passive or aggressive. Fear makes you focus all your efforts and energy on your emotional survival because it has convinced you that it is at risk. It becomes "all about you" even if you are pleasing others because even then the only reason for your pleasing is to be liked and accepted or to avoid blame and guilt. All fear-based behaviours create a negative dynamic between you and others, which bring everyone's negative beliefs into play.
Any life situation that triggers feelings such as being unlovable, unwanted, unacceptable, judged, entrapped, anger, resentment, guilt, fear, insecurity, powerlessness, submissiveness, inferiority, inadequacy, exclusion, rejection, abandonment, worthlessness, inadequacy, embarrassment, shame, dismissed, invalidated and so on, prove that your fears are about to take control through the negative beliefs make them real for you.

If you look closely at the dynamic of a negative event between you and a partner or friend and even a total stranger, you would recognize that one person's issues are complimentary to those of the other. Even though each of you may be using contrasting behaviours they are actually mirrors of the same or similar negative belief systems — fears. By one playing out their issues on the other, each individual turns these beliefs into a reality experience for themselves. Your understanding of the dynamic between yourself partner, parents and others will make it easier for you to recognize what issues you have taken on in childhood. The need or habit to go into specific behaviours over and again in fear that you might certain consequences are an indication that it is strategic and build on fear. Be prepared to question the validity of your feelings at all times until you understand yourself better because of their capacity to deceive you is always present.

Always try and be aware of HOW you feel, WHEN you feel it and in WHAT context you feel it in order to realize the reasons WHY you feel it.

Once you recognize that you are behaving out of fear than you need to look at the nature of your feelings and the context in which they are experienced. It is important to also identify the consequences you believe you will be subject to should you fail to meet the conditions your negative beliefs imply. Pay attention to feelings of — aggression and anger, criticism or judgement, abandonment or rejection, being ignored or forgotten, being unlovable or unacceptable, not being good enough and so on. Making notes of how you feel, behave and think can be really useful because these allow you to relate them back to your history. It gives you the chance to analyse and compare all the elements involved and correlate them to what you may be going through at this time. It will add to you capacity to develop greater clarity and understanding of your sense-of-self. Also be aware that as it is for you so it is for others including those you share the experience with.

Negative Life Events

The things that upset us in life, frustrate or make us angry always represent issues within us. Your impatience with other drivers in traffic, annoyance with your work associate, your criticism of yourself and others all point at you being the issue because you are the constant factor in all of them. Dependent on the fears of your sense-of-self, every encounter can turn into a negative event. Imagine you always get over-looked by shop assistants causing you to feel insulted and frustrated. Who is responsible? The obvious answer would be that it is the person serving you. Off course they may need to be more observant to see whose turn it but there is more to this than what the eye meets.

Ask yourself: Why does this happening so frequently to you and with so many different shop attendants — is there perhaps a secret conspiracy against you? You may note that you are the constant figure in all these encounters, which could be taken as evidence that somehow you must be involved. The question is: How do you generally behave around others and what do you feel? When you are in a social group do really want to be noticed and approached or do you like to take on the cloak of invisibility and avoid contact? Do you fear having to express your feelings, opinions or meet the expectations you believe others have of you? Are you worried that others will recognize and notice all the shortcomings and failings you believe you have? These could be many of the reasons why you may have developed the strategy of being invisible in the presence of others in order to avoid being noticed and approached. However, when you walk into a shop and wait to be served, you expect that this intent radiated by you has somehow disappeared. The truth is that you should not complain that you have created a reality experience consistent with your negative beliefs and behaviour — you do not want to be noticed for reasons represented by your fears and this is exactly what you experience.

The influential power of your energetic self is even more significant than that of your physical body. The quality of the energy of your aura is determined by the state of your being which is defined by your sense-of-self. Your belief systems play a powerful role in the nature of your presence, which speaks louder than your voice ever can. ***You "transmit" who you are through your energetic being.*** This influences the dynamic between you and others to the extent that it can trigger their fears and insecurities and cause them to react and respond with their strategic behaviours. All this can happen without any specific related dialogue. Such is the power of the presence of our consciousness and its dynamic interaction with others

The second aspect of our presence is our body and how it speaks to others through posture, movement and stance. Each aspect reveals something about you, which is subconsciously understood by others who tune into your physical state of being through the perception created by their sense of self. No matter what the kind of interaction you have and with whom, your belief systems and theirs — positive or negative — will play leading roles in the energetic, psychological and physical dynamic of your encounter.

Conditioned by Fear

Fear is an intrinsic part of negative beliefs and like a virus will contaminate everyone it comes on contact with. Its effect is like a contagion, in that once it infects you, it wants to be in control and take you over even if in the end it might sacrifice its own existence. Fear is neither kind nor benevolent and does not care about those who believe they have to depend on it to be safe.

The human response to emotional fears is distinctly different from that to physical threats because they are very different in nature. Once a physical threat has proven to be innocuous we generally no longer treat it with fear. We have much greater difficulty however in dealing with our emotional fears. Emotional fears are a creation of the mind and not real. Our belief in them makes them appear true and this deception goes unnoticed by us. Our fears are learned in childhood but continue to be played out throughout our life because they delude us into believing we will not survive without them. Every time we are confronted by a fear we are looking at a part of our own sense-of-self. Our fear of not qualifying for unconditional love and acceptance convinces us to take on a change of identity and behaviour in even though love will now be conditional. The emotional pressure that is created by being in disharmony with your essence creates force behind your need for emotional survival. The idea that we will only find love and acceptance through the approval of others becomes overwhelming and dominates all of our intentions, behaviours and feelings. At this point, ***we are flying emotionally blind because fear is in control and we have become passengers of its intent.***

Your perception of reality takes on a veil of truth beyond which you will find it difficult to see any possible alternatives. Unconsciously, you are likely to selectively ignore any information that contradicts your particular version of reality. With your perception corrupted by negative beliefs and convinced by what you feel, you will not recognise that your understanding of the dynamics you observe between yourself and others are based on illusions. You give your concept of reality the ring of truth by surrounding yourself with people — friends and acquaintances —who share your fear-based beliefs and values or complement them. Those of like or complimentary belief systems are naturally attracted to each other to avoid being confronted by others whose belief structures contradict their own. Once fear gets a hold of your mind, the illusionary security it provides causes you to avoid those whose beliefs contradict your own and your friendship circles reflect this.

Every element of an emotional experience is part of a mosaic that forms a picture of the nature of your sense-of-self. You do not need to worry about positive experiences because they will always support you but the negative influences need to be recognised and understood if you are to change. Most of us get to the point where we begin to realize that our strategies are failing us and our issues become intrusive, painful and limiting experiences in life. This is usually a critical period and how you deal with your feelings and fears can make an enormous difference to how you will transit this phase. Try and go back to your earliest memory of having the same feelings and context in respect to similar events in your life, preferably before the age of ten. That is where you are likely to find the answers for the causes of your current state of mind

Recalling the emotional dynamic that was active at the time between you and the parent or person involved can be the source for uncovering the information you need. Recognizing the fears and insecurities of your parents is an essential part in your journey of understanding your own issues. The dialogue you were exposed to is usually very significant because they reveal the nature of the issues of the speaker. As a child you would have been taken their words literally. Being called derogatory names as a child will cause you to label yourself for life. Labels such as stupid, hopeless, useless, worthless, and not good enough, a failure disappointment and so on become the words by which you will identify yourself later in life. If your parent's dissatisfaction with you was openly verbalised then remembering these moments makes it easier for you to establish the nature and context of your issues. Even if they have the best of intentions, parents can still have a negative emotional impact on their offspring, so do not feel you are judging or condemning them by exploring your emotional history with them.

Parents with high expectations of their offspring may not realize that potentially, they are imposing their values and standards and thereby dismissing or ignoring their children's innate talents, passions and desires. Should the child resist being steered in a direction that is not its own, the parents can make them feel guilty for not fulfilling their expectations. Children can be made to feel ungrateful by parents who feel they sacrificed themselves for them and cause them to believe that they are a burden and an unwanted responsibility. It is difficult for many parents to accept that their child has interests, talents, abilities or aspirations that are valid even though they totally different from their own. A sports focussed family may have a child whose focus is not physical and who does not excel in these areas. An academic family may have the reverse or have an artistically minded child. If the unique and innate gifts that a child brings into the world are not accepted it will feel that it does not fit in or belong or that it is unwanted. Note that parents who force their children to conform to their expectations were treated in a similar way in their childhood.

When parents get upset because of what their child does they generally blame the child without taking a moment to reflect whether they are the one with the issue. They will not see that the manner in which they deal with conflict causes their children to believe that "who they are" is the problem and not what they do. It is not uncommon for children to think that they must have been emotionally 'faulty' or 'dysfunctional' when they were born because of the way they are treated by their parents. The manner in which our issues become a part of us and the way we interpret and record them makes us feel and believe they are an intrinsic part of who we are and therefore unchangeable. This gives us the impression that the best we can hope for to change our life is to adopt new behaviours and thought processes to help us cope. Fortunately our minds are immensely flexible and resilient and we have not reached anywhere near our emotional intellectual potential. We were born with the capacity to literally change our sense of who we believe are by releasing limiting beliefs and illusions.

Negative attitudes such as criticism, transfer of guilt or neediness etc. can be hidden in behaviour, physical expression or unspoken expectations. For instance, parents who have an issue showing feelings and emotions may never articulate love and affection, discontent and criticism or other emotions openly. They may use facial expression, behaviours or obtuse comments to ensure that they communicate their fear of being confronted by negative emotions or even all kinds of feelings. Regardless how obscure their communication may be to others, as their child you will learn very quickly how to interpret their intent and be aware of what will get their approval and what will not.

When the suppression of any display of emotions is a strong part of the family paradigm you grow up in an environment in which this behaviour is normalized. This kind of dynamic is indirect and deliberately non confrontational and obscures that this behaviour is negative and harmful. The effect on a child will be can be emotionally damaging because the experience that that it is lovable, that it mattered, that it is interesting, that its feelings deserve to be considered is denied. The fear of upsetting others prevents you from being freely expressive of your feelings, turning relationships into an emotionally confrontational experience. You have come to believe that putting your feelings and emotions, needs and expectations on display is inappropriate and imposition on others and so you contrive to be emotionally appropriate by being restrained and controlled. Avoiding guilt by suppressing what you feel, need and want will cause you to attract and be attracted to partners who suffer similarly fears.

A New Perspective

It is not easy to look at a behaviour or attitude you taken to be normal with new eyes and realise that in reality it does not support you in being your authentic self. By taking a critical view of feelings and behaviour and extrapolating it back to your family history in order to discover the links you will find to the core reason for your issues. Your knowledge of what really drives you will make your search easier.

The following may provide some ideas on how to approach an issue:
You need to distinguish the experience of the child you once were from that of the adult you are. It is easy to forget that you begun life without any worldly awareness and that you were naive, helpless and dependent. Your earliest state of mind gave you a totally different perception of who you are compared to that of an adult you have become.

Imagine that if your mother had self-confidence issues and therefore does not trust her decision and choices nor wants to be responsible for anything. Even though you would not have intellectually understood what your mother's issues were, you would automatically be exposed to the consequences of her emotional behaviour — stress and anxiety, fear and worry and so on. Your mother's fears make it difficult for her to cope with raising you particularly if you are the first child. You will interpret her unconscious resistance to accepting responsibility for your life because of the fears this raises in her as unwillingness and resentment to be there for you. Consequently, you come to believe that you are the cause for her reluctance and fear. Your innate need for support and care, nurturing and unconditional love, acceptance and so on is now in your understanding a burden and intrusion in your mother's life and the cause of her stress and insecurities. As a result, you do not feel unconditionally acceptable or loved because you believe that you are responsible for your mother's negative state of mind. The only response that is available to you is to suppress and hide your innate expectations and need to be taken care off in order to protect her from you. As result you suppress your authentic self, your innate expectations to be unconditionally loved wanted and accepted, your innate need for care, protection and support. Guilt will drive you to be self-sufficient and self-reliant and emotionally self contained and even take on the role of your mother's emotional protector.

As an adult male you may subconsciously choose to take role of being the protector and caretaker of women in your relationships. You will attract and be attracted to women who come out of their childhood feeling insecure and unconfident and are needy and want to be taken care of, just like your mother. Guilt makes you feel responsible for their insecurities and cause you to believe you will only be worthy of their love if you save them from everything they fear. This makes you feel that you have to put their needs and expectations before your own and this will makes you feel denied. Your powerlessness to fulfil your own desires and wishes is likely to create anger and resentfulness and this can be the beginning of disenchantment in the relationship

A similar scenario will occur if you had an emotionally absent and disinterested father. Whatever the justifications or reasons are for why a father was not part of his child's early life, the child will come to the conclusion that it somehow to blame. A father's emotional and/or physical absence will cause a child to believe that it is not wanted. It will be convinced that its father is not interested, does not love it that it is unacceptable and so on because there must be something wrong with it. As the child, you will become critical of yourself to explain the reasons why your father is not there for you, resulting in self–blame and criticism. Your belief systems may read something like — I am not good enough for my father, I am a burden and a nuisance to my father, I am unlovable, unwanted, and unacceptable to my father, I am uninteresting and stupid in my father eyes and so on. Once you accept these beliefs as self-defining, they will impact the way you will create your life experiences and relationships. If negative thoughts and feelings trouble your mind and control you attitude, behaviour and choices, you have proof that you are subject to fears held in your sense-of-self.

Only by releasing these beliefs can you literally be a different person. In the absence of fear driven beliefs, your perception and feelings, thought and ideas will change and become more representative of who you really are. You will find that you will become more if not totally detached from external influences that would in the past have upset you, made you feel powerless and angry or just afraid. Your behaviour will also begin to change because without your fears your old strategic behaviours are no longer a necessary part of your self-expression. In the absence of believing that you have to be something you are not, your behaviour and feelings can now become spontaneous, genuine and sincere. Once your self-perception changes so will your goals and aspirations.

Without negative beliefs there is no negative intent, which was the cause for negative thoughts and feelings in the first place and so these too will wane and disappear. Your fear-motivated neediness will dissolve because there is no basis for its existence without negative beliefs supporting it. You are no longer looking to attain something from the world or others that is missing within you because the negative belief that created this desire is no longer present. In short, without negative beliefs at the core for your issue, there is no basis for negative perception, thoughts and feelings or strategic behaviour. The negative intent projected by the beliefs that hold it are no longer the centre of your focus and attention because they are absent and this sets you truly free from fear. In the absence of negative beliefs new doors will open inside your mind, expanding you potential and your capacity to fulfil it.

Chapter 22

The Power of Harmonious Intent

If you really want to change your life, your focus needs to be on ***letting go of who you are NOT, instead of trying to become who you think you should be.***

Reality is that if you are really serious about solving the problems you are experiencing you will not get a permanent solution by totally ignoring the core reasons why you manifested them in the first place. Once you have accepted that you are the creator of your life experiences it does not make any sense to rely on a superficial analysis of an event on the basis of 'who said this' and 'who did that' in order to pin the blame on someone. Without understanding the causative factors involving you in the manifestation of your issues, you are not solving your problems.

Understanding WHO YOU ARE is the path to realizing the problem and coming to a solution.

That part of your sense-of-self that does not represent your unique and authentic self is kept in trance through the power of fear. Dominated by fear you are kept in a permanent state of emotional imbalance that can keep you on edge of depression and anxiety. The extent to which fear pushes you out of your centre of balance, mirrors the level of emotional disharmony. When you are in a situation you find difficult or confronting you are constantly faced with an inner-conflict between your reasoning intellect and your fears. By each individual being an emotional mirror for similarly affected others, we collective play out our fears that appear to us as issues. We create both friendships and conflict in this way. Like-minded people will be attracted to share time with each other while those with strategically opposite behaviours will entice conflict.

Releasing our fears will have the effect of transforming the dynamic of the relationships between ourselves and others. While you have changed, they have remained the same and may find that they can no longer interact with you on the same basis because the fears you shared with them are missing in you. As a result they no longer understand you and you may feel detached from them. It is only then that you may realize that the central reason why you spend time together was due to the issues you had in common. Without your fears you can no longer relate in the way you used to. Feeling greater confidence, emotional stability and inner-harmony does not resonate with the fears of the past. The illusions that were created by fear will be replaced by an increased awareness and clarity of who you truly are.

The key to how all of this works lies in our understanding of why and how beliefs determine our intent and provide us with the capacity to create and manifest a positive or negative reality for ourselves.

Beliefs and their intents are to our creative minds what a lens is to a spotlight — just like a lens focuses light, beliefs are an instrument of the mind that determines, focuses and shapes our intent.

The mind facilitates the expression of the innate, unique and creative forces of our spirit in order to evolve through experiencing itself through its manifestations in physical reality.

The capacity of consciousness to give it exclusive focus to the intent of a conviction held by the mind and gives it the power to create and manifest its own experience of reality. Take for example light that passes through a clear lens that concentrates it to a specific point with great brightness, just like clear harmonious intent would. However, if the lens were distorted, the focus of the light would be corrupted and the clarity lost and the light defused just like intent contaminated by fear.

It is little more complex with belief systems because light does not have the inherent predisposition that our consciousness has. If a belief contradicts the pre-disposed intent of our consciousness to be in harmony with its essence and instead creates and manifests with fear the outcome will reflect its origin. The capacity of fear based beliefs has over your perception should not be underestimated. Its presence in your sense-of-self can cause you to view your life as being completely subject to others and the world convincing you that you have no power or control in life. Instead of being the creator of your life experiences you are the victim of your own manifestations.

Our belief systems are a necessary construction by our mind so that we have a sense of identity and a framework to form our intents as creative tools to manifest through action, choices and decisions.

The beliefs that make up our sense-of-self and those we hold about everything in life and the world should be seen as a flexible program that provides us with

a level of predictability for our existence in emotional and physical reality.
We learn what is safe or dangerous for us and in relation to others, our environment and the nature of the world. Our initial experience with people, objects and food, situations or processes can result in our trust in them because they prove themselves to be safe or support us or distrust because they show themselves to be a threat and harmful. Our beliefs form themselves as a consequence of what we have learned so that we do not have to keep on testing the nature of everything we encounter in life as if it is the first time. Once we accept an experience as a safe and secure or dangerous and a threat we create emotional stability by accepting it in the form of a belief that defines our expectations of future confrontations. This allows us to be physically and emotionally involved in the world whilst maintaining personal security without having to constantly reassess every encounter that confronts us. We cannot exist without beliefs because they give us a predictable and dependable world to live in. By the same token, encounters that threaten our emotional and physical survival will cause us to accept beliefs that create a fearful and threatening world for us

Without beliefs our minds would be without the power to create a meaningful existence. In the absence of a delineated intent our consciousness cannot project nor attract the energetic states necessary to manifest its life experiences in concert with all other consciousness. The incessant innate force to create and manifest cannot be switched off and therefore in the process of living life we have no choice but to choose. Without exception, all of our choices contain intent created by our sense-of-self and so regardless whether it is harmonious or disharmonious, our intent will become our life experience. Generally, in the long term a consciously manufactured positive intent cannot override intent that is a product of fear. The nature of negative intent has to be realized and released in order to make way for positive and harmonious intents.

Because of this truth, *the only way to control what you manifest in your life is to be in control of the beliefs that define your sense-of-self* because these are the source for your intent. If you believe the sky is blue and you share that belief with others it will not have any negative effect on you because it is only an observation. However, if you believed that blue skies make you happy or you believe that grey skies are depressing, you have created a problem for your self. Your happiness and moods now depend on the colour of the sky and you have given the power over your feelings to the weather. You are no longer in control of your emotional state of mind and you may even act as a victim of the weather by saying; "Here is another grey day just to make me miserable".

You would be surprised how many beliefs you hold at this level that you think are not important but collectively have strong sway over the way you feel. Superstition falls into this category where certain signs are believed to have the power to attract negative or positive events into our lives. Giving your power to what is outside of you will never support the expression of your truth nor bring you to live life as your authentic self. Superstition is usually product of a desire to explain certain outcomes and events of which you cannot recognize nor understand the origin. Good and bad luck fall in a similar category. Accepting that we create and manifest our own lives individually and collectively, there cannot be any events or experiences that are accidental in the true sense of that word. It is however likely that there will always be circumstances we cannot completely understand as to how and why certain events happened to others or ourselves. Were we to gain insight into the reasons and causes for an event however it will no longer be a mystery or a product of either good or bad luck.

Creating Harmony from Within

One of the most amazing qualities of our consciousness is our capacity to see beauty and grace. Exposure to something beautiful can take our breath away and bring tears to our eyes. Beauty can present itself in just about any form and appear anywhere at anytime but when it does have the capacity to recognize it immediately for what it is. Our sense of beauty can vary from person but there are common qualities in our perception of what is beautiful. The harmony and balance between shape, proportion and colour all play a decisive role in our perception of beauty. ***One of the most remarkable qualities of our consciousness is that we have an innate sense for beauty, harmony and balance.*** And while our sense for beauty is more highly developed in some than others, everyone can be touched by it without exception.

Just like fear distorts unconditional love by turning it into conditional love, its effect on the mind can also distort our innate sense of beauty and harmony. Issues generate negative emotions such as anger, aggression and powerlessness for example to which we either give open expression or suppress and internalize. Our negative emotional state will draw us to seek out people, environments and even entertainment that exudes the kind of emotional energy that is in congruence with how we feel.
Anger or aggression of being a victim and powerless, being unfairly treated or low self-esteem will cause you to be unconsciously attracted to places, people and entertainment that justify your beliefs and feelings. Anything from

friends, entertainment or localities that have a negative, aggressive and confronting slant can serve us in our need to have our state of mind validated. We may choose to be alone but more than often we will seek out those with similar emotional signature.

Music is a great example of this as an expression form and a medium that can be presented in an infinite number of ways. Music and be melodious and soothing or be aggressive and disharmonious and anything in-between. The composer and lyricist are the first in a chain of people that are involved in the production of music that we will listen to. While the innovators of a musical score and lyrics — the musicians, the singer — and the listener may never know each other; they can nevertheless be connected through the beliefs each holds.

The act of creating music can come from a harmonious sense-of-self or from a mind in disharmony with itself. The music and lyrics will invariably come through the filter created by the beliefs each contributor holds. Their feelings and perception will determine what kind of music they like and how it will be written. Inner-harmony will generally drive the desire to bring harmony into the world, while inner conflict will be expressed as disharmony with the world. If you feel discriminated against, inferior and powerless and carry anger with yourself, life or others this will show in what you create. If you feel loved, wanted, accepted, confident in yourself and so forth, then this too will show in end product of your creative activity. Your sense-of-self is always deeply involved in every act of creation.

The music will find its place on the shelves of music shops and or if you are fortunate, it will be played on the radio and through other media. Whether by design or unconscious intent, those attracted to listen to your music are very likely to share similar belief systems with those who created the music in the first place. The fan clubs that are formed around certain performers provide a level of evidence for this. The same goes for those who feel attracted to perform or sing the music. There is a certain congruency when music created from inner conflict and disharmony attracts similarly emotionally troubled minds as an audience. This does not have to be extreme or because we all experience life situations that can take us through a range of emotions. Just going through a period of unhappiness or disappointment can cause you to be attracted to melancholic or aggressive music. Those who are lost in their issues and suffer from a consistent negative state of mind will often be fans of music that tell the story of their anger and powerlessness. The nature of the beliefs we hold can also cause us to be attracted to other things, such as a particular fashion, a specific type of entertainment or places we are attracted to frequent.

We may not be composers, musicians or lyricists but we all have the capacity to bring something special into the world through our choices and decisions. No matter what we create, harmonious or disharmonious, our sense-of-self is always at the source of our creations and therefore the outcome of our creativity is also always our responsibility.

Conscious Harmonious Intent

Looking into your own emotions and beliefs in respect to your family history is of primary importance in your search for the roots for your issues. While letting go of your negative beliefs is one of the best ways to change your sense-of-self, there are some other things you can do to support this process. By consciously choosing not to respond to emotions that drive your negative behaviour *in tandem with the release of your negative beliefs* will assist your transition. Recognition of the negative aspects within yourself may also cause you to realize the choices that cause you to manifest these negative thoughts and feelings. Remember that it is not possible for you **not to choose** but you have the power to take control over **what you will choose** by releasing the fears that the control your choices.

Once you release a fear driven belief system it will take a little time before you have integrated the changes as a part of your sense-of-self. During the integration period you may experience some emotional ambiguity. It is during this time that consciously selecting what you know to be positive choices will help speed up your changes. Your choices may well push you temporarily out of your comfort zone because you have chosen not to depend on your strategic behaviour, as you habitually would. This will actively support your transformation and will make becoming more authentic easier. Generally, however, releasing you fears will result in automatic changes in perception, feelings and behaviour.

You will progressively shift the balance from fear towards unconditional love by releasing more of your negative belief systems and this will move you sense-of-self towards a greater state of harmony with your essence. So, even if you have not as yet released all the causes for your issues, *every time you make a choice that promotes your inner-harmony you are reinforcing your trust in what is true and real within you— the essence of your spirit.* Conscious awareness of the causes for your issues and the intent they create will not be enough to make negative beliefs go away. However, once you enter the process of integrating your new state after you have released your negative beliefs, your conscious positive attitude will help to bring it to completion. Old habits will begin to fade away as will the feelings that used to drive them. The old disharmonious self in respect to the issue you dealt with will become a foreign to your mind.

Unconscious Creators

We manifest every experience — negative or positive — so effortlessly that we do not even know we are doing it.

We may have learned to believe that we need an extensive education, training and skill and therefore collect degrees and diplomas to quiet the fear that we do not know enough to be acceptable and successful.

Distrust in our innate resources, capacities and talents and abilities may keep us busy acquiring extensive and detailed knowledge, information and highly effective strategies to achieve what we want. Regardless of how much we learn our doubt and distrust our feelings, insights and inspirations, instinct and intuition, creativity and other resources of the mind will sabotage our best efforts. All our intellect, reasoning and logic will not overcome our fears and insecurities. The acquisition of knowledge and experience is always a positive but if you want to use what you have learned most effectively you need to deal with your issues. An axe is only as effective as the person wielding it.

The pictures and stories of beautiful and successful models, stars and their lives can become the unrealistic reference points for people who suffer from low self-esteem. They might measure the state of their lives by the unrealistic media presentation of the wealthy and famous. It can become convinced that to achieve the same life style, happiness and success they need to be physically and emotionally the same. In the case of women, they may compare their appearance and the body shape with those who get public recognition for being beautiful and attractive to men or in the case of men to women. Once they have accepted and believe that they are not good enough or slim and attractive enough no amount of commonsense dialogue will change their mind. The origin for this can usually be found in their early upbringing where they would have been exposed to criticism in respect to physical appearance. The perception created by their negative beliefs about themselves alters their perception to the extend that they lose all perspective in respect to their own appearance and lives. They will never be slim or beautiful enough to the negative beliefs they hold. Their obsessive focus on what ever they see as a flaw is expanded into critical significance to their lives. They are absolutely convinced that they will not matter, be lovable and acceptable unless they are super-slim and beautiful to others and themselves. The strategic behaviours they may employ in an effort to overcome their negative perception can lead to self-destructive behaviours, anorexia or — if passive powerless — become overweight.

There is no limit to the strategies that we will employ to deal with our fears. For example, we may look at historical data to eliminate steps that led to failure in order to avoid failure in our life. We can also study and examine methods, attitudes and behaviours that have led others to success to emulate their path. All of this appears on the surface to be sensible and a logical thing to do if you want to be successful and avoid failure. *However, we are so involve with what we should not do and what we should do by trying to understand every aspect of doing that we totally ignore the nature of the DOER.*

We forget that each person is unique and that all those who failed or succeeded will have their own particular issues and problems. Once you believe that your success in life is defined by the amount of material wealth you can amass you create a reference point for yourself that you have to meet to convince yourself that you are successful. It does not occur to you that the reasons and motivations for needing wanting and amassing material wealth and power can be highly dysfunctional. You might argue that as long as you are wealthy you do not care whether you are emotionally dysfunctional or not. You do not realize that regardless of your life circumstances, you will see and experience it through the beliefs that make up your sense-of-self. What is the worth of all of your material success or fame if your experience of life is marked by depression, guilt or powerlessness and so on?

When we work for others are told to put trust in meeting in the value systems and standards of those who employ us. Their ideas of what matters and what does not may be skewed towards profit and ignore base human values and standards in order to achieve their goals. If these values do not match those that are innate in us we may find ourselves dismissing our own to incorporate theirs in order to be accepted at work. Our idea of success and achievements has to become that of the company if we are to be part of their system and culture. We may gradually become an extension of the system we work under and substitute their biased concepts of what matters in the world for the trust in the innate standards and values, integrity and principles of our being — our authentic nature. By never questioning what we feel in respect to what is expected of us, we can become blind to reasons for what we do thereby unknowingly sabotaging our trust in the value systems inherent in our creative and authentic self.

The truth is that we are incredibly effective creators from the day we are born. ***Whatever intent we hold in our sense-of-self will become our experience of reality, whether consciously chosen or not.*** How much more powerful do you think you need to be? When we get lost on the path created by fear, we need to accept that we have not yet learned how to use the resources our consciousness is blessed with effectively.

Synopsis: We experience negative events in our life for which we have no explanation unaware that the process that manifests it is within us. In resentment of our negative emotional experiences, we cannot imagine that we could be at the origin of their creation. Our indoctrination into strategic behaviour is at the core of our emotional blindness. We are convinced that our behaviours represent who we are and are necessary in order to overcome our emotional issues in life. We define our identity by what we feel and who believe we are —negative and positive. Our strategic behaviours define us to others and who they believe we are. In the absence of trust in our innate capacities and resources and with only our strategies to depend on, we are under the illusion that we are unlovable and unacceptable, unwanted and powerless, cannot trust or be trusted. Our perception makes the quality of our life and its success or failure dependent on the effectiveness of our strategies.

With the best will and using all of our conscious efforts we still do not find it easy to manifest the life style and relationships we want. Instead of addressing the nature of our being — our sense of self, we find it difficult to break our habit of resorting to 'doing' to solve our life issues.
We fall into a pattern of asking ourselves the same old question:
WHAT do I have to DO to solve my problems?
While instead we should be asking:
WHO do I have to BE to BE without my problems?
If you cannot recognise or understand that ***the nature of 'who you are'*** is responsible for your issues then working on your sense-of-self will seem like an impractical and improbable way to solve your problems in relationships and life.

The logical reasoning part of your mind is drawn to address the tangible aspects of an emotional issue and use tactics, strategies and information to solve the problem. This will inevitably involve assessing the behaviour and responses of others, the analysis of every aspect of an event to try and understand why it turned out badly or wrong. Without realising we get lost in the superficial aspect of the issue and try to resolve it by figuring out who did what and how and so on. Taking this approach is not wrong in the strict sense of the word but is never the less extremely limiting if you are seeking a permanent solution. The trust in our logic and reasoning is supported by our tendency to label our emotional self as unpredictable and unstable. Our strategic logical approach can deceive is into believing that our solutions are permanent because they may function well in a particular instance. We miss dealing with our involvement as creators of this experience because have done nothing to change the fundamental cause — you.

You will only achieve true transformation of the self by changing the doer instead of what is done and by changing the thinker instead of the thought.

Confronting issues, especially personal ones, will require a change in your perception and awareness of what is illusion and what is not. Deeply ingrained habits and beliefs that exist in our consciousness need to make place for a liberated and spontaneous way of thinking and reasoning that considers our core values. We need to have a different relationship with our feelings by having a stronger awareness of their connection to the essence of our spirit — unconditional love, acceptance and trust.

Consider this:

What and how we feel do not necessarily define us.

We are not the victims of our feelings or the environment unless we choose to be.

We are the originators of all our emotions and perception, feelings and behaviour.

Consciousness creates the experience of itself through the life it lives.

Realising the truth in these concepts can help us to accept our essence as the reference point by which we judge the quality of our choices and behaviour because then, our physical and emotional life experience will make much more sense to us. Our negative feelings will no longer control our decisions and choices because the true reasons for what we feel will start to reveal themselves to us. Our new concept of who we are in relation to our self, others and the world will allow us to recognise and address our emotional issues at their core. In turn, this will free us to change who we believe we are and consequently alter the nature of all of our relationships. The absence of fear will have changed our sense-of-self and with it the nature of our intent, which will open up opportunities to manifest the potential of our consciousness.

By releasing your negative beliefs and fears of being present as your authentic self, you will expand the expression of your creative self, supported by your belief that you are unconditionally lovable, acceptable and trustworthy. The renewed trust in your authentic self will facilitate that its unique nature can gradually take a greater place in the expression of your consciousness. The acceptance of your innate standards and values, integrity and principles will help to affirm new positive beliefs and increase your self-confidence. You will find that you will only be comfortable in accepting externally defined values and standards of others if they are in congruence will those that are innate in you. This will change your all of your relationships in every part of your life. Life experiences will be representative of your unique nature and provide you with greater satisfaction and profound learning experiences that will translate into happiness. The unique intent of your authentic consciousness will vibrate energetically in harmony with the highest values of your essence.

As your fears diminish your positive qualities grow in stature and create and manifest a positive reality just as effortlessly as you created your negative life experiences. Your positive intent will shape your perception; influence your choices and decisions to create the outcome intended by your positive beliefs.

Evolving Your Consciousness

What does it really mean for your consciousness to evolve or grow? Is it not already all it can be as soon as it is aware of being or is it perhaps a blank space upon which your childhood and society writes an indelible program which you are destined to live out?

Consciousness has no limits other than those it applies to itself through how it holds the perception of its own being.
We cannot even imagine what it would be like to exist without limits because we do not fully understand the limits we have created for our selves. For now, we cannot imagine our existence without limiting fears and conditions. Our present perception of the nature of our consciousness is extremely contracted by the limiting beliefs we share. Our approach to resolving emotional issues bears this out because at best we can generally hope to cure our emotional issues with coping mechanisms, strategies or psychotropic drugs. None of these solutions show a profound understanding of the nature and capacity human consciousness.

Evolving your consciousness requires changes that represent an expansion of its previous state of being by release of perceived limitations and restrictions on its self-expression. You will only truly know what the effect on your mind will be once you start releasing your fears. Intellectual learning may seem like the obvious way for consciousness to become more than what it is but that is only partly true. Knowledge and skill are important contributors to our survival in life, at work and in relationships but our emotions easily overrule the commonsense that acquired knowledge is supposed to provide us with. Neither do they provide us with truly affective permanent tools to completely understand and release our issues. Depending on what you have learned, your knowledge can stand in the way of personal change. The principles used to resolve mechanical or business problems do not work with emotionally biased issues. In fact, having a high I.Q., academic achievements or logical reasoning provide no assurance against emotional issues.

The Creator Within

Consciousness has the innate capacity to create and manifest but that does not mean that whatever you want will just appear when you want it. It would be like putting a gun in the hands of a child. Just like an infant we need to learn to become responsible creators. Manifesting our reality experience has the characteristic of also generating emotional sensations — our feelings — that reflect its positive or negative nature for us. If we were aware, we would recognize that the emotions we experience tell us about the creator not just about what was created.

In order to manifest on levels currently beyond our imagination we have to develop an understanding of our consciousness and the rules or laws that apply to its function and self-expression. That is a big ask when even now most people do not even realize that they are the creators of the reality they currently experience. We are all on our individual journey to the same destination — to become conscious creators. Right now we are like children in the sandbox of the playschool of the cosmos learning how we effect and manifest the nature of reality. Know that all of us get there in a time that is right for us. There is infinite time for all of us to achieve this but if you make this your conscious intent, the process of living your life will become a learning experience like no other. Learning to live in the absence of fear and be in control of your being in a state of unconditional love and acceptance here and now is an extremely significant part of our education.

Our learning in physical reality falls broadly into two categories: The first two things we learn in life are **what we have to do and who we have to be** to be endorsed and approved off. What we have to do is made very obvious by our parents through the expectations and rules they impose on us. Learning ***who we should be*** is usually the inconspicuous part of our childhood experience and generally involves compliance with the values and standards of our parents.

We should be learning to discover and embrace our authentic self and be shown how to live in harmony with our essence — unconditional love, acceptance and trust of self. Instead, exposed to the fears and insecurities of our parents and society, we experience the rejection of our authentic self by those we depend on for our survival. We discover that we need to become what they expect us to be so that they can quiet their own fears and insecurities. Their distrust in us becomes our distrust in ourselves. With our emotional toolbox defined by these experiences we try to create and manifest our lives.

The growth of our consciousness can only truly begin if we release the negative affect our family experiences had on us. Once our sense-of-self no longer relates to the negative aspects of our family history we will accept who we truly are. Releasing the fear based limitations of our society are yet another level of change that will facilitate a return to our true nature and when shared by others, emotional healing on a grand scale. Only than can we truly say that ***we have changed who we are to a complete new level of being***.

You may have noticed that the outcome of an act of manifesting is usually not what we would have wanted it to be when fear is in control. Creatively manifesting a desire, concept or idea will not be a positive act if exercised in total disregard of the consequences for individual and collective consciousness. Every act by every consciousness affects all others and for the outcome to be a positive, it needs to be a gesture in harmonious concert with others. When it is not the case it creates ripples of distortion touches every consciousness and reaches much further and deeper than you might imagine. Wanting to create selfishly to satisfy your own fears and insecurities creates a raft of issues for everyone associated with it. Those who share similar negative beliefs will either capitalise on the opportunities the outcome creates or become its victims.

Confronting Change

Change is essential for a freely choosing creative and unique consciousness. Without change it cannot evolve through learning. Change is a big challenge for those with fear because there appears to be no certainty whether the outcome it creates will bring is positive or manifest more pain, more issues and problems. Avoiding change can become a skilful strategic behaviour tied up in excuses and justifications. For those who fear change it can be terrifying not to be able to predict how the consequences of change will impact their life. For example: how it will affect their identity, how others will judge them and the prospect of their strategic behaviours becoming ineffective.

Those who suffer from fear of change and the anxiety and stress that often accompanies it will already be aware of most of these issues but how can they transcend the fear of change in order to change? What might surprise you is that your fear of change is a negative belief system just like any other fears. Releasing the fear of change is exactly the same, as for example, dealing with believing that you unlovable, unwanted or unacceptable and so on.

Releasing your fear of change is a great way to take the first step towards becoming authentic and living in your power.
Here is a representation of a belief system that you may hold that causes confronting change to be difficult for you.

- *I have to live in fear* of unpredictable, sudden, unexpected, unplanned, unchosen changes —
- *For fear* of the consequences, *for fear* of being overwhelmed and become powerless, *for fear* of losing control over my life, *for fear* it will cause me pain and make me suffer, *for fear* it will cause me embarrassment and shame, *for fear* it will make me helpless and vulnerable —
- *It will cause me to be* — rejected, dismissed, excluded, unwanted, unacceptable, undesirable, insignificant, judged, criticised and so on.
- *and so because of that* — I have to avoid change, reject and dismiss change, invalidate change, ignore change, reject and dismiss change —
- *I have no choice — because if I don't* — I will become powerless, vulnerable and helpless — unlovable and unacceptable — insignificant and worthless — rejected and excluded — criticised and judged — ridiculed and shamed and so on.
- *Because it is always my fault — I am always to blame – I am the guilty one and I am powerless to change it.*

(Add or delete as appropriate)

The complexity and length may surprise you but every element that relates to you needs to be owned by you in order to be able to release it. Fear of change is usually passed on by one or both parents. Their fear of change will have been displayed through various behaviours that would have painted any confrontation with change as something to be avoided at all cost. Its expression is not necessarily explicit. Sometimes these fears reveal themselves through the length of time they live in the same house, stay in the same area or stay in the same job. It can be the consistent sameness of their diet or habits and repetitive patterns of behaviour. Fear of change usually goes hand in hand with the fear of decision-making, initiating new actions and choices or exposure to risk. The intensity of the fear of change differs from person to person as do the reasons for it. To ascertain what your fears are and how they became a part of you it may help to consider everything presented here.

Realistically, evolving your consciousness to higher levels of awareness and mental and emotional capability is a lifetime if not an eternal journey of the spirit. The importance of this exceeds anything else you may want to succeed in or achieve in your lifetime. Dependent on the nature of your intend anything you achieve will contribute to the growth of your spirit and consciousness. It comes down to your approach to living your life — self-responsible and without fear or in disharmony and controlled by fear.

Since your spirit consciousness already has the innate intent to evolve in all areas of its potential being, it makes sense to **live life with the conscious intent to evolve spiritually**. The intent to evolve will always be realized even if our consciousness chooses to exist and function controlled by fear. The outcomes that fear creates in our lives makes our experience of it unbearable, unhappy and painful. Sooner or later we begin to realize that we can only stop our pain and suffering if we do something to change something our sense-of-self. So far, our general response to the distortions and imbalances in our own life and those in the world, have been addressed in an almost time honoured way: through strategies or laws and rules. Looking at the world, as it is right now, it is clear that it is not working on any level of our civilisation. At best, we are constantly propping up processes, systems and laws to stop everything sliding from under us. We do much the same in our private lives by our use of strategic behaviours to deal with our emotional issues. Living with the knowledge that you are the creator of your own life circumstances alters our whole approach to living life. Accepting full responsibility for our choices and the outcome they manifest alters our relationship with our self, others and the world. If we were to share this intent and the responsibility that comes with it with others of like mind we would automatically be creating a new and very different world.

Imagine a world where a large portion of people lived with this intent and what the outcome would be.

Changing your self is a step-by-step process. Expecting that all life's issues will suddenly disappear after a couple of sessions, will only lead to disappointment. It is however realistic to expect that each time you let go of a negative belief system you will have made a definitive change within your-

self. A persistent and consistent self-responsible approach to self-change will always bring positive results. Your changes will reveal themselves in the way you feel, in how you behave and change your perception and in how the world and others respond to you.

Your very first goal should be to release the negative issues taken on in your childhood, which are a part of your life right now. Releasing these will already transform you substantially and alter how you feel and see yourself and with it your experience of life. Secondly, there are fear based cultural and potentially restrictive religious influences that may have a suppressing influence over you. The third level would be existential in nature but it is unlikely you will be ready for this until you have made substantially transitions in the first two.

The incessant drive to evolve is an indivisible part of your consciousness and by using curiosity, exploration and learning to create and manifest you will continue to drive the fulfilment of your unique potential. Using all of your faculties — talents and abilities, inspirations, imagination and choices and so on to explore and try something new or to challenge the unknown are natural processes for us. Our consciousness seeks constant stimulation in its quest to know itself through the act of creating new experiences for itself. You could say that physical reality is a testing ground for consciousness where the inherent limitations of the environment and the existence of other expressions of consciousness are a challenge to its creative potential and capacity for spiritual growth. In this environment every act of expression is immediately mirrored back as an experience.

Without fear to hold you back, you will attempt challenges you would have previously shied away from and initiate ideas and concepts that never came to mind before. Your first efforts to create and manifest new concepts and ideas may not immediately bring the results you thought they would because you are always in the process of learning and expanding your consciousness. If your new ideas are a radical departure from convention they can generate a new set of challenges for your mind and for those exposed to them. If that were the case in the past, a negative response might have made you critical of yourself. However now, with a new perception of who you are, you feel confident to step back and examine the result from the point of view of a self-responsible creator. ***Without judgment and criticism you can view your manifestations in the light of its creator — you.*** Your exploration of outcomes that do not reflect expectations will be undertaken with curiosity and interest, not self-condemnation. Everything is now a learning experience and in the final analysis, all you would want to know and understand is ***what you need to change within your self*** to achieve the outcomes you strive for.

Your perception will have altered so dramatically that it will seem as if you have entered a different world with different people while ***in reality it is you and not the world that has changed***. Letting go of your fears alters the intent of your being and thereby opens the path towards achieving inner and outer harmony and this will form the basis from which you will create and manifest your new life. The new dynamic between you and others will change your experience of them and vice versa. Until now, this way of being has been foreign to you and yet it is the path towards clear realization and enlightenment of your spirit and to being empowered and authentic in life.

Chapter 23

The Voice of Your Authentic Self

Others may see your dedication to self-development as an act of selfishness but you should not allow this criticism to create feelings of guilt in you. Their response comes mostly from the belief that we need to support each other in our pain and suffering and it is than expected that you put others before yourself. In their eyes you will seem self-indulgent, only caring about your feelings, issues and problems and not about theirs or others. This judgment frequently comes from those who could be classified as aggressive-victims. These are people who because their belief in their own victimhood feel entitled to use aggressive strategic behaviours to get support, help and sympathy. In their world, nobody has suffered more than they have and therefore they will not allow their issues and problems to be overlooked or ignored. Their victimhood has become a dominating part of their sense-of-self and controls all of their relationships. They will attract friends whose inner-identity is steeped in guilt in order to have their victim state validated. The dynamic in this type of relationship feeds the general notion that we are victims of our environment and that therefore others or this case: you — need to take responsibility for his or her issues and problems.

When we manifest issues that make us feel that we are victims of life, we generally expect others or the world around us to change as a solution for the emotional distortions we feel. We disregard our innate capacity as creators and the reject responsibility that it carries by primarily seeking resolution for our emotional imbalance through others.

Every act of creation in our desire to manifest has the potential to cause feelings that are in contradiction with our natural propensity to exist in a state of inner-balance and harmony. Once we give into these feelings, we generally do not realize that our intent will be dominated by fear.

The truth is that were we to give our desire for balance and inner peace absolute priority we would be on the path of becoming conscious and responsible creators without fear.

Our proclivity to create and manifest would continue to propel us to challenge the capacity and capability of our inner being in order to evolve the potential of who we are and what we can be.
Our innate desire to grow from new challenges will always cause us to experience outcomes, which do not match our expectations.
In that way every new learning experience is an opportunity to move the perceived limits of our potential being to a new level.
This may appear to juxtapose our continued quest to exist in balance and harmony with our essence but it actually prompts us to realize the nature of our sense of self.

We can only be sure that the path we follow is in congruence with the intent of the Essence of Spirit by continuously comparing the outcome of our acts of creation and manifestation with the nature of our own essence as it parallels that of Spirit.

The state of true bliss is experience when our manifestations are in harmonious resonance with our own essence and with All Consciousness.

Realizing this for yourself requires you to become aware and introspective of the present nature of your sense-of-self in order to know what you need to change. **Self-transformation demands you put effort, attention and commitment into your process of change.** Superficially it may appear to others that you are totally self-involved but nothing is further from the truth. Your search for answers involves others with whom you had and maybe still have relationships. Others will not necessarily understand that your personal transformation will not only have a positive impact on you but will also benefit the relationships you have with everyone else in your life. Where in the past you would have played out an issue resulting in conflict, this will no longer be the case. Once you have released the fears at the source of your behaviour you will automatically stop engaging others on that level. You will no longer be attracted and attract those with issues complimentary to your own. The absence of these fears and their strategies will make those whose issues you used to engage lose interest in you.

True change — changing *who* you are — is of immediate and profound benefit to everyone you come in touch with. First of all there will be a shift in the energetic state of your being which then alters the nature of your presence and the dynamic with others. This results in changes in the relationship due to the difference in the emotional energy you radiate. A transformed sense-of-self will finds expression in your behaviour and posture, your attitude and gestures. The way your mind and body communicate your every emotional aspect is felt and understood by others. A higher state of inner-harmony makes a positive contribution to all who come in contact with it and the world.

Those who are depended on your expression of your issues to be able to play out their fears and insecurities may judge your desire to become empowered, secure and confident an act of selfishness. Until you start to work on yourself it is unlikely that you are aware that your circle of friends are people very much like yourself and therefore a match for your issues. Your changes will trigger or show up their strategic behaviours and insecurities, which can result in a re-appraisal of your friendships. The friends who unconsciously rely on you to facilitate the expression of their issues in order that they can feel good, safe or justified will feel most confronted by your changes but this cannot be your responsibility. Once the fears you held that made this possible are not present in you their strategic behaviour will no longer make you respond in the same way. Their time has come to become introspective about their behaviour, feelings and intent. All you can do is to support them to overcome their issues but this is something they must ultimately want to do for themselves. **You can never allow the issues or fears of others deter your personal growth.**

The Right to Be Authentic

Expressing the belief that you are the creator of your own life can invoke the idea in others that you consider yourself to be a god or godlike. They might ridicule you for being under the illusion that you can create something out of nothing. Religious minded individuals might even be offended by the concept because it may seem as of you are blaspheming by saying that you are appropriating power that can only belong to God. Their response is predictable because they come from a place of powerlessness. Having made the choice to give the responsibility for their lives to god, the idea that they could be responsible for their life experiences will very confronting. Once you see yourself as powerless, it is difficult to accept that you are not only the creator of your own experience of reality but therefore also responsible for everything you manifested.

The concept of being the creator of your own life would seem completely ridiculous to someone whose life has been filled with pain, suffering and disappointment. The truth is that it is not always easy to recognize and accept how you are complicit in your own negative life experiences. Accepting that you are a victim of life leaves you with no way out of your emotional state of helplessness and powerlessness. Choosing to be a powerless victim will in all likely hood condemn you to a continuation of past and present pain and suffering into the future. It is the very reason why **understanding your own role** *in the process of manifesting your life is the most important awareness you can attain.* Only then can you appreciate the nature and potential of your own consciousness in respect to the reality in which you live you existence. What matters is that you learn to understand how and why you create and manifest your individual and collective reality within the realm of the present capacity of your consciousness. *We need to remind ourselves that every unique gift our consciousness contains comes from the Source from which we originate.*

As a manifested consciousness you can never be more than the Universal Consciousness that manifested you. However that does not mean you that you are not responsible for creating your own life. Quite the opposite, human consciousness has been instilled with all the resources and capacities to do just that. We can only evolve our consciousness if we are the creators of our own reality experience and it is the reason why we are endowed with the mental and emotional faculties and resources. Our life experiences — negative or positive — are our teachers and allow us to accomplish personal and spiritual growth. We need to learn how to live our own life to the fullness of our potential and still be in harmony with collective consciousness. Our learning always begins with us as individuals first and then as a collective consciousness second. When the first changes the other must follow.

Earth is home to an incalculable number of life forms from microbes to whales and birds and anything in between, not forgetting humans. Unique diversity exists within the same species of life, plants, insects and microbes. Even though it is not obvious, there is not a grain of sand on any beach in the whole world completely identical to another and even every droplet of water on our planet would vary in some finite way from another. We cannot necessarily recognise the unique differences in everything that exists but that does not mean it is not so. Our senses are relatively easily fooled and the sameness and physical consistency that we believe we see in our world is an illusion and hides the unique state of everything in reality. The point is that being unique and different is normal and being truly identical to others is more than likely rare.

The problem we have with accepting the individuality of others arises from our own belief that our own unique nature — *authentic self* — is not wanted. When who we authentically are does not match the expectations our parents, we become convinced that the failure lies with us for not being who we are supposed to be. The inner-conflict this creates generally results in the suppression of much of our authentic being. A child has no choice but to adopt beliefs and behaviours that conform to our parent's expectations. This is such a surreptitious process that overwhelmed by feelings of fear we do not realize that we are dismissing who we really are in order to avoid rejection or abandonment. The fear we carry of being our unique self can have the effect of making us reject unique and different qualities in others. As a consequence, when we are confronted with the unique nature of others, we may find that we judge and reject their individuality in the same way our unique self was treated by our parents. Without realizing we may have become part of a generational cycle of suppression and discrimination that is negative for us as well as others.

The unique nature of our spirit is the one thing that is common to all of us and instead of creating separation through judgement, should bind us together because each is an intrinsic part of Universal Consciousness. It has become a fundamental challenge for each human being — to exist in the absence of fear to be free to express the capacity and potential of their unique and authentic being. Not just out of fear of being our authentic self but also because of fear-based beliefs we already hold.

Unconditional acceptance of who you truly are will allow you to accept the true and individual nature of others without fear. You can be your authentic self without denying others or feeling denied with the understanding that it is the same for you as it is for others. Once you take ownership of who and what you are, you also take control over your existence by being the determining factor in the creation of your life. You are meant to be different from everyone else in the world, so celebrate and be proud of the individual nature of your consciousness and its potential and give it free and unlimited expression. And while you are at it, help others celebrate theirs.

Being Authentic

The fears that caused us to reject our authentic self in the first place have the affect of blocking us from giving it unconditional expression later in life. We get so hooked on the strategic behaviours that are a product our fear driven self that we unwittingly create chaos through the voice of our negative beliefs. Every now and then there is a moment in most peoples lives where everything seems to fall magically and gracefully into place and they get a glimpse of what it is like to live life without fear. This may be momentary but it is a taste of being the person you know you were always meant to be. We need to record these highlights in our memory because these become new emotional reference points for who we can potentially be as an individual. Our innate yearning to live life in harmony with our essence will always direct us to discover our true nature.

The idea of becoming your authentic self often raises new fears.
If I do not know who my authentic self is:
- How will I know that the person become is who I am meant to be?
- Will I like who I am becoming and will others like me?
- Will the person I become be nice or nasty?
- Will others still know who I am?

The answer is that your authentic self is an intrinsic part of your consciousness and spirit and cannot be lost, disappear or be taken away. The fears and their associated strategic behaviours and negative feelings that you have taken on as a substitute for your unique authentic self also serves to actively suppress it. You have become convinced that if you do not respond to your fear you will be unlovable, unwanted or unacceptable and so on. You then are in fear of letting go of your fear-based beliefs and this keeps your trapped in your dependence on your strategic behaviours. Consequently releasing the negative beliefs represents a fundamental challenge to you in your quest for personal change. Remember that all of your ***fear is based on the conditions you believe exist for being loved and wanted, accepted and trusted.***

By peeling away each layer of fear, you will ultimately be left with the core of your being — your authentic self and its innate potential. There is no need to worry about the nature of your authentic self because it will be a positive in nature and intent. Your authentic self emerges out of the essence of your spirit and therefore can never be unlovable or unacceptable, bad or inferior. Instead in its purest form it exists in the vibration of unconditional love acceptance and trust, which corresponds with the state of consciousness we all innately, seek within ourselves.

Even though you may believe that you have never given your authentic self has free expression, there will be instances where your fears and strategic behaviours fell away and allowed aspects of your true self to appear and be expressed. This usually happens when you least expect it and when you do not feel under emotional pressure by your surroundings, fears and insecurities. These small glimpses of inner and outer harmony are very significant examples of the capacity of true nature of your being and potential. In the future they can serve as inspirational reference points on your journey to release your fears and become who you are truly meant to be.

Escape From Illusions

We all aspire to practice our passions and desires to earn the income we need to exist. In the absence of passions and interests we often struggle to know what kind of work we want to do. The prospect of a life without direction and without a sense of purpose is not motivating and inspiring. Not ever knowing your passion feels for some frustrating and des-empowering and can underpin a lifelong sense of dissatisfaction. In the absence of a passionate desire or a dream to fulfil we often feel there no other choice but to find a job that makes us enough money to survive and perhaps buy entertainment to occupy our time.

Without a particular focus or direction in life we may let family tradition and the issues that come with them make the choices for us. It is not unusual that parents who were never given this option when they were children, to dismiss the idea of doing work that is exiting and compelling for its own sake. The option may not even occur to them and they do not realise this attitude can alienates their offspring from their innate potential and talents and abilities. Other criteria concerning status and financial expectations can override what they consider to be folly. Once parents have convinced a child that the invalidation of its passions and fascinations are well founded, it usually begins to dismiss these innate qualities within itself. Once an adult, it will dismiss its attractions and desires without knowing why and at the same time cannot find anything that stimulates or excites them.

The unconscious automatic dismissal of their passions and attractions can cause them to pass up opportunities they might have otherwise considered. Many find themselves following in their parent(s) footsteps often mimicking their career choices as part of our desire to please them to be accepted and validated. Conforming to their expectations, values and standards at the cost of the potential of discovering our own passions and desires, talents and abilities. Often, they finish up studying for degrees they will never use or work that is unfulfilling. This can lead to dissatisfaction and a search for something different later in life.

When there is a consistent lack of interest by the parents in the needs and expectations of their children, they may feel motivated to follow a career for the power and influence or fame and recognition it appears to offer. This can be acting, public speaking, being an entertainer, become a manager any position where recognition, adulation and power can be experienced. This career direction can frequently be attributed to beliefs in their own insignificance, powerlessness and unworthiness of recognition.

If for example you have been ignored and forgotten and your presence is treated as being of no consequence, your fear of insignificance may drive you to find a position in life that will make you the centre of attention. This can make you strive to become an actor or a performer or perhaps a public figure in the media. Finding a place in the public eye will fulfil your need to find significance through the recognition by others to convince your self that you are special. You do not see that your need to create this response in others makes you totally dependent on their recognition and validation. You have effectively given them the power over your personal sense of worth and significance. Once you have chosen this strategy, your fear of being worthless and insignificant will always be with you.

As it waxes and wanes throughout your career it can drive you to take risks that can overextend your capacity to be in control. Any failure, no matter how small, will intensify your fears and can cause you to become more desperate to maintain or rekindle your success. Constant fear of losing public recognition and adulation will make it easier for you to justify compromising yourself or try and find something that will give you emotional reprieve from your anxiety. The only way to get out of this is to resolve your fear-based beliefs at the core. Given that you have the desire and talent to meet the expectations of your career, it will be more likely that you become and stay successful without negative beliefs controlling your choices and decisions.

Compared to those who are passionate about their work there are many more who have chosen their career to survive, because of family influences or for particular emotional issues. We need to be aware that the emotional issues at the core of each of these choices are in actuality illusions.

You can confuse your search of your passions and fascinations by following needs that portray themselves as intense interests but are a product of negative beliefs. Unknowingly committing yourself to a fear driven interest can cause you to spend your life chasing a goal that often stays out of reach or of which the outcome is difficult to maintain or keeps you failing. The need to achieve often relates to the feeling of having to prove something about yourself to others — to be in control, be successful or to be wealthy and so on. Your real motivation for your apparent passion is the fear of the consequences you believe exist if you should fail — being powerless, being judged to be a failure or being poor and so on.

The fear of failure and losing control, embarrassment and shame can turn the need to succeed into an obsession. The consequences generated by our negative beliefs give our fears a sense of reality that make anxiety and stress the dominating emotional forces that propel our behaviour. Fear can convert ambition into a ruthless motivation to succeed at the sacrifice of principles and values. The present psychological working environment of western society makes this kind of behaviour easily justifiable and as such is often celebrated because the importance of the bottom line outweighs any other considerations. It could be said that we have to be ruthless in business and live our humanity in our private lives. This contradiction can result in inner-conflict when it becomes the central focus in the way we live life, work or do business and conduct our relationships and our general interaction with the world. Our commitment to be successful can become a justification for making decisions that disregard the effect they have on others in order to achieve our aim. Superficially it may appear as if we are passionate about our goals but in actuality we are trying to fulfil a fear driven need to avoid being and being seen as powerlessness failures.

That is not to say that you might not have the talent to be a businessman, an actor or a singer or a good speaker. If your innate talents and abilities are bound up in fears and insecurities they will distort the manner in which you express them. Your behaviour will then become strategic because you begin to imagine all manner of consequences, should you fail.

As long as the central reason for your what you want to do in life is driven by negative beliefs, you will be tied to the negative consequences you believe they hold. It may surprise you that the nature of your goals and expectations will often change once your fears have been transcended. Characteristically, when fear is the motivation for your aspirations, the destination will always be more important than the journey. The emphasis of your effort and attention will be to achieve the ultimate state of security, wealth, recognition, power and so on. The step-by-step process of getting there does nothing but frustrate. You cannot wait to get to your goal because in your mind that is the only thing that matters which makes having to work for every step of your journey a nuisance.

Your resentment of the process actually works against you because you cannot commit yourself to the attention to detail each step requires. The chances that your lack of commitment to each part of your journey will cause you never to get to your goal get higher each time you fail to apply yourself. It should not be surprising that people with this mindset are unlikely to succeed. Rather than savouring the experience that each incremental triumph provides, avoidance of the work it takes to get there will cause them to never reach the pinnacle of their aspirations. Discovering the deeper reasons for why you want something so badly allows you to discover your fears and is a good beginning to get your priorities right. Releasing the original issues at their core may give you access to the full capability of your talents and abilities and get you to discover your true passions.

When the journey becomes more important than the goal interesting things begin to happen in our minds. Every time we are successful in achieving our incremental goals the solutions and learning experiences we are expose ourselves to have the power to transform us. These inner-changes will influence our perception and expectations and how we perceive our goals and aspirations and alter what we ultimately want the end of our journey to be.

Love Without Fear

Being authentic goes hand in hand with being truthful to yourself in your emotions and the expression of your feelings. Being emotional sincerity can only be truly achieved in the absence of self-judgment and guilt and this applies in particular to relationships. In the process of change you need to acknowledge all of your feelings good or bad, positive or negative without judgment. Self-criticism actually diminishes the relationship you have with yourself first and than with others. Your self-criticism proves you do not accept who you really are and seek to prove that you can be who you think you should be to get the approval and endorsement of others. The affect this will have on your behaviour is unavoidable because you do not want others to see what you believe are shortcomings and faults. The result will make your behaviour strategic and therefore contrived and because of that, sincerity, truth and spontaneity will be lacking not just in your relationship with yourself but also with others.
Without being aware, your relationships with others are subject to your issues and not unconditional love or friendship. Elements based on the fear of being unlovable and unacceptable or unwanted and not being good enough and so on have crept into your involvement with others. Even though you may be in the throes of love and attraction, your fear of rejection, being a failure or inadequate and so on will already influence the way you present yourself and communicate with your prospective partner. You try so hard to present your self as someone you believe fits the expectations of the person you are attracted that you are not at all who you really are or could be. Your fear of the consequences — that you will judged to be worthless and not good enough— will keep you from having a real relationship that is sincere and honest, spontaneous and unconditional.

Te strategic behaviours and responses that are freely and fluently used by you were learned long before intimate relationships of this kind were even in your imagination. They may have become more sophisticated but at their core they are the same as were when in childhood. You do not even realize you acting out of second nature because your behavioural response to your fears feels normal and natural. With fear in control your relationship lacks the foundation it needs to make it successful because your issues will rule your thoughts the feelings.

Intimate relationships are in many ways your proving ground for the state of your sense-of-self. Trust issues of any kind concerning love and intimacy, gender or acceptance will definitely reveal themselves once you are in a relationship. Loving unconditionally means to have as few conditions as possible on your relationship and that will not be realized until you have dealt with your own fears and insecurities concerning love, acceptance and trust. You need to be largely without the fear of giving, receiving and allowing yourself to be vulnerable in love to acquire this state. Releasing fears in respect to being authentic and sincere in the expression of your emotions in particular will have a big impact in creating greater freedom and self-confidence in revealing the true state of your emotional self. Your true sense of trust in love is only as strong as the love and acceptance you have for yourself and there is no alternative to this.

Being in a constant process of resolving your fears may cause you to believe that you have to clear all your issues before you can start a relationship but this is fortunately not true. Although there will be always a part of mutual attraction that is founded in issues, it is not a requirement to be clear of all your fears before you can allow yourself to fall in love. *The key factor in being in a successful long-term relationship does not only depend on the absence of fears.* Certain issues — that cause you to feel passive-powerless or aggressive powerless — will attract abuse or make you be abusive in their expression and these must be released before you embark on a relationship. The reason for this lies in the reality that you will always attract a complementary counter part of your issues. Once you have released the most paralysing of your issues it is relatively emotionally safe to make yourself available again even though your constant alertness is required.

The key quality to look for in a partner is their willingness to accept responsibility for their feelings and behaviour and be prepared to search for the causative reasons within themselves. Emotional self-responsibility that is not a product of self-blame, guilt or fear of confrontation is the lubricant that will allow you to maintain dialogue in times when issues come to the surface. *Emotional self-responsibility will support individual growth and maintain the love between you.*

Conflicting Needs and Expectations

On the surface, the dynamics of relationships in stress and conflict appear to be very complicated. The main reason for this is not in the actual complexity of it but because of the habitual thinking and feeling patterns we have developed over many generations. Our perception of our own consciousness and being is distorted by many centuries of influence, which have gradually convinced us that reality we perceive has nothing to do with our own conscious being. In this view, reality exists completely independent and separate from us by its own set of rules and laws. We have become programmed by the idea that most of what we experience is caused by external forces and influences, effectively turning us into victims of life most of the time. This 'program,' which has become the basis for our perception of our selves in life, is also the reason why relationships are generally experienced as difficult and problematic. Disagreements and conflict usually result in mutual blaming and therefore finds no resolution other than perhaps compromise.

It difficult to know what is really going on when you are in the middle of a relationship conflict and you are subject to the negative experience of your own issues. There are fundamental principles that hold true in every relationship whether they are friendships, intimate or in the work place. First of all, **all relationships are a dynamic** and that means that both parties are involved and contribute to what is being played out between them. In this respect when there is conflict, **there are no innocent parties in relationships**.

The attraction that people have for one another can be broadly divided into our innate and authentic qualities and our issues or fears.
Our original and authentic self also seeks its complimentary counterpart through a relationship in order to grow and evolve.
Our fear-based self does the same but if unresolved has the effect of stunting our spiritual and emotional growth.
The complexity of our psyche reveals itself more clearly in conflict when we act out our negative self-beliefs instead of being authentic and true to our essence. Once fear has become a dominating force in our minds it also defines and controls our attraction and interactions with others. At the same time, we set ourselves up for emotional conflict and disharmony because the issues each brings in the relationship will eventually surface and dominate.

Reality is that every conflict with others is evidence of an inner-confrontation between our authentic sense-of-self and the fears we have accepted as our substitute identity. If it remains unresolved, the contradiction between the fears our consciousness feels compelled to obey and its core intent — unconditional love and acceptance — becomes an inner-conflict we have to live and experience everyday. This causes fears that each partner holds to feel as if they are real and then these become the dominant forces in the relationship. Remember that we are at the centre of our own life experiences and that ***we can only change who we are by letting go of who we are not.*** This is what will manifest a new and different experience of life and relationships

Each emotional transformation is an incremental step revealing a new sense of what unconditional love, acceptance and trust represent to you. Its influence in the form of positive self-esteem and self-trust will gradually become a greater. Once your accumulated changes reaches a point where your positive or authentic beliefs out-weight the negative part of your sense-of-self, your self-confidence will grow exponentially. The ever-increasing presence of your unique, spontaneous and authentic self and your sense of personal power will become a natural part of your self-expression. Your need to be validated by others to create proof that you are lovable and acceptable will completely vanish. Your unique authentic self, supported by your essence will grow in stature and prominence as your fears diminish.

The transformation of your sense-of-self also affects the nature of your conscious and subconscious intent and with it, your perception and values, standards and feelings, thoughts and behaviour. Your world cannot be other than very different place from the world you used to know because the person you have become will be very unlike the person you once were.

Chapter 24

Unconditional Being

Do we really have the capacity to create the life through our choices or are we destined to live our existence through our fears and insecurities? Is it possible for us to be so out of touch with who we truly are that we are convinced that that our environment determines how and what we choose in life? If we are conscious of being and the reality of our surroundings, is that not proof enough that our experience of everything is real and valid?

Even though you may never have even thought to ask these questions up until now it should be clear that they are extremely relevant to how your life will unfold for you. If you are to have a life that makes sense of your existence, you need to have them answered. Once you realize that it is just as possible to exist in the illusions created by your beliefs and emotions, as it is to be in the reality of your spirit you have choices you were not even aware of. We will not realize the control our inner-identity exercises over every aspect of life until we let go of the negative mental states responsible for this distortion in our perception.

The incredible flexibility of human consciousness and its capacity to adapt allows it to survive in even the most negative of emotional circumstances. Unfortunately, this very same flexibility and adoptive capacity can also lead to self-deception and living in illusions. Once the mind accepts emotional fears as if it is the same fear for survival as for instance standing on the very edge of a cliff, your consciousness is held by illusions. This deception, as product of fear, is shared by humanity across the world. This state of mind is not the product of one lifetime of human existence but a result of countless generations being subjected to a creeping indoctrination of fear based ideas and beliefs. In many instances these fears have been delegated by controlling forces and institutions within various cultures. Once fear gets hold of one individual it can be transferred to the young and germinate within them to be passed on to the next generation. On a fundamental level this has created a not always subtle but an extremely persistent fear-based intent that has led humanity away from its innate connection with the essence of its Origin. The further our consciousness is disconnected from this the more we begin to view ourselves and therefore others and living life with fear and suspicion. Once enmeshed by these fears, we can see no other way and believe we have no other choice but to depend on our strategies to survive them.

Fears and insecurities create a negative dynamic with others and the physical world that take us into an ever-expanding circle fear — of distrust and aggression, neediness and guilt. The fear-based expectations and strategies they generate then dominate our lives. The apparently logical and statistically proven official explanations for the ills society suffers do nothing to reveal the core reason for their existence and do little to improve the emotional wellbeing of humanity. Instead of providing a clear insight into the nature of our consciousness, existence and life, the conclusions that are reached commonly go no further than noting the circumstances and the behaviour of those involved. The solutions offered by society are generally no more than advice on strategies, the institution of rules or laws as a means to control the individuals who appear to be the source of the problems.

Knowing what is right or wrong with us can be confusing when our issues are welcomed in some environments and judged in others. When our behaviours serve to build wealth, success or make money for yourself or corporations, they are celebrated. Displaying the same behaviours in our personal life and we may create conflict and issues thereby confusing who we think we should be. The inconsistency with which human behaviours are judged by society and in particular through the media only serves to create confusion in people and in particular in the young.

The real 'battle' that humanity needs to win is not within the physical world but within our minds — *that of unconditional love, acceptance and trust over fear.* With fear increasingly becoming the dominant and controlling force in the world, humanity is pushing itself towards a crisis of consciousness. The strategies and behaviour that come from fear are either justified or condemned or treated as a psychological disorders. Many believe that there is no reason to question their own behaviour and feelings if it matches that of the majority of the population. *Using general consensus as your frame of reference for what is normal and acceptable is a grave error in judgment when you consider that everyone is subject to their own fears and those of others.* The general concept of what is normal and what is not usually comes from statistical consensus that finds confirmation by comparing numbers rather than appreciating the unique qualities of our consciousness. We try to define normality by counting commonality, not taking into consideration that the overall state of human consciousness is a product of many thousands of years of progressively distorting influences. The level of misconception of our consciousness is difficult to measure because it is obvious that we are at the present psychologically so far away from its highest possible state. Without specific reference points we cannot trust our perception to determine what that can be. We are caught in a bind that denies us absolute clarity of the true potential of our consciousness until we release our fears because they are the very reason why we cannot recognize who we can be in the first place.

The truth is that because of fear, we all suffer from different levels of distortion in our perception of our selves and the world. That distortion ultimately translates into pain and suffering on a personal level and collectively, on a world scale.

Once the mind is caught up in these often subtle but never the less commanding negative beliefs they control how we are in life. Extracting our selves from their gript can then become extremely difficult because it requires us to change our perception of who we believe we are. We fundamentally need something about our selves we hold to be true. Our issues present themselves in such a logical manner through our interactions with others that on the surface our interpretation of the experience appears totally real and valid. We do not question our reality experience because we do not even realise that we live our lives disconnected from the Essence of our being — *unconditional love, acceptance and trust.* Yet, these are the very elements that *form the cord that connects us with our spiritual origins, to each other and All Consciousness.*

Unaware of the innate reference points provided by our inner-essence, we lack the capacity to discern inner and outer harmony and disharmony. The capacity of fear to dominate our thoughts, feelings and behaviour ensures that we lose the ability to separate the illusionary-self from our authentic being. Without these reference points, our consciousness becomes like a ship without a compass and rudder and will lack the direction and focus our fundamental being should furnish. Instead, fear readily becomes the driving force that will control our self-expression, choices and our destination in life.

You may think that making superficially different choices or developing new strategic behaviours, will help you to step out of this illusionary psychological framework but that is not so. Your strategic behaviour may be temporarily successful and get you the result you hope for but you will not have changed *you*. Only changing your sense-of-self will produce a change in your fundamental perception and sense of being.
Remember that changing the thought and not the thinker, the doing but not the doer and the strategy but not the strategist will ultimately NOT work. Like everyone else, you are functioning on the illusion that by influencing or changing people and the material world, you are dealing with your

issues. None of what you have done has addressed the core reasons why a negative situation arose in your life in the first place. By **not confronting** the creator of these events — which is **you** and your negative belief systems in your sense of yourself — you set the stage to repeat your past issues in the future.

The distortions that we live with may appear subtle but the consequences they have for our consciousness are certainly not. Every time you do not accept responsibility for your life in some way your are disempowering yourself and giving fear validity and justification. It adds to the drift away from living in the essence of our being as it is presently manifested by collective human consciousness. Instead of being in a state of personal empowerment our state of consciousness moves us to that of victimhood, powerlessness and aggression and from being self-responsible to blaming others and guilt.

As long as we are conscious of being we will incessantly create. We cannot ever stop manifesting our reality whether our belief systems support or contradict our essence. It is not something you can ever stop doing or even apply selectively— you have no choice in this. **You cannot choose not to choose.** Therefore life, as you experience it, will always remain your responsibility.
We are clever at manufacturing justification, reasons and causes for our ills but do not realize that we disempower ourselves in the process. The mechanism by which we have come to experience life is opposite to what we think it is — *instead of others and the world doing it to us, we are doing it to ourselves.*

Living consciously begins by becoming aware of your behaviour, emotional responses and feelings. In the beginning it is a process of continued questioning of every part of your self-expression as if you have a mini-me sitting on your shoulder, watching your every thought, feeling and move. Observing and questioning yourself objectively can reveal many negative facets in your behaviour, attitude and needs.

Developing a clear understanding of any negative belief systems that run your life is an essential step in becoming conscious in life. Arriving at the determination that you have had enough of being subject to a particular issue does not make the causes disappear. Similarly, the core reasons for your problems will generally not magically reveal themselves. The connections between a negative experience and the beliefs that created them can initially be obscure and difficult to recognize. You need to become conscious of every emotional step your mind goes through that led to a behaviour or/and action, a choice and feeling. Developing self-awareness is the journey your consciousness needs to take in order to sophisticate your mind. Any detail you uncover will contribute to your understanding of your sense-of-self and empower you to change.

If you have never questioned your own behaviour, feelings and nature before you could find this extremely challenging. But, if you can accept that blaming others and the world for your emotional experience of life will never permanently change anything, you will realize that you really have no other choice. You will be amazed what there is to learn about yourself and others by becoming conscious of the difference between who you believe you are and your authentic self. Patient exploration of the reasons for any behaviour and feelings associated with negative events through self-interrogation and self-reflection will bring insightful results. Persistence will always pay off as long as you apply the principles described in earlier chapters.

Your Evolution

Media in all its forms ensures that you will always hear or read about some terrible event and experience people go through. The reasons or causes for these disasters are really difficult to explain on the basis of each individual being the creator of their own reality. Therefore it can be hard to accept and for that matter for an outsider to explain the reasons why awful things happen to people of all ages and walks of life anywhere in our world. Violent death through war, hunger, poverty and illness are just a few scourges that cause unimaginable suffering. The presence of all manner of pain and suffering in the world is not accidental or bad luck. Individually and as a national and international collective, we are all creative and active contributors to what happens in the world. Our personal and collective fears, distrust and greed are the core contributors to these manifestations on our planet. Understanding the nature and capacity of mankind's collective mind and that of Universal Consciousness is still a new frontier in mankind's journey into consciousness. At this time there is no doubt that we create our life experience not just on a personal level but also as a collective and that this propagates to all levels of our existence. If one can recognize that fears of all kind are at the root of these miseries then the absence of fear in each individual can transform this universally.

Our understanding of human consciousness is still very limited. Science is still not sure where our consciousness resides let alone its capacity, origin and nature. We are a long way away from understanding the way all consciousness is interconnected. The lack of an official understanding of what it is and how it functions handicaps us as individuals in developing awareness of the nature of their own being and recognizing what having issues is all about. Even if we had clear insight of our own consciousness, we would not necessarily know the emotional state of mind of that of someone else. Explaining the reasons why someone loses their life in a tragic event is difficult if you do not know the exact and intimate emotional nature of their thoughts and intent of their belief systems and so on. Science is on a constant quest to know the universe and beyond— including human consciousness as new discoveries particular in quantum physics and astronomy show. What they find raises more questions about the nature of consciousness and reality and than they can presently furnish answers.

It is reasonable to assume that the nature of reality and consciousness are inter-related and are interdependent even though from our perspective, physical matter and life appear very different and separate from thought and intent. However the concept that their energetic relationship binds them together in a web of inter-connective consciousness is far from new.

To recognize what is real and what is not depends on our clarity of perception and so the question arises how we are to achieve that. The evidence is that our inner-identity — the beliefs we hold to be true — determines much of our perception because it influences our interpretation of what we experience. This is as true about the physical world as it is about concepts, ideas or facts. We struggle with this because just like we have learned to believe that our emotional issues are caused by what is out side of us, we also are convinced that the experience we have of an object is solely determined by the object itself and not by us. Presently the clarity of vision most accessible to us is what we can achieve by dealing with our fears and insecurities. This will enable us to see why and how we as individuals and as a collective, contribute to the state of reality we experience. ***The ultimate truth is that 'it' all begins with you.*** 'It' is living life true to the authentic nature of our being and allowing acts of creative manifestation to expand the nature of our consciousness.

We need to remind ourselves that we are consciousness-energy clothed in flesh- and that our physicality is a disposable part of our being. Life and death are nothing but transitional phases for our spirit consciousness. ***Existence in material reality puts us in physical bodies in order to have an intense and focused creative experience of our being by manifesting who we are in physical reality.*** In being physical in a material reality we have a tangible experience of what is created by our intent — consciously or subconsciously. Our experience of reality is then a mirror of who we are. If we are open to it, this will allow us to recognize the nature of the intent within our beliefs through what we create and manifest. If you make the mistake of believing that there are exceptions to this — you will be disappointed. Anytime you exclude the essence of your being — unconditional love and acceptance — from your life, your consciousness will create from fear and this will be mirrored in your life-experiences.

We are all on a personal journey to evolve our being but how we walk this path will always be our choice. What we experience on our quest of personal development is therefore also always our responsibility. Our relationships with others play a definitive part in our self-education. Relationships that present us with emotional conflict are subconsciously chosen dynamics that provide an opportunity to recognize the nature of our own being. Each party has their own reason for creating the issues that each plays out but our underlying and innate intent to evolve our consciousness is always consistent.

Growth and change in a relationship are easier if both parties can address their contribution to a negative dynamic without blame or criticism in a framework of self-responsibility. This can take a relationship to another level of intimacy and understanding.

In the spirit of the idea that 'what we teach we need to learn', we need to be aware that we all have something significant to share with others. **Each of us has an innate responsibility to help and lift others to higher levels of awareness and resolution thereby supporting the fulfilment of their potential and interestingly enough, our own.** Assisting the growth and expansion of another consciousness without taking control over their life choices and without sacrificing your own brings benefit to all consciousness. However the influence of fear can make us selfish and therefore insensitive to this. If we do not allow ourselves to receive this gift from others it will be because we harbour reasons for wanting to prove that we do not need any help or support. **Our destiny is to know how to create and manifest our existence in the absence of fear and in complete awareness of consequence to our self, others and the world.**

Fearless Self-Questioning

Even though the process of creating our own reality experience is real and tangible, the reasons and causes for what is manifested can be invisible to our senses because it so intrinsically interwoven in our life experience. We need to change who we believe we are before we can integrate a new perception into our life. Our greatest learning is the understanding of our own consciousness and how we affect others through the dynamic that our sense-of-self creates. As we gradually grow from within we will see how each consciousness is intermeshed with all others to create the fabric of world consciousness we individually and collectively experience. The concepts in this book represent an understanding of a small corner of spiritual consciousness, the actual capacity of which is probably beyond our current comprehension.

Knowledge of the nature of your issues and fears and how and what it manifests in your life gives you the power to change it. You become a mindful creator when you take ownership of your issues by being self-responsible and cease to be a victim of others and your surroundings. In the knowledge that your life is a product of your choices, you are left with two options: You can choose not to do anything and keep living out your issues and put up with the outcomes you create or you can choose to confront, accept and release you fear based beliefs and thereby transform your sense-of-self.

If you choose to change, you need to keep track of every part of your involvement in any negative experience in order for you to understand how it came to be a part of your life. From here on, when something negative has happened, you have to ask yourself why and how.

Always hold yourself accountable and responsible for your part in it by asking:
- *What* did I say or do and *why* did I say or do it?
- *What was the intent* behind my behaviour and *what was my behaviour primarily trying to achieve?*
- *What did I feel before, during and after the event* — Was I anticipating a negative response or confrontation? Was I afraid, angry or offended, embarrassed or ashamed, powerless or in guilt and so on and if so **why**?
- *When was the first time I had these feelings. What caused them at that time and why were they triggered now?*
- *What is it about the present circumstances or the people involved that create this emotional effect in me?*
- *Who were involved and what do you see as their part in the incident?*

These are just some of the questions that you could ask yourself but there are always more. Keeping notes is a good way of measuring your progress and perhaps marking changes in your understanding of your self and others.

Your Authentic Truth

You will find that the first 10 years of your childhood hold the core reasons for most of the negative beliefs you hold. All of these beliefs represent different levels of powerlessness or helplessness. Your experience of your childhood has become your idea of what is true and that is exactly how you should work with. Even though others in your family including parents and siblings may have a different or even contradictory understanding of your life, it is your version of the truth that counts. The only way to find answers that are meaningful and specific to your issues is by recognizing how you experienced your relationship with your family. It is the only truth that will explain the negative beliefs you have acquired. You will see that each of your siblings and your parents has had a different experience and will therefore see events from their unique perspective. The effect their childhood had on them and formed their sense-of-self will not parallel yours and your issues will not be identical to theirs. Your understanding of the unique nature of your own mind — negative and positive — is essential to your process of change.

In childhood, your unique interpretation of events was the defining force that determined the nature of the belief systems accepted by you as the truth of who you are.

In your quest to find resolution for your fears, the particular interpretation your naïve self gave to your emotional experiences is the only truth that is relevant regardless of what others believe.

Each family member will have their own take on events through the lens created by their issues and while they are definitely worth listening to, you need to be aware that no one can be truly objective including your self. Your primary goal is to have a non-judgemental understanding of the effects the emotional paradigm of your family had on your sense-of-self. You should always consider and respect the opinions of your family members even if their view does not agree with yours. You are the only one who can validate or dismiss what you believe to be your personal truth. Once you conceptually understand how you came to accept your negative beliefs you need to structure these into a belief system in order to release them. The words that ultimately make up these negative beliefs must reflect the interpretation you gave it as a child. To create a belief statement that is an effective means for releasing your fears they need to contain intent, context and consequence. Try and imagine what it would have been like for you to be subjected to the issues your parents expressed and use it to get a better insight into the nature of your beliefs.

Our unique nature ensures that the dynamic between us and our parents is different from that of our siblings and this means that our version of events will not be the same. Getting it right is obviously very important if you want to be sure that the negative beliefs are at the core of your issues. Just keep in mind that all negative beliefs are based on fear and therefore creators of your illusions. Recognizing context, intent and consequence in one negative belief can help you to realize those in others associated with it. In this way you can unravel beliefs that are related to the same issue. The answers you find can be somewhat confronting and you may at times feel reluctant to accept that you are causing your own problems. However knowing your issues and understanding their nature puts you in control and gives you the power to change them. Just remind your self that no matter what **the source for your issues** looks like it ***is not representative of whom you truly are — your authentic self***.

Dealing with what you will see as the negative 'truth' about yourself is never going to be easy to begin with but persistence and being honest with yourself will pay off. Habitual thinking patterns can cause you to go back to the idea that the causes for your issues are outside of you when they are really not. This would prevent you from recognising the real answers even though they may be right in front of you.

In your search for personal truth there can be no place for an ego mentality that needs to prove itself right or wrong or for criticism or judgment. Neither is misplaced responsibility in the form of guilt. The resolution of your issues through the release fear and thereby building a new and harmonious relationship with yourself is all that matters. Your reward is the continual growth of your spirit mind towards its original destination and thereby manifesting a rewarding life. Discard nothing of what you discover because every bit of information will eventually add up to an answer to an unresolved question. Everything you find out about yourself has significance, purpose and meaning and will ultimately lead to an explanation why your life the way it is.

Self-discovery can be like collecting the pieces of a puzzle that seem totally foreign to you. Sometimes it only makes sense when you get the final piece(s) and the puzzle of questions comes magically together to create and answer that is relevant. Have trust that every bit of knowledge stored in your mind is significant in your process of becoming aware even though its significance may not immediately clear to you. From beginning of your life, your mind has stored the memory of every beat of your heart and every breath you have taken and naturally each and every childhood experience you have ever had. At the start of your journey into your own consciousness it may take time for the necessary information to come to your awareness but this will become much easier as your knowledge grows.

Unnatural Behaviour

Your own behaviour is a perfect place to begin looking for clues for how you influence the creation of your world. How you behave in situations that are challenging for you is a usually a telltale of the underlying fears you hold.

Once you begin to pay attention to these feelings and associated behaviours, you will recognize that you have difficulty exercising control over your responses to certain situations and people. Your aversion or avoidance, aggression or criticism, anger or resentment in response to the behaviour or attitude of others or particular situations actually says much more about you than it does about them.

Behaviour that seeks to prove a point, demeans others, is abrupt and aggressive, is superior and dismissive of others, is excessively pleasing and accommodating, seeks to draw attention, vies for acknowledgement and approval are all out of balance and expose issues. Behaving in a dominating and controlling fashion is not an asset but an issue — a product of fear. Contriving never to upset anyone in order to avoid conflict and guilt suppresses any form of spontaneity.

When fear controls our behaviour there is nothing natural about the way we interact with others. Everything we do and say is likely to have an agenda of sorts. By attracting and being attracted to those who complement our issues — fears — we engage in mutual behaviour that accommodates them. This parallels the way our parent(s) related to us and this suits us because it continues the emotional environment of our childhood and therefore feels normal and right to us. Our behaviour and that of others is big part of the outer façade that we subconsciously create in order to overcome our negative beliefs. You try and fool your self and others that you are someone other whom you believe you are.

Without your fears and in unconditional love acceptance and trust with yourself and others your presence would adopt behaviours that would honestly sincerely allow others to see who you really are. You may actually have had moments in your life when you felt safe to be yourself and display your true self. If you have, imagine these moments to be the consistent state of your mind and self-expression. The absence of fears and insecurities creates an ease of being that will open the doors to life's experiences and sensations without placing conditions on the experience itself and thereby limiting and distorting your involvement and participation.

Generational Transference

The effect the 'emotional DNA' of your parents has on your sense of yourself is as significant as the physical DNA they passed on to form your body. Their fears in the form of issues and insecurities will have played a deterministic role in the formation of your sense of self. Should they have been fearful of making decisions and choices, be overprotective or controlling, critical and judgemental, distrusting or fearful, anxious or stressed and so on, it will impact your sense-of-self and therefore how you are in life and what you will manifest as a life experience. It is inevitable and should not be doubted. The question you should ask your self is not whether your parent's issues had a negative effect on you.

The real question is: In what way did their fears influence my sense-of-self?

The dynamic of relationships dictates that the issues of one parent will compliment that of the other and this makes the effect they will have on a child inescapable. Often their issues are so interrelated because they share the same core fears for their behaviour, which then forms the family paradigm that all family members are subjected to. This is usually not recognized in new relationships because their behaviours appear often opposite creating the illusion that they are different personalities. The complementary nature of their contrasting behaviour actually forms a strong part of the fascination and attraction they have for each other. If physical attraction is also present, these behavioural patterns create the impression that one will fulfil the needs and expectation of the other adding to the desire to get involved with each other.

Not Becoming Your Parents

At an early age our consciousness absorbs all impressions that come through the senses of the mind and the body. These sensations are at first totally new but always referenced by the innate expectation of being unconditional loved. When a child is required to meet conditions to receive love and be accepted, it provokes the feeling that it will be rejected or abandoned should it fail and this we call fear. Once these conditions have been established in the relationship with the parent, the potential for exclusion or rejection is ever present for the child. The beliefs it then forms and the alternative behaviour it takes on inspired by fear are a protective measure to avoid rejection and exclusion. Whenever anyone acts out of fear they do so to create conditions that secure their emotional safety. By the time adulthood is reached they will place these conditions unconsciously on others to avoid realizing their fears. In doing so are likely to parent their children in the way they were raised by their parents. Unfortunately we are all guilty of this in one way or another.

If your parents are harbour fears of being emotionally present they are likely to have difficulty showing or expressing, giving and receiving love and affection as well as other emotions they feel confronted by. You will leave your home environment with similar fears that will turn you into an emotionally inhibited individual or potentially excessively expressive.

Your parent's issue with the expression of love and affection will leave you to believe that you are not lovable and acceptable and this is vey likely to make you needy for love and affection. Your yearning to feel love and acceptance can make you very needy of your partner or it this is unfulfilling look at your children as a source for your need to be loved. Either behaviour will distort the relationship with your children and creates conditions on your love for them.

Your need to feel love and wanted can also result in anger because of the powerlessness you experienced by being denied by your parents. This anger may be directed at your partner when they do not fulfil your expectations. You can also make you children the target for your frustration because they naively demand from you what you never received — unconditional love. There are many different dynamic and scenarios possible but it is important to realize that these fears and complementary behaviours do not disappear the day you become a parent. Your own issues ensure that they will be unconsciously expressed in your parenting.

Parents who aggressively or passively control their children by choosing and thinking for them can render them powerless. They make their children physically and them emotionally dependent by teaching them that they cannot trust or depend on their own judgment, choices and resilience. Over-concerned because of their own fear of living and confrontation they are likely to be overprotective and controlling of their children. Their offspring will adopt the parent's fears and become fearful of life, decisions and confrontation and so on. They will not have any trust in their own capacities and resources and constantly need validation and support before they do anything. They will live in a constant state of powerlessness and vulnerability because being overprotected made them believe they are fragile in an aggressive world.
The caring protective nature of the parent's behaviour hides they are behaving and acting from fear and powerlessness and not from trust in their own capacities and power.

In most family dynamics, one parent is the aggressive powerless victim while the other is passive powerless victim to one degree or another otherwise their personalities could not co-exist. The children will be made powerless by both parents — generally through intimidating aggression by one and guilt by the other parent. From this dynamic various behavioural scenarios are possible. The main point to be made here is that as a product from this kind of environment you will have issues to content with. Many of these issues will become visible when you have children and the demands of parenting take your relationship and your role into an entirely new direction. There will be demands on you that you are not prepared for and for which there is no formal training. What follows is a potential scenario for you to ponder over.

The aggressively controlling parent has the tendency to choose and decide for the children and set the standards and values for behaviour in the family. They are also likely to be critical and judgemental of their offspring. The behaviour of this parent has the effect of taking away the power of their children and their trust in them selves. The parent's distrust in their choices and decisions will cause them to distrust in their own thinking, reasoning and judgement. This will result in the fear of making choices and decisions independently and being independent when they are adults. They will not develop trust in the personal power, resources and abilities they were born with. Instead, their fear of the potential of negative consequences will make them try and avoid any situation where critical decisions have to be made. Entering a cycle of avoidance in decision-making will result in constant procrastination. The belief that they cannot trust themselves makes them depend on others for support and advice for fear that if they were to decide themselves they would experience failure, loss and disaster.

Alternatively a child's intense fear of making bad decisions and choices can trigger the need to prove its mental capacity and power to go it alone by demonstrating that it can make its on choices independently and be successful. This will usually result in conflict and confrontation with the dominant or controlling parent who feels they are made wrong and criticised by their own child. However, by emulating the dominant parent, the child is on a path of becoming the parent it resents the most. The need to prove they are right and know better does not stop when they become parents and so the outcome for their children is predictable.

Even thought both the aggressively behaving child and the passive child have similar basic issues their contrasting behaviours cause their parents perceive them very differently. The passive child is usually seen as the acceptable one and the aggressive child as being difficult and unacceptable. The parents do not realize that these behaviours are responses to their own and which have made their children feel disempowered, have no control and feel guilt about their innate needs and expectations. It is their children's way to protect themselves from feeling vulnerable and powerless in the world. Both the children see themselves as powerless victims of their family environment — one believes it has to wait for permission and approval to do what it wants and to be who it feel it is. The other tries to achieve the same by using aggression to proactively be independent from the parents. Emulating the attitude and behaviour of its parent is an innate strategy employed by consciousness for its emotional survival. Commonly the dominating parent is at loggerheads with the aggressive child but can be in a relationship of sorts with the compliant one. The passive child is likely to be closer to the passive parent who fears confrontation through the guilt feelings and beliefs that she has passed on to her child.

Children who grow up in this kind of environment may already show this kind of behaviour at school in the form of bullying or by being the victim of it.
Potentially, the aggressive sibling may become the bully who needs to push others around in order to feel powerful and in control. Unconsciously they will seek passive powerless children to dominate in order to deal with their fears of powerlessness. Both victims and aggressors are likely to come from similar psychological environments where they are either aggressively or passively disempowered. (Intimidation, aggression and control or/and guilt, victimhood and powerlessness) However when intimidating and dominating personalities are aggressively confronted they often default to their fundamental issues of powerlessness and start to behave, as of they are the victims.

A dysfunctional family paradigm does not necessarily have to be physically or emotionally aggressive or abusive. Any emotional environment that is consistently oppressive and controlling will have a disempowering effect on the development of a child's sense of itself. Parents who create guilt, use passive criticism or have a passive victim attitude are just as powerful an emotional influence on the mind of naïve child, as parents with aggressive and controlling intimidating behaviour. Either way, a child will always naively assume that it must be responsible for the aggression or the guilt it is subjected to. Any form of suppression or guilt will educate a child into negative strategic behaviours that will either be only harmful to it self as well as to others.

Growing up with parents who are physically present but do not have the capacity to give and receive on an emotional level is like being abandoned on a daily basis. This kind of emotional environment has deep-seated consequences for the emotional development of a child. The absence of emotional connections leaves a child guessing whether it is lovable or not, acceptable or not, trusted and wanted or not and so on. It experiences a consistent lack of validation of its innate emotional self which leaves it in deep doubt and insecurity about the value and significance of its own being. In the absence of emotional signals endorsing its innate expectation for unconditional love, acceptance and trust from the parents, it will feel that the expression of its authentic and emotional self is unwanted.

Communication in such a family is generally impersonal and only concerns the generalities of physical life, avoiding any direct reference to each other's emotions, issues and personal opinions. Revealing emotions in a direct personal context is usually taboo, as is holding one another emotionally accountable and responsible. These subliminal rules are learned very early in life. However, the process of living life will always manifest what we fear and so frequently a family with these issues will produce at least one sibling whose perception and behaviour contradicts the prevailing family paradigm. The presence of an emotionally expressive child confronts those who live by the unspoken rules of emotional suppression and this can result in favouritism and conflict. The majority has learned not only to suppress their emotional expectations such as the desire for closeness, affection and love and a host of other feelings but also those of others. Their fear of being emotionally present and expressive and respond to the emotional needs of others causes such parents to employ behaviours and activities designed to avoid this. Being dutiful, physical caring such as providing and cooking or the giving of gifts are often used as a poor substitutes for love and affection, closeness and intimacy, interest and involvement with their children.

Censorship of your unique and authentic self, dismissing its spontaneous creative potential and suppressing spontaneous thoughts, feelings and emotional truth will have a devastating effect on every aspect of your life. To protect yourself from being guilty of upsetting or offending others, you will censor yourself by putting everything you say through an emotional filter. This effectively kills any spontaneous expression and emotional truth.

You are likely to choose relationships that repeat your childhood experience. You will feel an attraction for personalities that are emotionally unavailable and tend not to be emotionally present and involved. They are attracted to you because you will never emotionally confront them or make demands because you are afraid to be guilty for upsetting them. In the long term, this kind of relationship will not satisfy you but your fears may keep you there.
Alternatively you may choose a relationship where the potential for confrontation and guilt is minimal because they have similar issues to your own. You may not realize that a relationship like this is like an unspoken contract where each promises the other never to make any emotional demands. Unfortunately this often includes the sincere expression of love and affection. If these are your issues than they will be a significant part of your relationships that are essentially a continuation of the family paradigm with which you both grew up.

To live consciously means becoming aware of every emotional element in your life that acts as a restriction, suppresses you and stops you being who you truly are. It also means becoming aware of who you truly are, your capacities, gifts and individual powers. You can only make choices with the awareness of the consequences if you recognise the nature of your limiting beliefs and the capacity of your unique and authentic self. Making choices and decisions with awareness of consequence — positive or negative — is the way to you can begin to assume control over your life. Awareness and knowledge of your negative beliefs are the first steps towards releasing them to transform your sense-of-self and your life. Discovering and becoming aware and accepting your authentic self and its unique nature will take you to a new life experience.

Your Reality Is YOU

It cannot be emphasised enough that your experience of reality is a representation of whom you believe yourself to be — your sense-of-self. By now you may realize that getting to know your self in depth is a process and requires commitment. There are four distinct levels at which we can sense our being.

- *The essence of our spirit* — unconditional love, acceptance and trust, our innate and unstoppable drive to express, create and manifest the nature of our being — our authentic self — into reality where it becomes our life experience. Our experience of our reality is actualized through the incessant stream of decisions and choices that we have to make in order to survive emotionally and physically.
- *Our unique and authentic self* — the person we truly are and an intrinsic and defining part of our being — represented by qualities and gifts that define the potential of our consciousness, our innate talents and abilities.
- *Our subconscious sense-of-self* made up from all previous elements with the addition of fear-based beliefs and programmed strategies. These are given unconscious expression through all the emotional and physical means available to you: your behaviour, your feelings and perception and so on. This is where you hold all of your beliefs whether rooted in unconditional love or fear. The negative beliefs contain your fears and insecurities, your sense of powerlessness and vulnerability.
- *Our conscious sense-of-self — ego self* — can contain any kind of belief or conviction about anything. There will be a collection of superficial belief systems that commonly reflect you're the desire of how you want to be seen by yourself and by others. On this level you will be aware of certain fears and insecurities that directly relate to world experiences but the source for their existence in you usually escapes you. This is where

you experience and respond to feelings that reflect the belief systems that are either in or out of harmony with our essence. Here you experience the product of your fears through anger and powerlessness, anxiety and stress and so on and draw on your subconscious strategies to survive.

Your conscious self is also the place where you experience the outcome of your positive and harmonious beliefs without fail.

Out of these, the self you are most aware of and best known by to others, is your ego self with all of its fears, represented by your behaviour and emotional expression. The stories you create for the benefit of yourself in relation to others allows you to hide the fears you hold and to convince yourself that others will see you in the way you want to see yourself.

The perception you have learned to accept and believe to be true by default can also keep you blind to the actual reality of your sense-of-self. This can cause you to be unaware of the deeper intent that drives your strategic behaviour and feelings. Your vision of life and the world will on the surface appear to be logical and clear but taking into consideration that your fears will distort your perception of reality, it may well not be what you think it is. The concept of love, acceptance and trust that you currently hold to be true are formed exactly in this way. Although you may think that you know what love is, your understanding is likely to be highly distorted because of the distorting beliefs you may hold. Your accepted idea of normality makes it difficult to see and recognise that is not unconditional love. Until we realize that we are the problem we will blame the failure of relationships on one another.

It is important to accept that you are the one choosing your partner that you agree to date them and become intimate with them. If you want to understand why you are in a relationship and not happy or why you are being abused you need to look at your self first. As a constant figure in all of your relationships that you engaged in by choice you only look at your self as the responsible party. This may seem like a tough concept to face up to but accepting it puts you in control. Becoming aware of your negative emotional contributions places you in a position of strength because **you are the only one that has the power to change you.**

Here are some examples of complimentary issues:

For example:
- A convincer and liar will choose someone who is distrusting and suspicious.

- A suspicious and distrusting individual will seek someone who can convince them to trust.
- A controlling dominant person will find power by choosing a needy, insecure and powerless partner.
- A needy, insecure and powerless partner will seek someone who will take control and protect them from their fears and insecurities.
- The blamer and accuser will choose someone who feels constant guilt and responsibility for everything in order to avoid having to be responsible.
- A guilt driven person will attract someone for whom they will take responsibility.
- A person who believes they are unwanted and unlovable and gives love to get love will attract a selfish partner needy for love and acceptance.
- A selfish person, incapable of giving love but needy for love and affection will choose a partner who will give love and affection in order to be loved because they do not feel entitled to it in return.

We may believe that we are aware of all the elements that define our choice of partner but this is rarely the case. Without knowing the nature of our issues we are inevitably drawn towards the person who is in reality a mirror for our own fears. Our emotional issues redefine our concept of love, sexual attraction and emotional intimacy and each contributes to the nature of the dynamic of the relationship we engage in.

We often confuse our attachment to someone with unconditional love because we have no understanding of reasons why we are attracted in the first place. When issues appear in a relationship this lack of awareness becomes a problem. When the conflict in a relationship escalates to an unresolvable level, going your separate ways is not always easy. Unresolved and still active issues can cause the separation process to become extremely difficult, painful and drawn out. When partners are unaware how their own issues have contributed to the failure they will assume that they are victims of one another. Letting go of each other can than become difficult because they are in a sense not finished with each other. Outstanding issues still bind them together even if on the outside it looks like they cannot stand each other. The anger they hold on to is mutual blame for disappointing the unspoken expectation that each would provide emotional compensation for the others fears and insecurities. This translates into anger and resentment for not being who and what they expected each other to be. This can than feel as if they cannot live with or without each other and therefore cannot move on. Each has to find resolution independent of the other because the real problems lie within.

Your understanding of the dynamic in the relationship and the emotional part each of you play can provide clues to how your early family environment influenced your mind. The emotional patterns of behaviour that are active in your relationship will mimic those experienced in childhood. When issues appear in a relationship there are no innocent parties —*what each individually experiences is their own responsibility.*

Your own behaviour in relationships is a good starting point for self-realization.

From the point of view of being a contributor to the issues you experience in a relationship these may represent some of the behaviour and attitudes you may have:

- *Blame:* You make your partner or others responsible for the issues, fears and insecurities you feel and thereby avoiding being held accountable and confronting your own shortcomings.
- *Expectations:* You expect your partner or others to be or provide those things for you that you feel powerless, incapable or too vulnerable and so on, to deal with yourself.
  You feel entitled to expect your partner to accommodate your fears needs, wishes and desires etc. without you having to ask or explain.
- *Guilt:* You suppress your needs, truth, beliefs or power to avoid being blamed for upsetting your partner or being a burden to them. As a result you monitor and filter everything you express to avoid eliciting a negative response from others for fear of attracting guilt, criticism and rejection. Whenever something goes wrong you fear that somehow you will be seen as the guilty-one.
  You can never do anything right for your partner and others and always fail them and blame yourself for your shortcomings
- *Creating Guilt:* You aggressively hold others or the world responsible for your negative life experiences — nothing is ever your fault. Or, by acting the victim of everything and everyone, by default others and the world are responsible for the negative emotional events in your life.
- *Dominance and control:* You expect your partner or others to listen to you and be obedient and subservient to your choices, ideas and expectations and to accept your determinations and expectations as right and justified without question. If they do not, you feel your power is threatened and you may become aggressive for fear of losing your position of power.
- *Criticism and judgment:* Your partner or others disappoint you constantly and cannot do anything that is right or good enough to deserve your approval no matter how many times you point this out to them. You are obviously vastly superior to them.

- ***Anger and aggression:*** You get upset whenever things are not the way you expect them to be. You feel others deliberately oppose and contradict you in order to undermine you need for control.
- ***Emotionally unavailable:*** You find it difficult if not impossible to show what you feel for your partner and others. You expect them to "know" that you love and care for them and believe that all the things you do and buy is enough to prove this. You avoid any situation were you may have to reveal what you really feel. Your strategy is to withdrawal and become emotionally and physically unavailable. You feel like a victim of the emotional needs of others because you never received love and attention in your childhood.

Start by asking yourself the following questions about your own behaviour and that of your partner:

- ***Am I taking responsibility*** or am I holding my partner responsible for what I create in my life and how does my partner respond to this?
- ***Do I apply the same standards*** and values to myself as I do to my partner and vice versa?
- ***Do I complain***, nag, criticise and am I judgemental or do I feel my partner is?
- ***Do I feel needy***, powerless, dependent and inferior in my relationship or is my partner that way with me?
- ***Do I support my partner*** to evolve into their best self and do they support me in the same way? Or, are we competitive and/ or envious of one another's achievements and success, popularity and significance?
- ***Can I be open and free***, honest and truthful in my communication and the expression of my feelings with my partner and can my partner be so with me? Or, do I have to tread on eggshells whenever I want to speak my truth in fear they get angry, upset or cannot cope? Or is it the other way around?
- ***Am I free to fulfil my potential***, passions, and desires? Or do I put others before myself because I believe that will only be loved if I nurture and protect others from their fears and insecurities?
- ***Do I have the expectation*** that my partner or others focus all of their attention on me and put me before themselves? Or, do I put others before my self in order to please them and be loved and accepted?
- ***Does my partner have to meet my expectation*** of what I want them to be so that I feel safe and in control? Or, does my partner expect me to be that way for them?

- *Do I expect my partner* never to emotionally confront, challenge me or hold me accountable because will make me feel powerless or a failure? Do I therefore demand that my partner accepts my ideas, beliefs and choices as the only option? Or am I the one always complying to my partner ideas and expectations because I fear I cannot trust my own decisions and choices or that I will be rejected if I do not?
- *Do I feel the need* to constantly point out my partner's failings and inadequacies? Or, does my partner always criticise me and cause me to feel inadequate, hopeless and dumb?

Being truthful with yourself is paramount if you want to get the most out of questioning yourself. *The basis for living consciously lies in learning to understand who you believe yourself to be as distinct from who you really are.* Distinguishing the illusionary part from the authentic self creates the awareness of who you really are. Not just with yourself but it also changes your capacity to see what is real and what is illusion in the world. Being able to recognize or predict the consequences of your negative or positive intent within your actions and choices makes you aware of how you create your life experiences. Once you know how your own belief systems affect your relationships, success or happiness, you have the option to alter the outcome by changing who you are. Releasing your negative beliefs allows you to begin to create and manifest your life from a place of ever-greater authenticity and inner-harmony. Supported by an enhanced awareness of the nature of unconditional love, acceptance and trust you will become conscious of your different intents and their effects in your life.

Living consciously requires you to constantly monitor your own state of mind, emotions and behaviour. You might imagine what you might call a mini-me sitting on your shoulder as an objective observer whispering in your ear.
Your mini-me might ask you why you just said something or the reason why you reacted in anger or guilt. It will question your feelings and behaviour, actions and choices in response to every situation. This mini-me will act as a more objective observer of your emotional or impulsive self by using your reasoning mind.
The conclusions extracted from your self-observations can raise the awareness of the nature of your thoughts, feelings and behaviour. You can use it as a temporary tool that allows you to become aware of the deeper motivations behind your behaviours and self-expression that have led to negative outcomes. This can take you to a useful realization of the negative beliefs you hold, the fear that drives them and their intent.

The process of living life will invariably present all of us with emotional events that are actually a mirror for our emotional issues. You will lose your fear of negative outcomes once you realize that each negative experience gives you the chance to discover more about the nature of your mind and the opportunity to change. ***The path towards self-realization and transformation is littered with opportunities that present themselves as failures, disappointments and pain.*** Changing your perception of a so-called negative experience brings you a step closer towards the expansion and transformation of your consciousness. This change will make life in general a very different journey. Keep in mind that ***you are the only one that can raise the bar for the person you want to be and the life experience you want to have.***

Chapter 25

Living Unconditional Love

Although we are coming to the end of this book we are still very much at the beginning of all there is to learn about our consciousness and the process by which we create our reality. This is in many ways an introduction to the different elements that are involved in this process that we call life. How the expression consciousness creates the reality it experiences is fundamentally very different to what you have been led to believe about living and life. It should be no surprise that these new ideas will challenge many of close held beliefs of who or what is responsible for what we feel, how we behave and ultimately what we experience as a consequence. Accepting that the point of power in life actually lies within your own consciousness can be difficult to accept when you have been blaming others or the world most of your life. The realization that the power to manifest our own life experiences lies within allows us to embrace the potential of becoming self-responsible creators of our own lives and more. Everyone's journey in life is to set their mind free from perceived restrictions by transcending your fears in order to take your place as a positive and responsible creator.

Positive Interventions

The loss of the authentic self together with conditional love and acceptance are the most intense negative influences on our incredible minds. Once a child has lost one through the other it has no choice but to confront and resolve these issues. The idea that you do not have to do this is just another illusion because the consequences of their presence will manifest throughout its life. Their expression does not just affect you; it will also resonate in the lives of those closest to you and adds to the negative state of the collective.

Recovering and discovering the authentic-self is a journey within itself. Realizing new qualities, interests or abilities is a joyful experience that builds self-confidence and trust. The process of getting there is incremental but your baby steps can become big strides. Even after many fears have been released it can still feel that being unconditionally loved and accepted and authentically your self have not been completely embraced. Your different fears are layered in order of priority and significance by your knowing mind. Trust that whatever the fears you feel drawn to deal with are the right and appropriate issues to confront. They usually present themselves to you because they are a priority to you at this time.

Sometimes the strong identification with certain issues can cause the absence of them to create a sense of emptiness. It can feel as if a certain purpose and meaning in life has been lost. This is because you have spend so much of your mental and emotional time obsessing about these fears that their absence leaves your mind with nothing to occupy itself with. On the positive side you can put your mind to creative use by exploring new possibilities in your life
In order to create and manifest a life that is positive and in which we will evolve, we all need to be in the belief that we are entitled and deserving to be unconditionally loved and wanted, accepted, trusted. Consequently we must be unconditionally lovable and acceptable, trusted and wanted to our selves and others. This state of being reflects our innate and unconscious aspiration to exist in harmony with the true nature of our essence. By the fact that we exist and conscious we are entitled to be unconditionally loved and lovable, accepted and acceptable and so on.

The experience of a childhood excluded from love, acceptance and trust from the very moment they became conscious to the physical world can cause the concept of unconditional love to be a foreign and therefore difficult to realize. If this is the case you can remind yourself of the true nature of your spiritual essence by accepting the following statement:

I now know, believe and accept and I am unconditionally convinced
that I was born, that I came into existence, awareness and consciousness
with the entitlement, right and deservedness
to feel and experience, receive and give, exist and live in unconditional love, unconditional acceptance and unconditional trust,
to be unconditionally wanted and included considered and praised, listened to and heard, recognized and appreciated, acknowledged and validated,
and so because of that I am free to unconditionally express, reveal, articulate, demonstrate and give a voice to my authentic and unique self, my true nature, my spontaneous self and my truth,
this I know, this I believe, this I accept, trust and believe unconditionally.

Obviously, this will only be effective after you have released your fears — negative beliefs. You have the option to do this and it can be useful to repeat this after every release of negative beliefs.

This can act as a conscious reminder of how you are entitled to be in the world. However, you need address your negative beliefs systems first and separately and to accomplish change within yourself.

The potential of our spirit-consciousness is immense and so is its capacity to manifest through intent. Humanity's addiction to fear is the greatest obstacle to overcome. ***Our indoctrination in the culture of fear has made us believe that we are powerless in life. This belief makes us respond with strategies that have turned us into helpless victims or controlling aggressors in order to survive emotionally and physically.*** This has grown into an adversarial mentality that acts as an overriding restriction on the perception of our options for personal and world transformation.

You do not have to wonder what that world would be like if humanity lived in the grip of fear because it is happening right here and now. The state of the world, the systems and institutions we live under are generally based on all manner of fears. The suffering caused by crime and violence, war and famine are first of all a result of individual and then collective fears. We are all involved — the bystanders as well as those who are active in the process.

We will open doors to a different reality experience by leaving our illusionary fears behind and accepting unconditional love as the new core value of our consciousness. Sharing this with similarly evolving individuals who are on a parallel path to your own will have a positive effect on all of consciousness and ultimately on the very nature of reality. ***The intent within our sense-of-self will always find manifestation in the world whether from love or from fear.*** It is unavoidable because it is the nature of consciousness in the expression of the sense of itself.

Awake to Truth

Up until now you have effortlessly manifested your life without necessarily being conscious of how and why. This has allowed you to claim ignorance of the reasons for many of the things that have happened in your life. If you are fundamentally tired of reliving the same negative emotional experiences over and over again, you now know that you are the one who can change to bring an end to this.
Your inner changes will cause you to recognize that every relationship is actually two dynamics.
The inner-dynamic — between your mind (sense-of-self) and the essence of your spirit — determines the kind of relationship you have with your self. It

can either be the source for inner-harmony and strength or for fear, powerlessness and conflict within your self.

The outer-dynamic is your interaction with others and the world. It results from the expression of your inner-dynamic and will reveal the harmonious or disharmonious nature of your sense-of-self. Even though your inner-dynamic will be the origin for your attractions, feelings and behaviours, you will be most aware of the experiences of life and relationships created via the outer-dynamic.

In the absence of fear, the essence of your being and your sense-of-self will converge towards the same resonance. Your perception, behaviour and feelings will change in response to your new inner-state. Without the need for strategies you will attract and create relationships founded on positive beliefs and expectations. Your choices and decisions, behaviour and responses and thoughts and feelings will be different without you even trying. Your awareness will shift to a different level allowing you to see emotional elements in others that were previously invisible to you. The fact is that you will have changed your world by changing who you are and in doing so you have taken a significant step towards being who you were always meant to be.

Once in the awareness, that ***we are spirit-consciousness*** and therefore not limited in our existence by our physical body we also know that we are not victims of our surroundings, of others or the universe. We can then feel safe to connect unconditionally with others and all of consciousness. ***We will be in the awareness that emotional strength and the power come from within.*** Manifesting a world without fear, in which everyone can exist true to them selves, requires the unconditional contribution of each individual consciousness. Even though our potential is immense, much of it is unrealized because of fear. In many ways human consciousness is like a child, still playing in the sandbox of physical reality, limited by fear and unaware of its true potential and capacity.

The understanding of intent and consequence are central to our development of the awareness of the nature of our consciousness. Any belief — positive or negative — is not a just static energetic construct in our minds. It is a highly volatile energy pattern which resonance contains intent. It is an emotional program that will attract and be attracted to other belief system patterns that are in harmony with it. At this point, the very nature of the energy of belief system patterns becomes very significant. Should they resonate out of harmony with our core essence their vibration becomes representative of fear. If in harmony with the essence of spirit it core intent will be based in unconditional love and acceptance. The resonance of a negative belief will be reflected in fear-based emotions — guilt, and rejection, powerlessness and anger and so on. This results in attracting and become attracted to those whose belief systems or to manifest events are of a similar resonance. The consequences of conscious or subconscious intent that flows from our beliefs are familiar to all of us because they are the source for our experience of pain and suffering or positive, happy and fulfilling experiences.

The core resonance of positive beliefs and their intent are an indivisible aspect of everything that exists. When your sense-of-self creates from intent in harmony with its core essence, everything that exists gravitates to support its manifestations. All beliefs actively transmit the nature of their intent into the universe and then connect and interact with intent that is complementary in its vibration. Once these intents begin to relate to each other they create a dynamic that must find its own positive or negative conclusion.

The Essence of Being

To get a more philosophical perspective on this process it helps to understand what role pain and suffering and all other negative feelings play. Your mind manifests negative emotions such as sadness and loss, powerlessness and anger and depression as emotional signposts. The intent behind their presence is to make you aware that your belief of who you are, is distorted — driven by fears. Your negative emotions are a direct warning to make you aware that you are 'out-of–harmony' with who you really are. Your emotional stress is a signal from your mind to prompt you into reassessing the nature of your sense-of-self so that you can deal with your fears and insecurities — negative sense-of-self.

The experience of "Universal Consciousness" starts within us and is intrinsically connected to the nature of all consciousness. Generally we all live with fears but their particular origin, nature and how we experience them is very individual. This is the reason why we are collectively living much of our lives in illusion, first of all with ourselves and as a consequence with each other and with the world.

The simplicity of being in harmony with your true nature appears to be at odds with the enormously complicated emotional and psychological issues you experience when you exist in fear. We are so carried away by the river of fear that envelops every part of our lives that existing in the absence of it appears difficult if not impossible. That will change, once you realize that what you believe to be true about yourself and the world is source of everything your mind acts out, feels and experiences. Discovering that you are the source for everything that you create and manifest in your life is deeply empowering. As the owner of the beliefs that determines who you are, you are endowed with the power and control over what you choose to accept as a truth or reject because it is an illusion. This awareness is the power that allows you to achieve a state of being that finds its strength in unconditional love.

All consciousness innately gravitates to be at one with its essence and this propensity is far more persistent and influential than fear will ever be. Fear can at some level always appear as an influential aspect of our psyche but in overcoming it we evolve and in its absence we will find fulfilment of our being.
The existence of fear in others and how it controls them will become obvious once we become aware of our own negative beliefs and release them. This will expand your insight in human nature and realize that you are not the only one that suffers the consequences of fear. Judging others over the way they live their lives would be like being in judgment of your self. However, you may be able to help them understand the part they play in their issues by asking them questions they should be asking themselves in respect to their negative life experiences. Questions, that will lead them to realize that they are active contributors to the situations or events that cause them pain and unhappiness. It is unfortunate that most people are only prepared to look at themselves when they can no longer bear the pain their issues create in them. Commonly their strategic behaviours need to fail them before they are prepared to take responsibility for their lives.

You may find it hard to believe that the resolution of your fears can have a significant impact on the influence of unconditional love in the world yet it is the very force by which the world will change. By working on yourself you are not being selfish, self-centred or uncaring about others. The resolution of your fears will enable you to exist within the power and potential of your own being and then you will be able to make contributions that truly matter to others and the world.

The true value of your life achievements
does not only lie in your effect on others or on the world
but in how they changed the nature of your being.

The success of your life
is in the realisation
of the responsible creator
within.

Printed in Australia
AUOC02n0947210415
267108AU00001B/1/P

9 781457 516665